Bread Head

Bread Head

Baking for the Road Less Traveled

Greg Wade

with Rachel Holtzman

PHOTOGRAPHY BY E. E. BERGER

W. W. NORTON & COMPANY
Independent Publishers Since 1923

Contents

Introduction: The Birth of a Bread Head   7

Part I. Digging In   13
Helpful Stuff for Getting Started

Bake the Bread You Bake   15
A Glossary of Terms   19
Using This Book for Ultimate Bread Success   23
Better Flour for Better Bread   27
Say Hey to the Grains   37
What You'll Need   43
Everything You Need to Know about Sourdough   57

Part II. Digging It   65
Recipes and Other Tasty Things

Chapter 1. Like a Road Leading Home   67
Chapter 2. Golden Loaves to Unlimited Devotion   121
Chapter 3. Fire on the Mountain   189
Chapter 4. Long, Strange Trip   219
Chapter 5. Friends of the Devil   245

Part III. Digging Deeper   303
Troubleshooting and Taking Things to the Next Level

Fermentation Experimentation   305
Baker's Percentages and Building Your Own Recipes   313
Troubleshooting: Help, Everything's on Fire!   323

Acknowledgments   327
Index   329

The Birth of a Bread Head

THERE'S MAGIC THAT HAPPENS OVER THE AMBER WAVES OF southern Illinois wheat fields around sunset in the late summer. After a long day harvesting, I'm dirty and tired, but as I take a moment to rest, the light dims and the fireflies dance. Every time I'm visiting the grains that will eventually become the flour that will eventually become my bread, I take a good half hour to sit back, reflect on the day, reflect on the work, and just watch nature happen. I feel the same way about baking bread. It's a celebration of what has come and what will come; of earth, wind, water, fire; of life and death. When you make bread, you're nurturing this living thing, making sure it's getting what it needs, and putting a lot of time and care into it, up until the point you decide it's ready—when you send it to its beautiful death, into the fire. You stand next to the oven, transmitting all your good will into that bread—*Please rise; please be what I want*—followed by anticipation and, ultimately, as you crack into the crust and release the earthy, sour steam of resurrection, reward. The connection of soil and sun to wheat, and flour and water to bread, and living yeast to ashes is one the oldest, most natural cycles—one that I've found much inspiration and beauty in over the course of my thirty-odd years, and one that I've inked permanently down the length of my right arm in honor of our inevitable bond (in good company with another fifteen or so tattoos that, among other things, provide protection for travelers, wish good fortune and good spirits, and remind me that maybe we're all just living in a galaxy inside an octopus floating around in space). It's safe to say that it's made me a Bread Head, meaning I'm pretty much always thinking about how to make bread, and how to make it better.

Jerry Garcia and the Grateful Dead said it best: "Once in a while you get shown the light, in the strangest of places if you look at it right." For me, it was in the basement of Stephanie Izard's restaurant Girl and the Goat. Marty Travis of Spence Farm walked in to drop off an order, shook my hand, and said, "Hey, I grow wheat." I said, "Hey, I make bread." And it was pretty much love after that. At the time—about twelve years ago—nobody else around here in the Corn Belt besides Marty and his son Will were offering local, organic grains, and they definitely weren't growing the wayward brothers and sisters of common wheat—things like rye, sorghum, buckwheat, barley, millet. So we got to talkin', and by the time I took over the bakery at Publican Quality Bread in 2014, I was buying almost 100 percent of what they were harvesting and milling: six varieties of wheat, four varieties of corn, heritage grains aplenty, and pretty much anything else that their slice of good green earth would grow. Paul Kahan, executive chef and partner at PQB, shared my vision for providing Chicago with naturally leavened, long-fermented products made from locally farmed heritage grains, so we put our money where our love is, and I've been makin' Bread Head–approved loaves ever since.

I've always felt that there is a path to more delicious, more nourishing food and practices that support a healthier planet—and it starts with a different approach to making bread, the most elemental of foods. This bread is rebellious and willful, but also the product of careful method and consideration. It's an eff-you to the factory-farmed, industrially made versions that you see on every shelf in every grocery store across this country. It's decidedly alive, fermented for up to sixty hours, not pumped out in five. Its flours aren't "enriched" or spiked with conditioners and emulsifiers (the real causes of much of the anti-gluten epidemic), just milled wheat. Its deep, wild flavor is the product of nothing more than plants and time, fermentation and fire. It's kinder to the body and, ultimately, kinder to the planet. It's the kind of bread that will help heal our damaged foodways *and* our gut microbiome. Oh, and in case I didn't mention, it's damn fine bread—that kind that deserves to be on everyone's table, and definitely can be, no matter your skills. As I like to say when holding up my palm with the shovel tattoo, "Ya dig?"

Of the bittersweet things to arise after many of us closed our doors in March 2020, baking bread was one of them. Seemingly overnight, people who hadn't so much as cooked a meal for themselves in years were nurturing their very own sourdough starter pets and proudly producing boules and loaves. Sure, everyone had more time on their hands to experiment, but this was also an outgrowth of something else: tapping into the desire to create something nurturing and nourishing. And tasty, too. When we needed comfort, bread was there. Right off the bat, I got loads of messages from people asking all sorts of questions—*How do I know if my starter is still alive? How frequently should I feed it? Why are my loaves turning out flat?* And my favorite: *Can I use other flours if the store is out of regular bread flour?*

It made me realize that it was high time for people to have a resource that walked them through this process in a way that was accessible, useful, stress-free, and just a tiny bit more interesting than scrolling through a hyper-technical bread website. But most importantly, I wanted people to start to connect with bread baking on an intuitive level— to understand what is going on, why it's going on, and what they're going to do about it.

Like me, *Bread Head* is most definitely not the result of a classical education or the pursuit of perfection. I was never formally trained. I learned to make bread by reading and practicing, practicing and reading. I made a ton of mistakes, learned from 'em, and made some more. So at the heart of this book are the lessons I've absorbed during a career spent seeking to harness the great unknown:

- Baking bread sits at the intersection of science and alchemy, technique and intuition.

- When you bake, you must have a rich and robust conversation with the grain, and the bread you bake is something you both have to agree upon.

The significance of our connection with the farmers who grow our grains should be no different than the significance of our connection with the people who sit around our tables and consume our bread.

This book has a certain amount of me nerding out over gluten chains and open-cell structure, but I promise to keep everything as simple and user-friendly as possible because bread baking shouldn't feel like homework. I'll talk about basic ingredients and what happens to your bread on a cellular level as it ferments and bakes, as well as introduce the components of flour, why each is important, and how it can affect your dough. There will be a (chilled-out) master class on fermentation (including permission to not feed your starter every day, plus instructions for how to be successful with commercial yeast because I want this to be available for people other than just super serious "dough-nuts"). Ultimately, I'll provide the tools necessary for consistent success, the kind I implement in our bakery. I'll also walk you through different types of grains, describe their flavors, and shed some light on how they behave and what can be substituted where. I'll give you direction for what to look for at the grocery store and, more importantly, who in your area to talk to about getting such products locally.

The bread I'm going to teach you to make is a little rough around the edges, a little louder than is polite, and stupid good. When you're using grains beyond straitlaced white wheat, your bread goes to a much more unruly and interesting place. There's buckwheat with its dusty, barnyard vibe that pairs really well with chocolate (cool side note: buckwheat produces more nectar per plant than any other commonly grown crop, which is why we get all that awesome spiced honey from it); deep, funky sorghum that somehow got relegated to animal feed; quintessentially Midwestern corn that is so much tastier in butter-slathered breads and baked goods than in ethanol and plastic (a major reason to reach out and make friends with anyone who's growing heritage varieties); and not-just-for-birdseed millet, which has a mild sweetness, earthiness, and soft, dense cooked-grain texture.

The recipes that I'm giving you are time-tested applications of whole grains in all their glory, and they'll be rolled up into breads, pastries, and other baked treats sweet and savory to round out your daily baking rotation. There are staple breads like **Farmhouse Sourdough** (page 125) and **Marbled Rye** (page 169), and also hearth breads—crusty, chewy loaves that are baked directly on a stone or clay baker versus in a loaf pan—that feature less-familiar combinations like **Honey-Oat Porridge Loaf** (page 162), **Sorghum and Rosemary Ciabatta** (page 179), and **Buckwheat and Thyme Loaf** (page 138). You'll find new places for familiar faces like **Oat Dinner Rolls** (page 73) and pizza dough (sourdough, wheat Neapolitan, and whole-grain Roman), and reintroductions to global offerings like **Injera** (page 223), **Volkornbrot** (page 233), and **Whole-Wheat Parathas** (page 235). And in tribute to my grandmother, who was always spending time in the kitchen with me baking, we'll hit the bakery classics ranging from the humble—**Buckwheat Brownies** (page 89), **Oat Doughnuts** (page 100), **Whole-Wheat Sponge Cake with Honey Buttercream** (page 117)—to the humbling—**Bacon-Rye Cheese Rolls** (page 253), **Wheat Brioche** (page 250), **Buckwheat Canelés** (page 267). When it won't affect the integrity of the product, many of the recipes take advantage of alternative sweeteners such as sorghum syrup, maple syrup, and honey in all its essential varieties like acacia, alfalfa, buckwheat, wildflower, and clover. And yes, there will also be ice cream (page 300).

My goal for this book is the same one we have at PQB: that people can tell that the bread comes from *us*. I love getting texts saying things like, "Hey, I'm out at Lula Cafe—this is your guys' stuff, right?" It means—first and foremost—that you can taste that it's made with craft and dedication, and that it lets the grains and fermentation speak for themselves. Our rye bread isn't made with caraway or onions because straight heritage rye is freakin' delicious, especially when used in its cracked, malted, and freshly milled states. And secondly, there's a *signature* to the bread. There's something just a little bit special and different and thoughtful about it. That's why I wanted to write this book—not to teach you how to make *my* bread, but how to discover *yours*. And every step of the way there will be notes, asides, and sidebars coming from pretty much all angles as I walk you through what is essentially a game of trial and error. I share many of the lessons I've learned from royally screwing things up myself, plus other commonly made mistakes, and explain how you can solve them—including how to rouse sleepy yeast or reverse the curse of the hollow loaf.

The path might be wandering, and the uncertainties many, but just as I have put my faith in the process, I believe that this book will get you there too. Here's all the knowledge you need—the science and technique—to connect with your own instincts and feel for the transformation of flour and water into golden loaves.

Go forth—make mistakes, make a mess; make flattened loaves and too-crispy cakes. Because once you do, you'll be one step closer to making the kind of food that you can feel good eating every day. And if you get tripped up, just remember that, yes, we may in fact be living in a galaxy inside an octopus floating around in space.

PART I

Digging In

**Helpful Stuff
for Getting Started**

Bake the Bread You Bake

I DIDN'T WRITE THIS BOOK TO TEACH YOU HOW TO RECREATE the product that I make in a professional bakery. Granted, if you follow these recipes, you're going to make a great loaf, because the techniques I've learned over the years at Publican Quality Bread will get you the most hydrated, flavorful, structurally sound bread. And going that route is totally fine. But I also want to give you the confidence and tools to bake *your* bread at home. This means a few things:

Bread is a living organism. And because of that, it's a product of its environment. The heat, the cold, the humidity, the altitude, heck even the vibes in the room—they all conspire to make a loaf of bread unique. Learning how to adjust to those things has been the key to running a production bakery—not to mention becoming a better, more intuitive baker. I've made a lot of bread in a lot of different places—in home kitchens, in bakeries, on farms—and I've learned how all these shifts can affect the final product, even though the ingredients and the process largely stay constant. So while a recipe can tell you how to make the perfect loaf of bread under ideal conditions, what happens when you live in the real world?

You can either try to manipulate your environment to be perfect for making bread (inadvisable) or adjust your bread for the environment you have (much better idea). This will happen naturally through trial and error as you learn more about your unique baking space—does it run cold? Maybe on the humid side? You'll start to notice the ambient temperatures around your home, and you may even start paying attention to the weather a little bit more, get a little bit more in tune with the environment. If you know it'll be a hot and sticky day, then you might short-mix your bread and add a little bit less water. Conversely, if it's really cold out, you might give it a little bit more time, mix it warm, and keep it in the warmest area of your house. I'll teach you how to read these signs, but you have to learn to look for them. It can be helpful to use a log as you bake to keep track of these variables, which I'll talk more about on page 306.

Bread is personal. Usually you're making it for your family and friends, and there's a lot of dedication attached to it. So it only makes sense that you get personally involved in making it. My goal for you is to begin using these recipes as guidelines, then supplementing them with your intuition and preferences. I encourage you to play around with different flavor profiles through things like spices, seeds, and herbs, and to change up the inclusions (such as dried fruit and nuts). And of course, there's experimenting with the grains themselves, lending each loaf of bread its own unique signature.

Bread is not about an ego trip. I'm telling you right now: You're going to have a lot of failure. Get OK with it! It's about the journey. Even people who are extremely devoted to their craft and have a ton of skills are never going to step back and say, "I made the best bread. I'm the best." Every time we bake, we're manipulating this or that, trying a little more salt or a little less starter, with the ultimate reward

being that we're making the best bread we can. I've had it both ways—I've made exceptional loaves of bread and then come back the next day to replicate it and it's a dismal failure. You just have to revel in the inconsistency and know that it's part of the process. Then, when the bread gods are smilin' on ya and everything has aligned in your favor and you make amazing bread, you'll know that it's possible —even if it's not every time. And in the event of complete meltdown, I've got you. (Check out "Troubleshooting: Help, Everything's on Fire!" on page 323.)

Sometimes it's just about having bread right now. We artisan bakers are constantly trying to challenge ourselves to hydrate our doughs more fully or push our fermentation time. But there's plenty of very valid loaves of bread out there that are not super hydrated and don't contain sourdough starters. *Sometimes you have to make bread for the purpose.* Do you need to be spending three days making bread to have a bun for pulled pork sandwiches? No, you just need a vehicle that's going to be super soft and delicious. Sometimes you need a special loaf for a holiday or a birthday or something you want to celebrate, at which point you'll take the extra time to really take care of it and make it into something super nice. But most of the time, you need bread tonight. Or tomorrow morning. And that bread can be made with the same integrity and intention and pride as the loaves that you take two days to make.

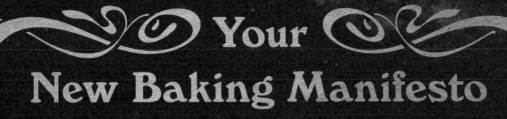

Your New Baking Manifesto

From here forward, in the name of a lifetime of great bread, let's agree to a few guiding principles, which the Dead summed up best:

I need a miracle every day.

Pretty much the most appropriate statement about making bread ever.

Without love in the dream, it will never come true.

Bread can actually feel when you're having a bad day and will turn out in kind. Do it with love.

If you plant ice, you're gonna harvest wind.

Same sentiment: You get out what you put in.

Watch each card you play and play it slow.

Be deliberate in your decisions about how you are going to make your bread.

Talk about your plenty, talk about your ills; one man gathers what another man spills.

Don't be afraid to talk to people about your experiences in baking. Sometimes a discussion can lead to a revelation in your process.

Hang it up and see what tomorrow brings.

Sometimes you just gotta see what happens when you bake it tomorrow. It might just turn out! And if it doesn't, learn from your mistakes and move on.

Sometimes we live no particular way but our own.

Bread should be personal, intimate. Make your own bread; live your own way.

Nothing left to do but smile, smile, smile.

This is when all your hard work finally results in a great loaf of bread!

A Glossary of Terms

You might stumble upon some of these throughout the book. Here's what you need to know:

Crumb: The fluffy interior part of the bread. Particularly with hearth loaves, you can judge your fermentation by the internal structure of the bread, or the crumb. Those holes that you're looking at when you crack open a loaf are called alveoli. They can be uniform or irregular, large or small, and different breads are going for different things. For sandwich breads, you want them tight with a closed face, versus a sourdough where you're looking for the open, irregular structure (sometimes called honeycomb) that you get through the mixing process, the hydration of the dough, and the use of a sourdough levain (more on that later).

If you're cutting into your sourdough and it's really closed in structure and dense, it means you haven't trapped all the gas you need to leaven the bread, so you're relying on just the existing yeast to spread the gluten web. What does that mean for next time? (1) Your starter may not have been as active as you wanted it to be, and/or (2) You probably didn't bulk ferment for long enough, and/or (3) You may not have individually fermented long enough.

If you've overproofed the bread, you'll know because your loaf will have what's called "flying crust," meaning there's a significant gap between your crust and your crumb.

Crust: You've certainly heard of bread crust, but it is something we bakers identify, judge, and grade. A good crust is an outer ring of bread that gets nice and caramelized through the baking process.

Elasticity: How much resistance you'll get when you're stretching your dough.

Extensibility: How far dough will extend when stretched. This'll tell you how the gluten's been developed. If your dough snaps and breaks when pulled, then it's not extensible enough and needs to be mixed more to develop more gluten. There's also such a thing as *too* extensible, or flaccid and stringy, meaning you've likely overmixed. You've developed so much gluten that it's to the point where you've deteriorated your dough. At that point, best to scrap things and start again.

Elasticity versus Extensibility: These two qualities have an inverse relationship—you can have a dough that's not elastic enough and too extensible. Or too elastic and not extensible enough. What you want is for it to be both. You want it to stretch but also give you some resistance.

Gluten: Gluten is an elastic substance that is formed when two of the naturally occurring proteins in wheat—glutenin and gliadin—are allowed to commingle and combine in the medium of water. Gluten is what provides bread with its structure and its ability to be leavened. It's that simple. Unfortunately, gluten has become synonymous with a lot of health issues, but that has more to do with the flour and processes you're using to bake (more on that on page 33).

Inclusion: Think of inclusions like inside-the-bread confetti—nuts, seeds, fruit, and herbs.

Preferment: A portion of dough that's allowed to ferment with yeast before it's added back into the mix. This will not only deepen the flavor but also start to break down the complex sugars of the wheat, giving you the health benefits of a fermented bread. Preferments are so called because you are fermenting a portion of the flour before you make your final mix. There are different types of preferments, but the benefits are all similar: You are developing structure and enhancing flavor while also reducing your final dough mixing time. That said, you will get different flavor profiles and structures from each type, particularly whether you use sourdough or commercial yeast. It's kind of an "all squares are rectangles, but not all rectangles are squares" situation. All sourdough starters/levains are preferments, but not all preferments are sourdough, ya dig?

Types of Preferments

Levain: The proper French term for your sourdough starter.

Poolish: A preferment made with commercial yeast, typically 100 percent hydrated or more. Bread flavors will be more complex, with a moderately open cell structure in the crumb.

Biga: A preferment made with commercial yeast, typically 40 to 50 percent hydrated. Bread flavors will be more "yeasty," with a very open cell structure in the crumb.

Proofing: Also called proving or bulk fermentation, proofing is the step in the bread-making process when the dough is showing proof that it is alive. The one indication of this that we can see is it's growing in size. What we don't see during this time is that your dough is establishing the building blocks of its internal structure, becoming more extensible and workable, and developing flavor. I like to say that bulk fermentation is what allows your loaves to express themselves during final or individual fermentation. If you don't bulk ferment to begin, the loaves will never reach their full potential.

Using This Book for Ultimate Bread Success

THE RECIPES IN THIS BOOK ARE DESIGNED TO INCREASE THE tools in your toolbox one by one. It comes back to practicing—again, and again, and again. Seeing what you like and what you don't, what works and what doesn't. And I'm going to help you out, too.

First, start with a recipe that is good and simple, preferably from "Like a Road Leading Home" (Chapter 1). Maybe it's a no-starter or no-unusual-flour-required loaf like **A Good White Bread** (page 68). Or a recognizable recipe that's a riff on something you know and doesn't require much by way of assembly, like **Buckwheat Banana Bread** (page 86) or **Sorghum Blondies** (page 103). See, nothing scary here.

Then, build on that confidence and enthusiasm with "Golden Loaves to Unlimited Devotion" (Chapter 2). Maybe try out a simple porridge bread—it's no different than what you were doing in the previous chapter, but now you're pre-cooking some of the grains before mixing and baking. The **Carolina Gold** (page 141) will check that box, as will the **Honey-Oat Porridge Loaf** (page 162), in addition to providing you with tasty table bread. Maybe now you start adding some inclusions, a fancy word for things like dried fruit and nuts that get folded into the dough. **Millet Porridge and Cherry Loaf** (page 135) and **Peach and Cashew Loaf** (page 130) might have your name on 'em.

Next, on to things like **Farmhouse Sourdough** (page 125), **Seeded Pumpernickel** (page 149), or **Sorghum and Rosemary Ciabatta** (page 179). You'll be making what sounds tasty for your next sandwich, stew sopper, or fettunta while also picking up the basics of working with a sourdough starter, keeping an eye on dough and water temperature, and shaping your loaves.

Feeling frisky? Move on to "Fire on the Mountain" (Chapter 3) for recipes that are traditionally cooked with live fire but can also be made on the grill, in a skillet, or in the home oven, like **Wheat Pitas** (page 197), **Sourdough Pizza Dough** (page 209), and **Rye Naan** (page 199). Basics stay the same, but now we're digging more deeply into the environment that the dough gets baked in and how that influences flavor.

"Long, Strange Trip" (Chapter 4) features breads that step outside the Western approach and are shining examples of grains used in their cultural and agronomical context. They showcase whole grains coupled with techniques that you don't traditionally find in the American bakery. Think

Injera (page 223), **Whole-Wheat Parathas** (page 235), and **White Wheat Tortillas** (page 241).

"Friends of the Devil" (Chapter 5) will bring you even further down the path with recipes that are indulgent and decadent, and take a little more hands-on time in the kitchen—**Sourdough Pizzelles** (page 299), **Bacon-Rye Cheese Rolls** (page 253), and **Whole-Wheat Croissants** (page 277), among others.

I know you may be tempted to jump right in and make those **Maple Rye Kouign Amann** (page 285), but let's start simple. Let's build a progression of skills. And in the process, let's fill you with the confidence that you too can bake great bread, and fill your bread box with an abundance of delicious baked goods.

Roasted Garlic and Mashed Potato Ciabatta (page 173)

If you've come all this way and you're getting super consistent results, we'll start talking about how you can manipulate the recipes using tools like baker's percentages and water temperature algebra, and even how to build your own recipes. In time, though, in time.

A Note on Baker's Percentages

You'll notice that all the recipes in this book contain what are called baker's percentages, or ingredients expressed as a ratio relative to the amount of flour used. (Or when there's no flour, to the main ingredient such as milk in pastry cream.) This is a metric that bakers use in order to scale their recipes up or down in order to suit the needs of production and have their product stay consistent. It's also useful when creating your own recipes.

This is not, I repeat, *not* a required tool for you to use, especially if you're just starting out. As I'll go into in much more detail on page 313, I've simply included them in the event that you choose to make your own recipes or find yourself wanting to scale up these recipes. After all, they're a crucial part of my outcomes as a baker and a handy tool to have at your disposal. So if you're a professional baker already, you're most likely familiar with using baker's percentages. And if you're an aspiring professional, they're something I recommend getting to know. But otherwise, feel free to ignore them entirely.

You'll also notice that I've included a section dedicated to "Digging Deeper" (page 303). This is where you'll, yes, hear more about baker's percentages, along with other techniques and know-how for adding nuance to your bread baking—how to manipulate fermentation, or troubleshoot where you might have taken a wrong turn. It's all about helping you understand the rhyme and reason behind the build of a loaf of bread, whether you're just starting out or adding new skills to your repertoire.

A Note on Yields

As you go through the bread recipes in this book, you'll notice that many of them yield more than one loaf. This is not because I couldn't be bothered to scale the recipes from my bakery. On the contrary: When you're learning to make bread, it's helpful to repeat the process a second time—often you'll learn something that next time around, whether it's getting the hang of shaping the dough or nailing the bake. But above all, excellent homemade bread can be repurposed in all manner of ways, freezes well, and makes a nice gift for a friend. So as you can see, there's no downside to that second loaf.

Better Flour for Better Bread

Perhaps the most important aspect of this book, aside from actually getting in the kitchen and making good food, is understanding where grains come from, how they're grown, and why this should matter—to your bread, to your health, and to our planet. Bread is what originally brought me back to the land, to the Midwestern farms that steward soil as it's meant to be nurtured, and grow the wheat and grains as they're meant to be grown. After meeting Marty Travis from Spence Farm, and then his son Will, along with a few other groovy folks like Harold Wilken at Janie's Farm, Jill Brockman-Cummings at Janie's Mill, and Lou Kozma at Hirzel Farms, I learned how much of a role small noncash crops play in a biodynamic farm system and why we all have a stake in driving the need for and use of these crops.

The truth is, not all grains are created equal. Some are grown season after season in tired, nutrient-depleted soil; raised and harvested with abrasive chemicals; and milled with additives to enhance the look of the final product (bleach, for example). They are grown for the bottom line, and the flavor and nutrient value reflect that. On the other hand, some grains are grown to actively nourish the soil, replacing what naturally gets depleted after supporting the nutritional demand of crops like corn, soybeans, and tomatoes. They come from seeds bred for integrity, not just to withstand pesticides. In fact, they don't need that extra junk because a good, healthy plant comes equipped with its own allelopathic protection, meaning it produces its own biochemicals that protect itself against things like pests and disease while not damaging the soil. And these grains in turn make a world of difference in how your bread tastes and how it makes you feel.

In my opinion—and in the opinion of my agronomist buddy, Gary Reding (because whenever possible I go to the most knowledgeable person I can, and in this case, it's Gary), there's bad farming, better farming, and best farming. And as a result, there's not-great flour, better flour, and best flour. Here's how it breaks down:

Not-Great Flour: Industrial Conventional Wheat

Although there are two different growing styles of commodity wheat (irrigated and nonirrigated) and two different types of wheat grown (spring and winter), by and large the conventional wheat grown for bread on an industrial level shares a few similarities:

It's monoculture farming. This is the modern industrial practice of planting the same species of crop on the same land, over and over again, in order to pump out as much of that crop as possible. This comes with a number of downsides, namely:

- Plant pathogens and diseases can adapt to the soil and attack the crops.

- The soil builds up a tolerance to pesticides from repeated use, requiring more and stronger chemicals to be used.

- The land's mineral value diminishes, leading to the necessity for adding inferior synthetic nutrients back into the soil.

The land sits bare between plantings. Regardless of the type of wheat these farmers are planting, there will be a lag of at least a few months between when one crop is harvested and the next one goes into the ground. And in that time, nothing is planted in the soil. You'd think that might be a nice rest, but according to Gary, "Mother Nature does not want land bare, ever. It's not natural; it's not how things go." Think about weeds—nature *wants* things growing at all times. That's because when earth is left bare, the soil gets compacted by the pounding of rain, snow, and wind, making it more difficult to grow future plants. Also, the organic matter in the soil gets depleted, including the beneficial bacteria that make plants healthy. Lastly, plantless soil can't effectively trap carbon dioxide, so it gets released back into the environment. (Mismanaged farmland is a big contributor to the climate crisis.)

It's not growing in healthy soil. Because of the repeated plantings of the same crop and the fact that the land is left barren for long stretches, the soil that's receiving these wheat seeds is already behind the eight ball when it comes to vital nutrients. As a "solution," commodity farmers have adopted Big Ag's "NPK mentality," or the belief that all they need to do is pump the soil full of synthetic nutrients—in this case nitrogen, phosphorous, and potassium—in addition to a host of pesticides, the blanket term for fungicides, insecticides, and herbicides. Nutritionally deficient soil also leads to a nutritionally deficient crop. So when we eat those plants, we're not reaping all the vital nutrients that we technically should be. In fact, researchers have found that the mineral deficiencies in our crops mimics the deficiencies in our own physiology.

It's delivering the glyphosate. Glyphosate is the most widely used pesticide in the United States. It's a suspected carcinogen and is also a registered antibiotic, which means that it's annihilating beneficial bacteria in both the soil and in your gut, which paves the way for a variety of chronic diseases. Glyphosate also happens to be the main ingredient in the herbicide Roundup. Commercial growers apply Roundup to speed the drying process of the wheat come harvest time, which would traditionally be left up to the sun, but that would take longer. It is strongly suspected that gluten is not to blame for the rise in wheat intolerance, but rather glyphosate. More on that in a bit. This also raises the issue of seeds being bred for ease of growth, versus selecting traits such as nutrient density.

It's milled in a commercial mill. This is significant because two things happen to commercial wheat in a large-scale mill that make it into less-than-ideal-flour:

- *They're not using the whole grain.* During the milling process, the grains are cracked open and separated into the germ, the bran, and the endosperm. The germ and the bran are discarded and occasionally go on to be used as animal feed. But that's where all your micronutrients and B vitamins are. The endosperm, on the other hand, is pretty much just pure carbohydrates. That's what's being pulverized into white flour.

- *They're adding bleach.* Seriously. It's not called bleach on the label, but "bromate" or "potassium bromate" are bleaching agents. They do this for two reasons: First, aesthetics. Back in the day, when the serfs were growing and milling the flour for the king, the royal kitchen would get the sifted flour, which was lighter, and the peasants would get the darker, heavier flour that was left over. Over time, whiter flour was prized—particularly for the lighter, fluffier cakes it yielded—and bleaching agents were added.

Second, these bleaching agents speed up the aging process of the flour. General consensus among all bakers is that freshly milled or "green" flour is relatively volatile and therefore more difficult to work with when baking. But instead of letting the flour age naturally, which would cost the mill money as the flour just sat in a warehouse for a month, a bleaching agent is added to expedite things.

For the record, we use some refined flour in the bakery. (Though, granted, it's a nicely grown product that is not bleached.) We mix it with freshly milled flour from local farms because then we get the best of both worlds: the integrity of dough from the refined plus the nutrition and flavor from the fresh.

Better Flour: Industrial Organic Wheat

Commercial, large-scale organic wheat is notably different from conventional in that it's being organically managed—that is, no chemical pesticides are used to grow it and no Roundup is being used to end the growing cycle. (Although there is a bit of wiggle room in the organic designation that allows for some pesticide use.) And instead of applying synthetic nutrients to the soil, farmers might use things like compost in order to naturally enrich the soil. Then, at the milling stage, an organic product isn't going to include a bleaching agent. So commercial organic flour is a big step up from conventional, but it's still not the best option out there, namely because many large commercial operations aren't able to steward the land in a way that smaller local operations are because of their volume of output, not to mention having a different relationship with both growing cycles and community than the folks I'll introduce you to in the next section. That said, grocery-shelf familiars like King Arthur, Bob's Red Mill, and Anson Mills are solid, easy-to-find options, in addition to any smaller regional outfits that might be represented in your baking aisle.

Best Flour: Locally and Sustainably Grown Wheat

The local food system focuses on soil health and plant nutrition, which leads to better crop quality. And you know what that leads to? The best flour for bread. Here's why:

There's more than one crop in rotation. Instead of growing only wheat or only corn, these farmers are rotating their crops. So while they may grow vegetables as their for-profit crop in the summer, they're going to follow that with a small grain, and then maybe a cover crop or grazing crop like clover or alfalfa. Then after a year, when the soil has had time to rest, it's back to planting veggies. A

common rotation that you'll see is corn, soybeans, wheat or oats, and hay. This rotation helps preserve the nutrients in the soil while also relieving pest and disease pressure.

It harnesses the power of the plants. As mentioned, all small grains have what's called an allelopathic effect, meaning they produce their own pesticides and herbicides. These are not detrimental to the other rotational crops, and they do not kill microbes in the soil. This is particularly beneficial to farmers when they're growing winter oats or winter wheat because there's always something green and growing in the soil, but it's not allowing weeds to take over. These plants are going to be the first things up in the spring, and farmers then have the choice to either grow the plants to maturity as an additional crop to use or sell, or simply turn them into the fields and send those nutrients back into the soil.

It's working with Mother Nature, not against her. Small-scale farmers also often rotate in livestock like cows and chickens to pasture over the fields. They keep the soil nice and loose by walking over it as they graze, as well as replenishing the microbes and nutrients in the soil (thanks, poop) and diminishing the pests (thanks, bug-eating chickens).

Healthier plants are tastier plants. The more successfully a plant grows and the healthier it is, the better it'll taste. That's because each phase in the growth cycle contributes different attributes to a plant. First, there's successful photosynthesis,

Using a tabletop mill to crack grains

which helps develop the complex carbohydrates in a plant. Next, a plant starts forming complete proteins, which helps it naturally defend itself from insects with simple digestive systems. If a plant can do that, then it can start storing energy in the form of fats and oils, which it uses to build strong cell membranes that protect it from airborne pathogens and UV radiation. From there, it goes on to produce secondary metabolites, meaning it's now resistant to insects and animals that have complex digestive systems. And then, as the grand finale, the plant starts producing bioflavonoids. These are what make a crop taste like what it is. So when you've reached this ultimate level of plant health, you're going to have a much more flavorful crop, no matter what it is. But if a plant is relying on pesticides and synthetic soil enhancements to do that job for it, it's never going to reach that tasty apex.

It's not about the strongest surviving. Whereas industrial farmers are incentivized to grow wheat from seeds that have been bred to withstand pesticides, smaller farmers aren't bound by that. Instead, they can choose what they grow based on things like flavor and function. When I first started working with Marty to figure out what kind of small grains he could grow and mill for me at the bakery, we started from seed. First, we looked at the genetics that would work best in the environment and type of soil where he's growing. Then, we looked at how they taste and how they perform. I had my friend Paul Spence (no relation to Spence Farm) send me a bunch of varieties of wheat from his farm in Ontario so I could bake

with them. Some were better for flavor, while others were better for baking, meaning that they lent themselves to a good rise and structure. Between Marty's need for a resilient agronomic crop and my need for a delicious and functional wheat flour, we chose our top three favorites: Warthog, Turkey Red, and Red Fife. Then, he grew those varieties in the same field, which is called polycropping. That meant that these plants each benefitted from the different biology of the others—some were more resistant to this, others to that. The overall effect was fewer pests, less disease, and a greater variety of nutrients in the soil. And when it was time for

Malted rye soaker

Marty to harvest and mill those grains, I ended up with a flour that delivered all the properties I needed—a blend we lovingly call "WTF flour," after the initials of the three types of wheat.

But the coolest thing of all is that Marty could save the seeds from that harvest—something conventional farmers are legally not allowed to do owing to their contracts with Bayer, who sells them their Roundup-ready seeds. Over the course of the growing season, all Marty's plants had cross-pollinated, leading to seeds that would go on to produce plants that not only combined the strengths of the three original plants, but were also completely unique to his farm.

It's a system based on trust. Marty put it best: "This model is better than organic because it's based on trust." For small farmers, the consumer is the regulator, not the government. These farmers rely on keeping their customers happy and knowing they're getting the best possible product—otherwise, they've got nothing. There's no incentive for betraying that.

What This All Has to Do with Gluten Intolerance

These days, it seems like everyone is eating wheat and feeling bad. And there's a reason for that—it has to do with the way in which the wheat is grown, managed, harvested, milled, and baked. Your body isn't built to be eating wheat that's been sprayed with pesticides throughout its life cycle, finished off with glyphosate, and treated with bleach at a commercial mill. All those chemical factors can wreak havoc on your gut health, which in turn affects how you're able to break down and digest food.

Another big problem is that most commercial wheat is being shipped off to commercial bakeries, where it's not fermented before it's baked into bread. Smaller bakeries, on the other hand, use a natural sourdough starter to create their product. This not only makes bread taste better thanks to its natural acids (lactic and acetic), but it also creates a chemical reaction that makes wheat easier to digest.

Dig this: Wheat flour is made up pretty much entirely by complex carbohydrates that are really tough for our bodies to digest. The scientific name for these carbohydrates is FODMAPs, which stands for fermentable oligosaccharides, disaccharides, monosaccharides, and polyols. Because FODMAPs aren't readily broken down by the small intestine, they tend to get fermented by your gut bacteria, leading to bloating, abdominal pain, gas, and IBS. No good.

But after just four hours of natural sourdough fermentation—way less than a loaf typically gets from start to finish—those FODMAPs are almost entirely broken down. Sourdough starters also create branch-chain amino acids, which regulate the intake of sugars into your bloodstream. So you're first breaking down the complex-sugar FODMAPs into simple sugars through fermentation, then the branch-chain aminos give the assist to get those sugars smoothly assimilated into your system. The result: no blood sugar spike.

And yet another great thing that happens with a sourdough starter is that you now have an enzyme

called phytase in the mix. Phytase breaks down phytic acid, which most grains contain as a way to preserve their own nutrients. The only problem is that phytic acid can actively block you from absorbing nutrients like iron, zinc, and calcium when you eat those grains. Enter phytase, which unlocks all those fiber-derived minerals and B vitamins that grain has to offer.

Just one more (pretty great) reason to vote for sustainably, responsibly grown, milled, and baked wheat.

How Do We Fit into the Growing Cycle?

Easy: Get to know your farmers. Seek out local producers and put your money where your mouth is. Ask if they're growing small grains—many farmers do and don't bring it to market with them. Or ask if they'd consider growing small grains in the future. Be mindful of the fact that many of these folks don't have access to the same large-scale distribution as their industrial counterparts. There are prohibitive hoops to jump through at almost every level, whether it's the cost of maintaining an FDA organic designation, not being in close proximity to the big milling and shipping operations that are mostly based in the West, or not meeting the food safety regulations in place by big grocery distributors, like being able to put all your product through an X-ray machine. (We run up against that all the time.)

The important thing to remember here is that this is about how we all work together to make something greater than the sum of the parts. Nobody can, or should, do everything themselves; we need to find good people to support us, and in turn, we support them. It's healthier for the soil, it's healthier for the environment, it's ultimately healthier for us, and it makes for more nuanced, more alive, more sustaining, and more delicious bread.

Where Can I Buy Better Flour?

When it comes to buying better ingredients in general—whether it's flour, honey, eggs, or butter—your local farmers' market is a gold mine because you can engage the farmers in a conversation about their growing and stewardship practices. And products that have not only been made with care but also haven't had to travel a long distance or sit on a grocery store shelf are going to taste better.

You could also enlist the help of the following resources, which I've curated through my work with the Artisan Grain Collaborative, Spence Farm Foundation, and other groovy cats who have put together some equally groovy information.

- *Small mills with online platforms:* A growing number of "local" operations now offer their products online. Some great options include Janie's Mill (JaniesMill.com), Cairnspring Mills (Cairnspring.com), and Farmer Ground Flour (FarmerGroundFlour.com).

- *Illinois Stewardship Alliance* has assembled the Buy Fresh Buy Local guide that lists growers, food producers, and bakeries from whom you can buy directly (ilstewards.org/wp-content/uploads/2013/06/2012_BFBL_Directory_reduced.pdf).

- *Artisan Grain Collaborative* maintains an interactive map that includes regional flour producers throughout the country (Grain Collaborative.com/our-network).

- *Challenger Breadware* keeps a pretty comprehensive, up-to-date list for flour sourcing worldwide (ChallengerBreadware.com/where-to-buy-grains-flours).

- *Simply Local* (SimplyLocal.io) is an app that lets you plug in your address and see local farms near you and what they produce. It's a great way to find not only grains but also proteins, eggs, milk, and produce.

Say Hey to the Grains

Types of Grains

Rye

Rye flour was like my local farm grain gateway drug. I got my hands on this fresh-ground rye and soaked it overnight so it would start to ferment naturally (aka my soaker method). Now, normally, when you open a bag of conventional commercial rye flour, it smells kinda like dusty cardboard. But this stuff? It had fermented so actively that the aroma coming off the bowl was spicy and floral and fruity all at the same time. There was no way I was going back, and now rye is one of my favorite grains to use. It's my go-to for bread, and it can work in some pastries, though you wouldn't want to soak it in those cases because it does ferment so well that it can weaken your gluten structure and overpower the flavor. That said, rye is perfectly suited for thinner doughs like phyllo (as you'll see on page 289) because the natural structure of rye flour makes it extensible, or able to stretch thin. Luckily you can find good-quality rye flour from local producers and from small mills who sell their goods online, such as Janie's Mill, or you can go with a larger organic producer such as King Arthur, Bob's Red Mill, or Anson Mills.

Note: Rye flour is interchangeable with cracked rye in all the recipes in this book except for the Volkornbrot **(page 233).**

Millet

This is a great grain for when you want to work with something that just sort of melts into your bread as opposed to taking over, flavor-wise. When toasted and cooked into a porridge, millet adds a mild cereal-y flavor. It's not super earthy tasting like rye or buckwheat, but it does add a subtle quality that enhances the overall product. Just keep in mind that if you don't toast it first, it won't add much flavor, and if you don't cook it first, it'll absorb so much moisture during the cooking process that the bread will be dry and crumbly.

Buckwheat

This one's not technically a grain, but we treat it as such. We use what's called a buckwheat groat and mill it into flour. It's kind of like rye's dusty, earthy cousin in flavor and performance, and it pairs incredibly well with "dark flavors," like baking spices, molasses, and chocolate. I particularly love using it in **Buckwheat Brownies** (page 89) because it deepens the chocolate flavor. And one of my favorite things to do with buckwheat is pairing it with buckwheat honey, which is kind of like a cross between honey and molasses if they were hanging out in a barn—kinda funky. You may or may not want to drizzle it on toast, but in a baked product, it's really nice.

As I mentioned earlier, buckwheat produces more nectar for honeybees per plant than any other plant, so it's excellent for pollinators. Also, this plant is a great nitrogen fixer, or more specifically it hosts nitrogen-fixing bacteria, meaning it puts nitrogen back into the soil, versus a grain, which takes nitrogen out. In my garden, I grow buckwheat in the late fall and winter as a cover crop.

Rice

Rice is just the thing when a baked good calls for a lighter flavor profile. It's also loaded with starch, so when you pre-cook white rice into a porridge (as these recipes call for), it adds a real richness and tenderness to the bread because those grains retain a ton of moisture in the finished product.

Corn

Growing up in the Midwest, I was surrounded by corn. But it was pretty much all used for animal feed or ethanol. Now, as a Midwest baker, I've made it a goal to add corn to my baking—but not just any corn. As a way of sticking it to all the not-good genetically modified corn that's grown on so many industrial farms in this region, I seek out heirloom varieties of dried corn such as Floriani and Bloody Butcher, which are deep red, and Orange Zdrowie, which is as acid orange as the name implies. I'm not only getting a superior product that has a much more intense flavor, I'm also able to use all the different colors to do something visually interesting. What's also pretty cool about the corn I get from Marty is that he was taught how to grow and preserve Iroquois white corn seed by members of the Iroquois Nation, who wanted to nurture this tradition and keep it alive on his farm. They also taught him how to fire-roast it, giving it a super smoky flavor that's incredible in bread, pizza, dough, and danishes.

In general, if using cornmeal in a baked good, you're going to want to cook it first into a polenta-like porridge before adding it to a dough because otherwise it'll suck up a ton of moisture. You could also soak it overnight in buttermilk to start hydrating and breaking down some of the starches (see **Heritage Cornbread**, page 91.)

Sorghum

Sorghum is a flowering grass grown for syrup, as well as for cereal and fodder for livestock. It's native to Africa, Australia, and Asia, but it's grown pretty much everywhere else, too. As a crop, it's a wise choice for farmers because it doesn't require much nitrogen and it's drought- and heat-tolerant—which is why you see it primarily grown in the South here in the United States. (Though I've seen it grown in Illinois as well.) Sorghum is another "lighter" flavored grain, but what sets it apart from millet and rice is its rich and buttery flavor. It's great in baked goods where that's exactly what you want—ciabatta, blondies, cookies, quick breads. You can also pop it like corn; it makes smaller and subsequently more adorable kernels than regular popcorn. This is another grain that you're going to be cooking or soaking before you use it so it doesn't steal the hydration from your final product.

Spelt

Consider this your Universal Whole Grain. For some reason, no matter what you're baking, if you sub in spelt 1:1 for all-purpose flour, it's going to work. Even if you go 100 percent whole grain. It's a flour that I really rely on: If I don't know what I want to be doing, I usually ask spelt. Because (1) it's going to work and (2) the flavor profile is one of those middle-of-the-road gamblers. No one's going to eat a baked product with it and say, "Oh, that's spelt." That said, as a naturally occurring hybrid between red wheat and emmer wheat, spelt is getting down into the earthy notes, flavor-wise, without being as spicy or floral as rye or as nutty as whole wheat.

Oats

I love the flavor of oats, especially when they're grown really well like Ron Ackerman—our bakery's supplier—does. It's the difference between the cardboard-like flavor and texture of what comes out of a canister from the store and something that has a deep, nutty aroma and a creamy, buttery quality. Night and day.

For the most part, I recommend cooking oats as a porridge before adding them to your dough because of how they retain moisture. Some people are into toasting oats first too, but I disagree—there's no need to mess with their natural flavor. I like working with oats in pie dough and other "dryer" pastry work because their natural quality of hoarding moisture inherently adds to what you're going for in that product.

Wheat

This is the big one because wheat is the most common grain grown pretty much everywhere. But why I really want to talk about wheat is because there are so many more varieties out there being grown by smaller farmers than what you'll find in the flour on the shelf at the store. Most of the time, if you need flour, that's what you're going to do—go to the supermarket and buy a bag of wheat flour, whether it's cake flour, all-purpose flour, bread flour, high-gluten flour, whatever. You're not choosing between white or red wheat, hard or soft, winter or spring. All those nuances affect flavor and outcome—white being lighter and less nutty than red, essentially the difference between an almond and a walnut. Still nuts, just a different intensity.

Harder winter wheat is higher in protein than soft spring wheat, and more protein means more gluten, making one better for breads and pizza dough (hard) and the other better for pastry (soft). (Fun fact: Soft wheat grows better in the South, which is why their foodways are filled with biscuits and pies and not so much with structured breads.) So while, yes, you could just go to the store and call it a day, why not see what the small farms around you are growing and figure out how to incorporate that into your baking?

Note: Wheat flour or bulgur can be substituted for cracked wheat in any of these recipes using the same measures. Cracked wheat is the whole wheat berry that's been cracked into a few pieces. Even though it can be slightly more difficult to source than other grains, I like to use it because I have found that when you make a soaker with it, the grain ferments on its own a little differently than if you make the soaker with wheat flour. Cracked wheat gets sweet as it ferments, and it incorporates into the final dough as more of an inclusion than into the structure of the dough itself.

Types of Wheat Flour

When choosing what kind of wheat flour to work with, it's important to know the differences, because they're not equal. Each is created with a blend of wheat that's intended to be used for a specific purpose, and you want the right product for the right application. Set yourself up for success from the get-go and use the kind of flour that the job (and recipe) calls for.

In the US, flour is graded by protein percentage. The higher the percentage of protein, the more gluten you'll be able to develop, and the "tougher" your final product will be.

Cake flour

Cake flour is generally between 3 and 5 percent protein. This is desirable for baked goods that should be light and fluffy.

Pastry flour

Pastry flour is between 5 and 7 or 8 percent. This is what you'd use when you want something to hold its shape but still be soft, like cookies, pie dough, and maybe biscuits (though I prefer all-purpose for biscuits).

All-purpose flour

All-purpose flour is 8 to 10 percent. They call it "all-purpose" for a reason—it's your go-to because you can use it for pretty much anything middle-of-the-road. Is a cake made with cake flour going to be better? Yes. But will it work with AP? Also yes. If you've got nothing else, AP will usually work in a pinch, but your product is going to be middle-of-the-road because you're not using the flour specifically designed for what it is you're making.

Bread flour

Bread flour is 10 to 12 percent. This is what you'll use for pretty much all bread. You're going to get good gluten development, which you need for proper fermentation and capturing the gases during that fermentation while still maintaining your loaf structure throughout the process. I prefer a bread flour that's 11 to 11.5 percent, and not the max of 12.

High-gluten flour

High-gluten flour is 12 and up. It is possible to have too much of a good thing, so while we want good gluten development in our bread, we don't want to go overboard. You wouldn't want to use high-gluten flour to make a "lean" bread—one that's just flour, water, yeast, and salt—because it would blow up like a torpedo (as in, more full moon than half moon) and be very, very tough in texture. But it does have its applications. Sometimes I'll add high-gluten flour to what we call high-ratio products— or things with a ton of fat: think brioche and panettone. It's also acceptable if you're blending it with a higher volume of a non-glutenous grain, like millet, oats, or buckwheat, because it'll add more structure to your bread.

To make sure your flour doesn't go rancid on you, store it in an airtight container at room temperature for up to a month (though in most cases, you could get away with two to three). If you have flour that you won't get around to using in that timeframe, you can store it in the freezer for upwards of a year. You'll want to bring it to room temperature before you bake with it, though, so the temperature won't affect your recipe.

What You'll Need

Equipment

Kitchen scale: Bread baking is all about precision, and a kitchen scale makes that possible. It also makes it easy. There's nothing fussy about throwing a bunch of ingredients in a bowl and checking the weight. You could use measuring cups—and I've given you those measurements—but especially when it comes to working with different flours that may differ slightly in how they're ground or how much moisture they retain, weighing your ingredients is going to help you nail consistency and recreate the kind of bread these recipes are meant to produce. I cannot stress this enough: If you are going to bake, buy yourself a digital scale and ditch the American standard system. You can get a decent model online for about twenty dollars.

Mixing bowls: You'll want bowls in a few different sizes, including one that's bigger than you think you'll need. Sometimes you just need a big fuckin' bowl. I like stainless steel.

Stand mixer (with dough hook, paddle, and whisk attachments): You could make a lot of these recipes by hand—especially the sweet stuff— but a mixer will make your life a lot easier. If you want to splurge, go for an Ankarsrum, which is one of the best table-top spiral mixers for hearth loaves that money can buy. Otherwise, a regular KitchenAid will do just fine.

Pizza stone: Find one that will fit in your oven and/or grill. Heavier is better because the heavier the stone, the more heat it will retain, and the more even your bake will be. If you're not in the store and picking these things up to compare, most websites will list each product's weight.

Clay baker or Challenger cast-iron bread pan: These are what you bake your bread in to mimic a clay oven. La Cloche makes a nice clay baker, but I'm a really big fan of the Challenger pan (full transparency: I'm a Challenger Breadware ambassador). That's mainly because it's designed specifically for this style of baking, as it retains the perfect amount of heat and steam. It's far and away the best product you could use for the job and is worth the investment. It's also worth noting that you could use a cast-iron Dutch oven, but with its deep walls and lack of handle designed specifically for lifting a very hot, very heavy item off a loaf of bread, it can be a little precarious.

Proofing baskets: There are many different types that you can find—especially online—and they all have different merits. The standard you'll see in most bakeries are reed baskets, and those do the job and serve the purpose. But really wet doughs have a tendency to sink into the cracks of the basket. There are also wood pulp baskets, which I haven't personally used, but some of the bakers I respect use them and their bread looks real pretty because the baskets are etched with different designs. But I think the best option is a wicker basket lined with linen. That way you get support and breathability, and the linen is stitched so tightly that the dough won't stick. Then all you need to do after you've used it is take a firm-bristle brush and

brush the whole thing out, or use a bowl scraper. If you do that, you won't have an issue with mold or bugs. Granted, I once worked with a baker who brought his own mold-caked baskets and said the French would "call this flavor," but I'm not into that. If you do catch some mold creeping in—and it can happen—just throw your baskets in a 500°F oven for 2 or 3 minutes.

Do not, however, under any circumstances buy a plastic proofing basket. The whole point of using a proofing basket is to allow the dough to breathe while it's proofing, and plastic isn't going to let you do that. And the wetter doughs will just stick to them. They'll try to sell you on them being dishwasher-safe, but you're not saving any hassle.

Linen: This is used for covering your dough while it rests and assisting with shaping, in the case of baguettes. You can find unbleached linen cloths specifically for this purpose (called couches, pronounced "kooches"), but you could also use any sort of clean kitchen or tea towels that don't have the fuzzies, if you know what I'm sayin'. Most of the time your dough won't even stick to these cloths, or you can use a dry brush to get everything off, but if you're dealing with something a bit wetter, take a bench scraper and carefully scrape off any dough, taking care not to rip the cloth. Don't just throw the cloth into the wash, or you'll end up with a caked-on mess.

Digital thermometer: This is the easiest way to determine dough and water temperature. Any digital probe thermometer will do.

Bench scraper: This comes in handy for pre-shaping your dough, moving dough from place to place, and taming unruly/wet dough.

Bowl scraper: I like using this to get up under my dough after it's been mixed to ensure that there aren't any pockets of flour hiding at the bottom. It also helps coax dough out of the mixing bowl, especially if it's on the wetter side.

Pastry brush: You'll want one not only for brushing egg wash onto loaves and pastries, but also for removing excess flour from your laminated pastries.

Ruler: This is extremely useful when it comes to laminated pastries.

Lame (pronounced "lahm"): This curved razor is what you'll use to score the top of your loaves before you bake. Chefs get to buy really nice knives, but bakers don't really have fancy stuff made for them, so a lot of us like to treat ourselves to something nice like a wood-handled razor where you can change out the blade. Check out a site like Etsy to find some good people making unique lame handles, then just buy a pack of razor cartridges. I use a brand called Derby.

Spider: This is a small straining tool that you'll use to scoop things from hot water or oil. You can buy super cheap ones from restaurant supply shops, but they're often aluminum. Especially when you're dealing with pretzels and the lye solution they get boiled in, you absolutely cannot use aluminum

because it will cause a chemical reaction. Get a stainless steel spider instead, or go with stainless steel tongs.

A Note on Salt: Salt isn't technically "equipment," but it's no less essential and will get used just about every time you reach for this book. I use fine sea salt in the bakery and in these recipes because the finer the salt you use, the better it will incorporate into the dough. A coarser salt like kosher will eventually dissolve, but it'll disperse less evenly. It'll also throw off your measure slightly if you are using volume measurements—just one more reason to go pro and use a scale!

Techniques

The beauty of every recipe in this book is that while some may involve multiple steps, none of the steps themselves are that difficult. To make it even easier, I'm going to break down some of the techniques that you'll find in a number of these recipes, in addition to some general know-how that will come in handy, such as how to know when your bread is done and how to store it once it's baked.

Mixing Your Dough

Mixing is one of the simplest but arguably the most important step in the bread-making process. For me, it is the most engaging and rewarding step as well. The way the flour, sourdough starter, and water come together to become something greater than the sum of its parts is nothing short of miraculous. Much of that has to do with what's called autolysis, a process first described by a French baker, Raymond Calvel. What's happening when you mix these ingredients together is that the flour is hydrated, which allows the two proteins in wheat, glutenin and gliadin, to intermingle and create gluten. Gluten is the elastic web that provides structure to dough and chewiness to bread. So even though combining flour and water is a fairly straightforward process at first glance, it is one of the greatest tools in the sourdough bread baker's repertoire.

We'll get to how to mix in just a moment, but before we do, I'd like to further illustrate the alchemic magic that is autolysis. When you first mix together a dough and all the flour has been absorbed, tear off some pieces to examine. You'll notice how easily the dough pulls apart. Now, let the dough rest for 15 minutes. You'll see how much farther you're able to stretch the dough before it breaks. That's your gluten chains at work! Ever notice how open and irregular some bakers are able to get the crumb of their bread (or those nice little air pockets that you see when you break into a loaf of sourdough)? This is a big reason why they're able to achieve those results—long gluten chains.

Salt—or lack thereof, I should say—also plays a pivotal role in this process. I never call for adding salt before autolysis is complete. Rather, it gets added during your final mix step. This is because salt, along with seasoning your dough and regulating fermentation, strengthens the ionic bonds between gluten chains. It's what bakers call "tightening" the dough. Remember those short, easy-to-break gluten chains you saw when you first mixed together your flour, starter, and water? If you add salt with your initial mix, it will lock up those short chains. Waiting to add the salt will shorten your mixing time, which is gentler on the dough and, in turn, gives you those nice, irregular air pockets inside the loaves.

How to Mix

The short version of how to mix is: Simply add water and starter to flour, and let it rest for 15 minutes up to 1 hour. That's it!

The slightly more nuanced version is divided into two basic methods: (1) mixing for lean doughs (doughs that only contain flour, water, yeast/ sourdough, and salt) and (2) mixing for enriched doughs (doughs enriched with things like milk, butter, or eggs).

Lean doughs (or bread you want to have an open, irregular crumb structure). The recipes themselves will provide detailed, recipe-specific instruction, so follow them for any deviation, but the process is going to look something like this: In a medium mixing bowl, add your warm water (called "water 1" in the recipes, since water 2 gets withheld along with the salt), sourdough starter, bread flour, and whole-grain flour. Mix until thoroughly combined, about 2 minutes. This process can be done in a mixer or by hand. Let the dough rest for at least 15 minutes, or up to 1 hour. Sprinkle the salt over the dough, then squeeze or mix it in until it is very even. Continue mixing until the dough is smooth, shiny, and strong—meaning it doesn't tear easily, another 7 to 10 minutes. Once the dough is strong, start drizzling in water 2 while the dough is mixing. Keep mixing until the dough has absorbed all of the water and is once again smooth, shiny, and strong.

Some bakers, myself included, add starter to the dough in this initial mix, while others start with just flour and water and then add their starter when they finish mixing the dough. This comes down to personal preference—neither method is right or wrong. I will point out that if you're going to allow the bread to autolyse for a long time (over an hour), then it's best practice to wait to add your starter. If under an hour, feel free to add it to the initial mix.

Enriched doughs. Enriched doughs generally have tight, smooth crumbs. Since we are not aiming to achieve an open, irregular crumb structure

Initial Mix

in a soft roll, we do not need to employ the auto-lysis process. Instead you're going to combine all the ingredients in a stand mixer and mix on low speed for 2 minutes, or until the dry ingredients are absorbed. Increase to high speed and mix for another 8 to 10 minutes, or until the dough is very smooth and strong.

Shaping Your Dough

This is the name for the process that happens after you portion out your dough. Each recipe will tell you how big your dough pieces should be, whether it's two equal pieces for two loaves of bread, or a number of them for buns, pastries, and so on.

Step 1: Pre-Shape Your Dough

Instead of jumping right into shaping dough like a boule, batard, baguette, loaf, bagel, pizza, or whatever, we "pre-shape" it. We do this for a couple reasons:

- Pre-shaping turns awkwardly shaped dough pieces into uniform ones. It evens out the cell structure in the dough, which makes it easier to shape down the road.

- You'll get a tighter final shape. That means that you're creating a tighter gluten web, which means more gas can be trapped, which results in a lighter, fluffier loaf.

- When you originally weigh your pieces of dough, you're likely going to have a large piece and then some smaller pieces that you cut to make your desired weight. Preshaping takes those pieces and forms them into one nice, even piece. This creates a more even starting point for your final shaping of the loaf.

When pre-shaping, what you want to do is work the dough until it is round with a smooth outer skin that springs back when pressed, which usually doesn't take more than a minute. What you don't want to do is work the dough so much that it begins tearing across the surface. This happens because, like a rubber band, gluten can get so tight that it snaps. If your dough tears, let it rest for 10 to 15 minutes so the gluten can relax, then gently reshape it.

Step 2: Let the Dough Rest

Now it's time to let the dough take a much-needed (much-kneaded?) break—namely so you don't work the gluten to the point of tearing it (remember that whole rubber band thing?). Best practice is to cover it with a non-nubbly tea towel or linen to keep it from drying out. As for how long it needs to rest, this will depend on how warm your dough is and how tightly you were able to pre-shape it. Your dough will grow by about a third in size, and when poked, it'll spring back but retain the mark for a bit. The wetter your dough, the more your dough will spread down and out versus getting lighter and fluffier. You should be able to feel air in there and meet some resistance, but not quite as firmly as just after pre-shaping it. Anticipate this process taking about 30 minutes for most breads. For some hearth loaves and baguettes, you can get away with 15 minutes.

Step 3: Final Shaping

Just what it sounds like: This is how you'll shape your loaf for baking. These are the common shapes that you'll find in most bakeries.

Baguette. Line a baking sheet with a large linen or tea towel. I recommend a linen here because their larger size is on your side.

The key when shaping a baguette is the size of what you're baking it in (terra cotta baker, Challenger pan, cast-iron pot), which will dictate the length.

Lightly flour your work surface. Take one piece of pre-shaped dough and place it seam-side up in the flour. Take the two top "corners" of the dough and pull them straight down, about halfway down the piece of dough. Now take the top edge of the dough and do the same, bringing it down to the middle of

Three Pre-Shaping Methods: Dealer's Choice

By hand: With each hand, grab two opposite "corners" of your portioned piece of dough and bring them down to meet in the center of the dough. Grab the remaining two opposite corners and do the same. (So you're essentially pulling from north and south, then east and west.) Flip the dough over so the seam side is down. At this point, you may want to press some flour onto your hands.

This next part is where you start to build tension in the dough and consists of four motions that, when put all together, become one fluid movement:

1. Keeping the heel of one hand in contact with the table and the dough, push the dough away from you. It should cling to the table slightly.

2. Next, keeping the heel of that same hand in contact with the table and the dough, shift the dough to the left (or the right, if using your left hand).

3. Now, with your fingertips reaching over the top of the dough to touch both the table and the dough, pull the dough toward you.

4. Using your thumb to guide the dough along the table, shift the dough to the left (or the right, if using your left hand).

Put those steps together until it becomes a rounding motion, and repeat. The dough should become tight and smooth in a minute or less.

With a bench scraper: This method works particularly well for wetter doughs that have a tendency to stick. Start by picking up a piece of dough—you'll see that it has a sticky side (the bottom) and a floured side (the top). Place the dough in front of you, sticky-side down. Similar to pre-shaping by hand, you're going to be putting together three separate motions until they become one fluid movement:

1. Hold the bench scraper so its edge is flush with the table and at a 90-degree angle to the dough. Push the scraper away from you with the dough.
2. Keeping your scraper in contact with the table and the dough, rotate the scraper in an upside-down "U" shape so that the edge of the scraper is now facing you at another 90-degree angle. Move the scraper and the dough back towards you.

3. Release the scraper from the dough. Push away, turn, release. Push away, turn, release. This will build the tension around the dough. You'll only need to do this a few times before you have a nice, smooth, tight ball of dough.

If you don't like either of the above: You can do this with your hand or a scraper. Place the dough on the table floured-side down. If the dough is on the wetter side and you plan to use your hands, dip them into a little flour.

Bring both hands up over the dough to form sort of "claws," keeping your fingertips in contact with the table just above the dough. Pull the dough toward you. Use your hands or a scraper to rotate the dough 90 degrees. Pull again. Repeat until you have a nice, smooth, tight ball of dough.

the dough. Give it a gentle press to seal it. Bring the top edge of the dough down once again, this time to the bottom of the dough. Flip the dough over so it's now seam-side down.

Use two hands to roll the baguette to your desired length. When rolling with your hands, think about keeping the pressure against the table with the palms of your hands—as though the dough just happens to be there. Continue pressing forward and back with the heels of your hands making contact with the table, while also working your hands outward to create length. If the dough starts to stick, dip your hands in more flour. The shape you're going for is one that is thicker in the middle and tapers to pointed ends. If the seam of your dough starts opening as you roll, just pinch it closed to seal it.

Transfer your shaped baguette to the linen. When it's time to add another shaped baguette, place it a few inches away, then pinch each side of the linen between the loaves and pull up. This will draw the loaves closer together while also creating a "wall" between them. Ideally that linen barrier will be an inch or so taller than the loaves, since they'll grow as they proof.

Batard. Pinch a 50-50 blend of rice flour and all-purpose flour between your fingertips and thumb and sprinkle it evenly over the inside of your proofing basket. Lightly flour your work surface and place your pre-shaped dough seam-side up in the flour. Use both hands to bring the bottom edge of the dough up to the top third and gently press to seal. Repeat that once more. Now bring

the top to the middle and gently press. Transfer the dough seam-side up to the basket. You can give the dough a gentle tug to encourage it to fill the length of the basket.

Boule (round). Pinch a 50-50 blend of rice flour and all-purpose flour between your fingertips and thumb and sprinkle it evenly over the inside of your proofing basket. Lightly flour your work surface and place your pre-shaped dough seam-side up in the flour. Collect the two sides of the dough and bring them to the center to meet. Do the same thing with the top and bottom of the dough. Flip the dough seam-side down and choose a pre-shaping method from above to once again shape the dough into a smooth, tight round. Transfer the dough seam-side up to the basket.

Ring loaf. As a general rule of thumb, you want to use a larger basket, a smaller amount of dough, or both for a ring loaf. You'll also need something to hold the ring's shape in the center, such as a cup, quart-size deli container, or tall ring mold—something that takes up one-quarter to one-third of the interior circle of your loaf, depending on the size

of your pan. Spray the center mold with cooking spray, dust lightly with flour, and set it in the center of the basket.

Lightly flour your work surface and place your pre-shaped dough seam-side up in the flour. You're basically making a large bagel: Pull the top edge of the dough with your fingertips, fold it about a third of the way down the dough, and press gently to seal. Repeat that again, taking the top edge and bringing it down about a third, and then another third until you've essentially formed a cylinder.

With the cylinder seam-side down, use the palms of your hands to roll the cylinder to your desired length (long enough to fill your proofing basket when it forms a loop). Bring the two ends together, press to join them, then use one hand to roll the seam on the table to seal. Arrange the loop of dough around the center mold seam-side up.

Scoring Your Dough

Scoring dough before it bakes—or slicing into it with a razor or lame—serves a few purposes:

- It helps differentiate your bread from anyone else's. Granted, this was a bigger issue when we were baking in communal ovens. Still, it's a nice touch.

- It lets *you* dictate where the bread splits. Anytime you shape bread, you automatically create weak points in the loaf. And when you bake bread, it essentially blows up like a balloon and can burst at its weakest point. By scoring, you're telling the bread where to burst, allowing your loaves to bloom or shred evenly.

You're complementing the shape that you've created for the bread. In the case of boules, you're scoring symmetrically so it keeps its nice round shape. For pretty much everything else—especially batards, sandwich loaves, and baguettes—you're scoring in the middle third of the bread to maintain its shape by preventing bulging and splitting elsewhere on the loaf. You'll also see that when you slice a loaf in half, the scoring accentuates the nice inner whirl you've created by tightly pre-shaping and shaping your loaves.

As for how to do it, apply gentle, even pressure so that your razor cuts about ¼ inch into the dough. You'll see below that you can get pretty

creative with your scoring, and in some recipes, I don't specify how exactly to do it because it's your call. For some types of bread, however, it's better to stick to some gentle parameters:

Batards and baguettes: You want to use a curved lame versus a straight razor. And you want to stay within the center third of your loaf. All you're doing is dragging the long edge of the blade from end to end of the bread, cutting in with the center point and dragging with the curved blade. For baguettes, I use a series of roughly 3-inch diagonal lines at about a 20-degree angle that overlap by about a third, but all falling within that center third of the loaf. Depending on the length of your baguette, you'll get in three to five cuts. In the case of batards, you could do a series of two or three diagonal lines, or just a single line down the center will do. (You can trace the line first with light pressure from your lame, if that helps.)

Boules: For these you want to stick with symmetrical scoring in order to preserve the perfect roundness of your loaf. But other than that, you can get pretty artistic. Common boule scoring shapes include an X, a square, a triangle, the classic San Francisco crosshatch, or a single line straight down the center.

Baking Your Dough

You'll notice that I call for baking your loaves "until the desired crust color is achieved." This is part of baking the bread you want. If you like a darker loaf, bake it dark. If you like it light, bake it light. You do

want to aim for an internal temperature of 200°F to make sure the bread is fully baked, but other than that, it's up to you.

Storing Your Bread

For the times when you don't manage to completely polish off what you bake—especially when a recipe yields two loaves, as they often do—here's how to keep your bread fresh for the long(ish) haul. You'll notice that I don't call for plastic wrap, which is because I'm not down with single-use plastic. Reusable airtight plastic containers are fine, but I highly recommend looking into reusable beeswax wraps. There's also a good old-fashioned bread box.

Soft breads: Store in an airtight plastic container, bread box, or beeswax wrap at room temperature.

Crusty breads: On the counter for a day is fine, otherwise store in a brown paper bag or beeswax wrap.

Cookies, cakes, and pastries: Store in an airtight container at room temperature once cool.

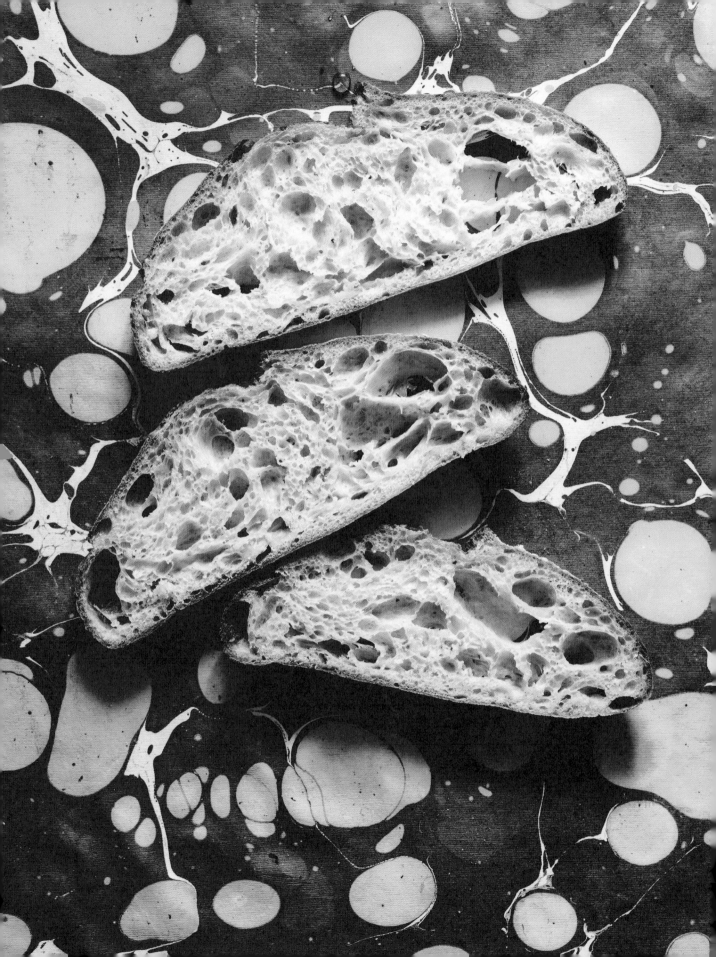

Everything You Need to Know about Sourdough

USING SOURDOUGH IN YOUR BREAD IS A WAY TO, QUITE SIMPLY, bring it to life. A good live sourdough culture brings both flavor and texture into balance, adding that signature, nuanced sourdough tang while also helping to leaven your bread—all by harnessing the power of wild bacteria and the natural acids they create. And because it's alive, your sourdough starter is a lot like a pet; you need to keep it fed and happy in order to yield the best bread. Behold, the basics to demystifying the creation, maintenance, and general understanding of your sourdough starter.

What Is a Sourdough Starter?

A sourdough starter, in the broadest sense of the term, is an active colony of yeast and beneficial bacteria that are living in happy, symbiotic harmony. Every starter is going to contain different strains of bacteria and yeast, purely because the wild yeast and bacteria you capture varies from environment to environment. And these different strains can and do have different flavor profiles, leading to a "terroir experience"—a major plus for creating your own sourdough starter. A most notable example is the "San Francisco sourdough," which contains a bacterial named for the region: *Lactobacillus sanfranciscensis*. You could find out which specific strains of bacteria and yeast are in your culture by sending a sample off to a lab such as the Sourdough Library, but it's not required.

What is consistent in all starters is that the bacteria will produce lactic and acetic acids, while the yeast will produce ethanol and carbon dioxide. These are the things that will flavor and leaven your bread. (As in, make it tangy, tasty, and nuanced and not flat and dense like a hockey puck.) Which leads me to . . .

What Does Sourdough Starter Do?

In short, a whole lot of eating and reproducing. The yeast will begin by breaking down the complex carbohydrates in the flour that makes up your bread dough into ethanol and carbon dioxide. The carbon dioxide is the gas that will be the actual "leavening" agent in your bread. As it's expelled by the yeast, the gas is contained by the gluten web developed in the dough. Think of this like blowing up a balloon—the gluten web is the balloon itself and the carbon dioxide is what's making it inflate.

The ethanol that the yeast produces goes on to become food for the bacteria in your starter. The bacteria then turn that ethanol into either lactic acid or acetic acid, depending on the temperature at which you ferment your bread. Lactic acid is produced in warmer temperatures and yields a smooth, buttery flavor. Acetic acid is developed in cooler temperatures and has a sharper, vinegar-like flavor. That's why if you choose to ferment your dough in the refrigerator overnight, you'll notice that your bread will be distinctly more sour.

But the starter isn't done yet! The acid produced during the fermentation process acts as a natural preservative, creating an environment that is harmful to other microorganisms, thereby extending the shelf life of your bread. Sourdough's naturally long fermentation process breaks down grains' complex carbohydrates, making the bread easier for us to digest. It also breaks down phytic acid, which is a naturally occurring nutrient blocker that's found in many grains and plant seeds. You can learn more about these groovy sourdough benefits—and why better flour plus sourdough baking is a nutrition game-changer—under "What This All Has to Do with Gluten Intolerance" on page 33.

Now the part you actually came to this section for:

How Do I Create a Sourdough Starter and How Do I Care for It?

There are a few ways to start:

Option 1: Flour and Water

500 grams organic whole-wheat flour +
600 grams water (80°F)

For this method, be sure to use organic whole-wheat flour. Your starter will be more successful than if you use conventional bread flour because organic whole-wheat flour still has the yeast and bacteria from the surface of the grain itself blended in with the flour. Before you get squeamish about that, remember that yeast and bacteria live on the surface of literally everything. If you choose to just use conventional bread flour for this recipe, the yeast and bacteria that float around in the air will eventually accumulate enough to turn your batter into a lively mix, but it will just take longer.

Mix the flour and water in a large bowl by hand until completely combined, 2 to 3 minutes. Be sure to use a bowl that gives the mixture room to double in size. Cover the bowl with a cheesecloth or tea towel. Do not use plastic for this—you want something semi-permeable so the bacteria and yeast in the air

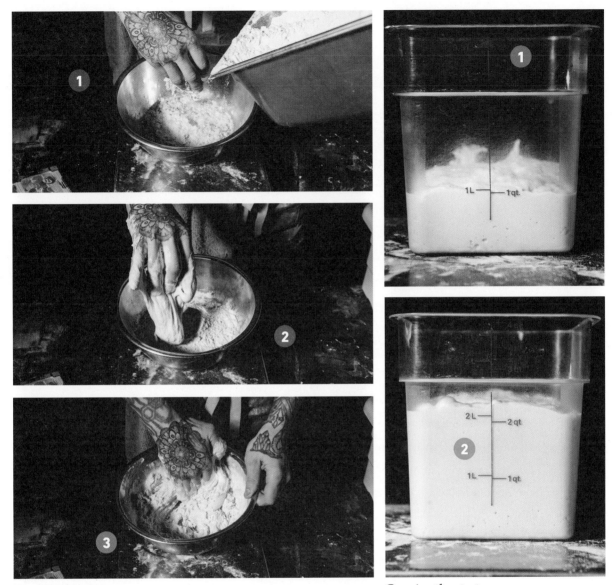

Feeding the starter

Growing the starter

can get at it. The purpose of the cheesecloth or towel is just to ensure that the mix doesn't dry out on top.

Let this mix sit at room temperature for 24 hours. At this point you may see some bubbles forming, which is exactly what you want! Stir the mixture either by hand or with a spoon to reincorporate the bubbles and to add some fresh oxygen into the mix. Cover again and let the mixture sit for another 24 hours. By now the mix should start to accumulate more bubbles and have risen. If that is the case, you've got yourself a sourdough starter! If you don't see a ton of bubbles, stir again and let the mix sit out for a third day; you should be good to go and can now use this as your "seed starter" in the methods outlined below. If you're still not in business, use the grape method (Option 2, see page 60)—you definitely want to go the extra mile to introduce the cultures you want.

Option 2: The Grape Method

500 grams bread flour + 600 grams water (80°F) +
1 bunch organic grapes (unwashed!)

Make sure you're buying organic grapes (any color) and not conventional, especially the ones that have that nice, white powdery substance on the outside of them—that's yeast! Whatever you do, don't rinse that off. Mix the bread flour (organic is better, but conventional will work too) and water together by hand in a large bowl until it's thoroughly combined, 2 to 3 minutes. Wrap up the grapes in some cheesecloth, then give 'em a good squeeze over the bowl to break the skins and release some juice. Shove the cloth-wrapped grapes down into the mix, cover with a cheesecloth or tea towel, and let it sit at room temperature for 24 hours. Again, you don't want to use plastic wrap since it's not permeable and won't allow any yeast and bacteria floating around to join the party. The next day, you should see plenty of activity indicated by bubbles in and on top of the starter, and the mix should have risen. Remove the grapes and cheesecloth and discard. You can use your "seed starter" in the methods outlined below.

Option 3: Your Friendly Neighborhood Bakery

If all else fails, or you are in a bind, contact your favorite local bakery. If they are anything like us, they've got buckets of starter kickin' around that they'd be happy to help re-home. Bakers, while largely an odd, soulful lot that gets up stupid early in the morning and likes jazz music, are actually pretty friendly if you strike up a chat.

OK, I've Got a Starter— Now How Do I Maintain It?

Here you've got a few options. But before we get into them, the point is to understand the mechanics of your starter in order to make the bread-baking experience easier for you. Some important things to note:

- The goal of each of these options is the same: to get your sourdough starter "active" and ready to use, meaning it's fed, revved up, and ready to (help your bread) rise. The timing depends on how much you feed your seed starter. The more flour you feed it, the longer it will take for your starter to digest and ferment all of that food.

- In addition to how much you feed your starter, you can also play around with hydration. Yeast thrives in a drier environment, bacteria in a wetter one. So if you're making a bread that has a wet dough or contains a lot of enrichment (butter, sugar, oil, etc.), it will benefit from a drier starter to give it more form—meaning you'll feed it with more flour than water. This will factor into how long your seed starter will need before it's ready, as drier starters take longer to ripen. (Think about it: more flour = more to digest.) On the other hand, if you want your dough to be more developed in flavor (that is, more sour), you'll want to use a wetter starter, so you'll feed it more water than flour. And if you want middle-of-the-road form and function from your starter, then you'll use equal parts flour and water by weight to feed it before you bake. This is what's called "100 percent hydration," because you are feeding it the same amount of water in ratio to the flour.

Scenario 1: I need my starter in 3 hours (100% hydration).

75 grams seed starter

75 grams water (80°F)

75 grams bread flour

Combine the seed starter, water, and flour in a large bowl and mix by hand until thoroughly combined and no dry flour remains. Cover with a cheesecloth or tea towel and let ferment in a warm (75°F) area of the kitchen (such as in the oven that has been preheated for 5 minutes to warm it up a bit, then turned off) for 3 hours.

Scenario 2: I want to use my starter first thing in the morning (12 to 15 hours after feeding).

There are two options here; choose one based on your personal preference and the kind of dough you're making. You'll want to choose 100 percent hydration if you want a more sour flavor, dry starter build for less.

100% hydration

10 grams seed starter

100 grams water (60°F)

100 grams bread flour

Combine the seed starter, water, and flour in a large bowl and mix by hand until thoroughly combined and no dry flour remains. Cover with a cheesecloth or tea towel and let ferment in a moderately temped (65° to 70°F) area of your house for 12 to 15 hours. I find the best areas in my house for this are the basement and closets that don't have heating vents nearby.

Dry starter build

15 grams seed starter

75 grams water (65°F)

150 grams bread flour

Combine the seed starter, water, and flour in a large bowl and mix by hand until thoroughly combined and no dry flour remains. This may take some work, as it is very dry. Cover with a cheesecloth or tea towel and let ferment in a moderately temped (65° to 70°F) area of your house for 12 to 15 hours. If that's not your kitchen, check your basement or closets where there aren't vents nearby.

Scenario 3: I'm going away for a week and want to make sure my starter doesn't die on me.

Before you leave

15 grams seed starter

15 grams water (80°F)

15 grams bread flour

Combine the seed starter, water, and flour in a large bowl and mix by hand until thoroughly combined and no dry flour remains. Cover with a cheesecloth or tea towel and let ferment in a warm (75°F) area of the kitchen for 2 hours. Transfer to the refrigerator and refrigerate until you return.

When you get back (you're going to feed the starter twice to revive it)

45 grams seed starter (all of what you refrigerated before you left)

50 grams water (80°F)

50 grams bread flour

Combine the seed starter, water, and flour in a large bowl and mix by hand until thoroughly combined and no dry flour remains. Cover with a cheesecloth or tea towel and let ferment in a warm (75°F) area of the kitchen for 4 hours.

Then, discard 100 grams of the resulting starter and repeat feeding with the remaining starter:

45 grams seed starter (what's left
from what you fed a few hours ago)
50 grams water (80°F)
50 grams bread flour

Combine the seed starter, water, and flour in a large bowl and mix by hand until thoroughly combined and no dry flour remains. Cover with a cheesecloth or tea towel and let ferment in a warm (75°F) area of the kitchen for 4 hours. It should now be ready to use.

When Do I Actually Use This Thing?

Your starter is ready to use when it has tripled in volume from your initial feed volume. You will notice lots of large bubbles on top and, if you look closely, there should also be a crack that develops right near the center of the starter, which will have developed tons of tiny bubbles. This crack means that your starter is no longer expanding, but is receding. In other words, your starter has reached its peak and it's time to use it! However, it's worth noting that this will be true only for the 100 percent hydration starter; a dry starter will not develop a crack. A dry starter is ready to use as soon as it has tripled in volume—you will feel lots of air in it.

Your starter should also have some structure to it when it is ready, and by that I mean that when you pull at it a little bit with your fingers, it should stay together in a clump and not be soupy. If it is soupy and very liquid, it is overfermented. In that case, you'll need to feed it again before using it. Another test you can do is called the "float test": Take a pinch of the starter when you think it is ready and drop it in a bowl or glass of water. It should stay in a clump and float. If that clump sinks, let it ferment longer. If it is stringy and soupy, it may float, but the runny texture is an indication that it is overfermented and should be fed again before using.

Starter Maintenance for Everyday Life

To give you some context for best practices in maintaining your starter, let me first walk you through how we do it at the bakery (don't worry, this is not what I'm recommending you do at home, unless you're baking all day, every day):

We feed our starter three times a day. We start with a 1:2:2 ratio (starter:flour:water) at 7 a.m. At 1 p.m., we refresh at 1:1:1 ratio (starter:flour:water). Then at 6 p.m., we feed for what we will need to use the next morning at a 1:10:10 ratio (starter:flour:water) and use it between 7 a.m. and 10 a.m. We never put our starter in the refrigerator because we are a sourdough bakery, and the more often we refresh and feed the starter, the more active and reliable it will be. We also always want forward momentum with our starter, and when you refrigerate the starter, the microbiome in the starter starts behaving differently. The yeast will go dormant, but some bacteria will still be active. We want the symbiosis between the microorganisms to be in full effect all the time.

That being said, if you are a home baker, feeding three times a day is a big ask. And it is completely acceptable to refrigerate your starter when not in use. The key is to feed the starter before you put it away for a cold nap, letting it get active before you do, then refresh it a few times before using it in bread. Follow the starter build using the "I'm going away for a week" (Scenario 3) instructions above and you'll be just fine. The point is, you always want to refresh as often as you can before you make bread, making sure to look for the signs of an active starter before you use it.

And remember:

- Your starter should be stored in a clean container, covered loosely with breathable material such as a linen cloth or clean, non-nubbly towel. Do not use a tight-fitting lid or you will run the risk of developing too much pressure in the container, which can burst, crack, or otherwise cause problems.

- When you feed, make sure you never fill the container more than a quarter of the way full, in order to account for extra growth in volume. I speak from experience; it sucks to clean up a fermented sour mess before you start making your bread.

- Store your starter on the counter if you feed it regularly or in the refrigerator if you don't. Do not store it in a place that will reach above 120°F or your yeast will start dying. At 140°F, all yeast will be dead.

Help! I Think I Killed My Starter

OK, so you really probably didn't. These things are pretty resilient. But if you've neglected your starter to the point of potential extinction (it's got the consistency of Elmer's glue, is very flat with only a few bubbles, has a layer of alcohol on top, or is discoloring from oxidation) try refreshing it every 4 hours with the following build. Feel free to let the starter ferment at room temperature overnight without setting an alarm in the middle of the night to get in an extra feeding. Just feed it before you go to bed and then start the refreshing process again when you get up.

50 grams seed starter
50 grams water (80°F)
50 grams bread flour

Combine the seed starter, water, and flour in a large bowl and mix by hand until thoroughly combined and no dry flour remains. Cover with a cheesecloth or tea towel and let ferment in a warm (75°F) area of the kitchen for 4 hours. Repeat until the starter triples in volume in the 4 hours and looks very active and bubbly. If you try this for a few days and it does not grow at all, then your starter is likely, in fact, dead.

Signs Your Starter Should Be Discarded

If your starter is growing mold on top or has a very "off" odor—keeping in mind that it is ultimately a bucket of fermenting goo—then it's time to scrap it and start fresh. Remember, if it smells bad, it's going to taste bad. For more information, see "Troubleshooting: Help, Everything's on Fire!" (page 323).

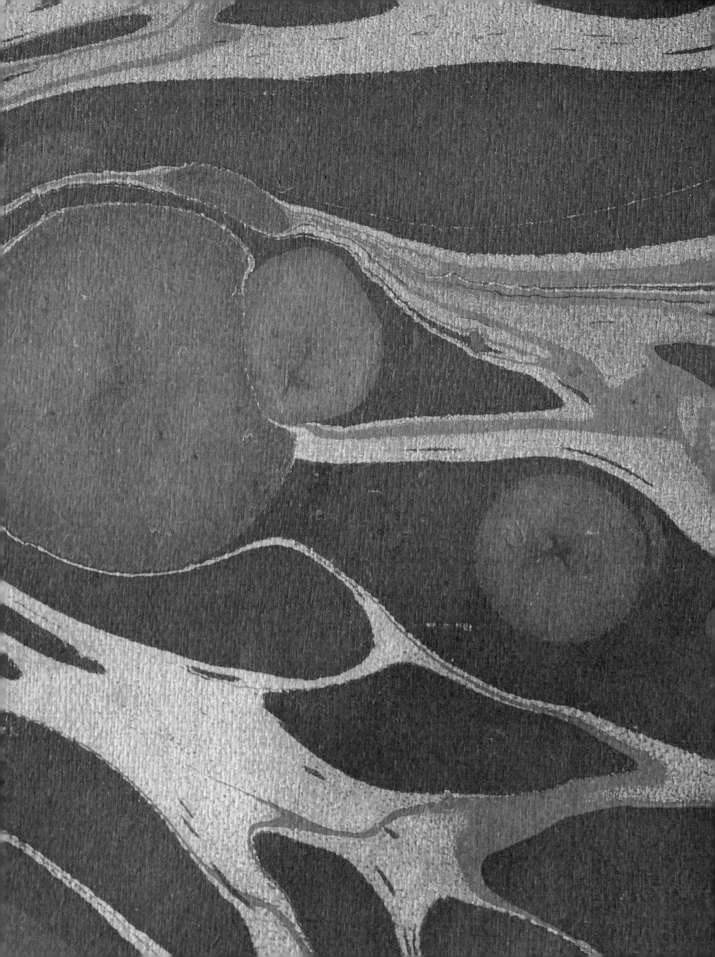

PART II

Digging It

Recipes and Other Tasty Things

CHAPTER 1

Like a Road Leading Home

A Good White Bread   68

Wheat Sandwich Loaf   71

Oat Dinner Rolls   73

Oat Cinnamon-Raisin Challah   77

Rye English Muffins   80

Rye Focaccia   83

   Sunchoke, Blue Cheese, and Rosemary   85

   Giardiniera and Goat Cheese 85

Buckwheat Banana Bread   86

Buckwheat Brownies   89

Heritage Cornbread   91

Cornmeal Whoopie Pies   93

Oat Galette with Seasonal Fruit   97

Oat Doughnuts   100

Sorghum Blondies   103

Spelt and Apple Muffins   105

Spiced Rye Cookies   107

Brown Butter Wheat Chocolate Chip Cookies   109

Honey Wheat Graham Cracker S'Mores   111

Whole-Wheat Biscuits   114

Whole-Wheat Crumpets   116

Whole-Wheat Sponge Cake with Honey Buttercream   117

Just like the road that takes you home, these recipes should feel familiar. They're goods that you've probably tried baking before or are at least recognizable—sandwich bread, cookies, waffles, muffins, biscuits, cornbread, and so on. The goal of this first chapter is to get you feeling in the groove while working with dough, playing around with fermentation, and introducing yourself to the new grains in your pantry. And there's no better way to do that than with simple, rustic recipes that you also can't wait to eat.

A Good White Bread

I like to call this "Look, You Made Bread!" bread. This recipe is about as basic as bread baking gets—the perfect starting point for getting a handle on the fundamentals before we throw fermentation into the mix. Which is also why I've chosen to make it white bread versus working with a whole grain as you might have been expecting. It's just a solid loaf of bread that is soft, fragrant, and great for sandwiches or for slathering with a slab of butter.

Makes 2 (750-gram) loaves

For the Dough:

Ingredient	Weight	Volume	Baker's %
Total flour			100.00%
>>Bread flour	800g	6 cups + 2½ tablespoons	100.00%
Water	500g	2 cups + 2 tablespoons	62.50%
Dry milk powder	50g	¾ cup	6.25%
Active dry yeast	7g	1½ teaspoons	0.88%
Sugar	75g	⅓ cup	9.38%
Unsalted butter, softened	40g	3 tablespoons	5.00%
Fine sea salt	17g	1 tablespoon	2.13%

For the Egg Wash:

Ingredient	Volume
Large egg	1 whole
Water	1 tablespoon

Mix the dough: Calculate your water temperature if desired (see page 310) or use warm water (80°F).

In the bowl of a stand mixer, add the water, milk powder, and yeast and whisk until combined. Fit the mixer with the dough hook attachment and add the bread flour, sugar, butter, and salt. Mix on low speed for about 4 minutes, until the dough is uniform. You may need to scrape down the sides of the bowl to ensure no dry pockets of flour remain. Increase the speed to medium-high and mix until a smooth, shiny dough forms. Remove the dough hook from the bowl and remove the bowl from the mixer.

Ferment: Cover the bowl with a tea towel or linen and let the dough ferment at room temperature for 2 hours. Fold the dough after 1 hour, then re-cover the bowl and let the dough rest for the remaining hour. When folding the dough, you will be stretching the dough from each side up and over the opposite side, tightening it into a ball.

Shape: Turn out the dough onto a lightly floured work surface and divide it in half; each half should weigh about 750 grams. Shape the dough as sandwich loaves (see batard on page 52) or choose a pre-shaping method to form as buns (see page 50). If you'd prefer not to bake both loaves now, you can stash one in the fridge and bake it the following day. Place the loaves on a baking sheet (if making buns, line the baking sheet with parchment).

Proof: Cover the loaves with a tea towel or linen and set in a warm area to proof for 1 to 2 hours, until doubled in size and very light and airy.

Bake: Preheat the oven to 350°F.

In a small bowl, whisk together the egg and water. Brush the loaves or buns with the egg wash and score (see page 53). Bake for about 35 minutes for loaves or 15 to 20 minutes for buns, until the bread is a deep golden brown. Allow to cool before serving.

Wheat Sandwich Loaf

This is pretty much the same recipe as **A Good White Bread** (page 68), but this time we're adding a little bit of wheat flour and replacing the sugar with honey—a match made in heaven, in my opinion. We're also going to use a preferment, or a portion of dough that's allowed to ferment with dry yeast before it's added back into the mix. This will not only deepen the flavor but also start to break down the complex sugars of the wheat, giving you the health benefits of a fermented bread. (Refresh your memory of all that good stuff on page 20.) You can enjoy this loaf as is, or garnish with rolled oats on top before baking it, just brush the loaves with a little water or egg wash first to help the oats stick.

Makes 2 (900-gram) loaves

For the Preferment:

Ingredient	Weight	Volume	Baker's %
Total flour			100.00%
>>Bread flour	110g	¾ cup + 2 tablespoons	100.00%
Water	110g	½ cup	100.00%
Active dry yeast	1g	½ teaspoon	0.45%

For the Bread:

Ingredient	Weight	Volume	Baker's %
Total flour			100.00%
>>Bread flour	550g	4¼ cups	66.27%
>>Whole-wheat flour	280g	2½ cups	33.73%
Water	515g	2¼ cups	62.05%
Dry milk powder	70g	½ cup	8.43%
Active dry yeast	7g	1½ teaspoons	0.84%
Unsalted butter, softened	55g	¼ cup	6.63%
Honey	70g	¼ cup	8.43%
Fine sea salt	20g	1 tablespoon	2.41%

For the Egg Wash:

Ingredient	Volume
Large egg	1 whole
Water	1 tablespoon

Continued

Make the preferment: Make this the evening before you bake. In a small bowl, add the flour, warm (80°F) water, and yeast. Mix by hand until completely combined, about 2 minutes. Cover with a tea towel or linen and let ferment at room temperature for 12 hours.

Make the bread: Calculate your water temperature if desired (see page 310) or use warm (80°F) water.

In the bowl of a stand mixer, combine the water, milk powder, and yeast. Whisk until the milk powder and yeast are dissolved. Fit the mixer with the dough hook attachment and add the bread flour, wheat flour, butter, honey, salt, and preferment. Mix on low speed until the mixture is homogeneous, about 4 minutes. You may need to scrape down the sides of the bowl to ensure no dry pockets of flour remain. When all of the dry ingredients are incorporated, increase the speed to medium-high and mix until a smooth, shiny dough forms and pulls away from the sides of the bowl, 10 to 12 minutes. Remove the dough hook from the bowl and remove the bowl from the mixer.

Ferment: Cover the bowl with a tea towel or linen and let the dough ferment at room temperature for 2 hours. Fold the dough after 1 hour, then re-cover the bowl and let the dough rest for the remaining hour.

Shape: Turn out the dough onto a lightly floured work surface and divide it in half; each half should weigh about 900 grams. Shape the dough as sandwich loaves (see batard on page 52) or choose a pre-shaping method to form as buns (see page 50). If you'd prefer not to bake both loaves now, you can stash one in the fridge and bake it the following day. Place the loaves on a baking sheet (if making buns, line the baking sheet with parchment).

Proof: Cover the loaves with a tea towel or linen and set in a warm area to proof for 1 to 2 hours, until doubled in size and very light and airy.

Bake: Preheat the oven to 350°F. In a small bowl, whisk together the egg and water. Brush the loaves or buns with the egg wash and score (see page 53). Bake for about 35 minutes for loaves or 15 to 20 minutes for buns, until the bread is a deep golden brown. Allow to cool before serving.

Oat Dinner Rolls

Now we're getting into the best of both worlds: a fermented bread (though still leavened with dry yeast in a preferment) that's made soft and supple by including a whole-grain porridge—a trick I use any time I want to keep a bread tender and moist for a long time. These guys are frickin' delicious, especially fresh from the oven when they're still steaming. Topped with some whipped honey butter or the like? Just get outta town. And we're still in nice-and-easy territory here. There's no real shaping involved, only making small rounds for the rolls.

Makes 24 rolls

For the Preferment:

Ingredient	Weight	Volume	Baker's %
Total flour			100.00%
>>Bread flour	85g	⅔ cup	100.00%
Water	85g	⅓ cup	100.00%
Active dry yeast	1g	¼ teaspoon	1.18%

For the Oat Porridge:

Ingredient	Weight	Volume	Baker's %
Total flour			100.00%
>>Rolled oats	75g	1 cup	100.00%
Water	225g	1 cup	300.00%
Fine sea salt	2g	⅓ teaspoon	2.00%

For the Dough:

Ingredient	Weight	Volume	Baker's %
Total flour			100.00%
>>Bread flour	400g	3 cups + 1 tablespoon	100.00%
Whole milk	160g	⅔ cup	40.00%
Unsalted butter, softened	100g	½ cup	25.00%
Honey	50g	2 tablespoons + 1 teaspoon	12.50%
Fine sea salt	14g	2¼ teaspoons	3.50%
Active dry yeast	2g	½ teaspoon	0.50%
Cooking spray, for greasing			

Continued

For the Egg Wash:

Ingredient	Volume
Large egg	1 whole
Water	1 tablespoon

Make the preferment: Make this the evening before you bake. In a small bowl, add the flour, warm water (80°F), and yeast. Mix by hand until completely combined, about 2 minutes. Cover with a tea towel or linen and let ferment at room temperature for 12 hours.

Make the porridge: In a medium saucepan over medium-high heat, add the oats, water, and salt. Mix with a wooden spoon until thoroughly combined. Stirring often, bring the mixture to a boil. Reduce the heat to low and cook until the porridge is very thick, 3 to 4 minutes after it comes to a boil. Spread the porridge over a baking sheet or plate to help it cool down completely.

Mix the dough: Calculate your temperature for the milk if desired (treat as you would water, page 310) or use warm (80°F) milk.

In the bowl of a stand mixer fitted with the dough hook attachment, combine the preferment, porridge, bread flour, milk, butter, honey, salt, and yeast and mix on low speed until fully incorporated, about 4 minutes. You may need to scrape down the sides of the bowl to ensure no dry pockets of flour remain. Increase the speed to medium-high and mix until a smooth, shiny dough forms and pulls away from the sides of the bowl, 10 to 12 minutes.

Portion and shape: Coat a baking sheet with cooking spray, line with parchment, and spray the parchment.

Lightly flour a work surface and turn out the dough. Portion the dough into 24 pieces, each weighing about 50 grams. Shape the rolls (see page 50), place them on the prepared baking sheet, and cover with a tea towel or linen. If you'd prefer not to bake all the rolls now, you can stash half in the fridge and bake them the following day. The rolls should have a little room around them, but they will touch once properly proofed.

Proof: Cover the rolls with a tea towel or linen and set in a warm area to proof for 1 to 2 hours, until doubled in size and very light and airy.

Bake: Preheat the oven to 350°F.

In a small bowl, whisk together the egg and water. Brush the rolls with the egg wash and bake for 30 minutes, or until they are deep golden brown. Allow to cool before serving.

These rolls freeze well. To reheat, thaw them first, then refresh at 350°F for 10 minutes before serving.

Oat Cinnamon-Raisin Challah

This recipe is a great way to show the new dimensions that whole grains can add to your bread both in flavor and in texture, and it's also the perfect example of just how good challah should be. It's a dryer dough, making it easier to work with and to shape (we'll go with a simple three-strand braid for this one).

Makes 2 (1-kilogram) loaves

For the Preferment:

Ingredient	Weight	Volume	Baker's %
Total flour			100.00%
>>Bread flour	100g	¾ cup + 1 teaspoon	100.00%
Water	85g	⅓ cup	85.00%
Active dry yeast	1g	¼ teaspoon	1.00%

For the Oat Porridge:

Ingredient	Weight	Volume	Baker's %
Total flour			100.00%
>>Rolled oats	50g	¾ cup	100.00%
Water	150g	⅔ cup	300.00%
Fine sea salt	1g	¼ teaspoon	2.00%

For the Challah:

Ingredient	Weight	Volume	Baker's %
Total flour			100.00%
>>Bread flour	760g	5¾ cups + 2 tablespoons	100.00%
Water	215g	1 cup	28.29%
Large egg yolks	180g	9 each	23.68%
Vegetable oil	90g	½ cup	11.84%
Sugar	90g	½ cup	11.84%
Large egg	90g	2 whole	11.84%
Fine sea salt	16g	1 tablespoon	2.11%
Active dry yeast	6g	1¼ teaspoons	0.79%
Golden raisins	150g	1 cup	19.74%
Cinnamon	10g	1¼ teaspoons	1.32%

Continued

For the Egg Wash:

Ingredient	Volume
Large egg	1 whole
Water	1 tablespoon

Make the preferment: Make this the evening before you bake. In a small bowl, add the flour, warm water (80°F), and yeast. Mix by hand until completely combined, about 2 minutes. Cover with a tea towel or linen and ferment at room temperature for 12 hours.

Make the porridge: In a medium saucepan over medium-high heat, add the oats, water, and salt. Mix with a wooden spoon until thoroughly combined. Stirring often, bring the mixture to a boil. Reduce the heat to low and cook until the porridge is very thick, 3 to 4 minutes after it comes to a boil. Spread the porridge over a baking sheet or plate to help it cool down completely.

Mix the dough: Calculate your water temperature if desired (see page 310) or use warm (80°F) water.

In the bowl of a stand mixer fitted with the dough hook attachment, combine the preferment, porridge, bread flour, water, egg yolks, vegetable oil, sugar, whole egg, salt, and yeast and mix on low speed until fully incorporated, about 4 minutes. You may need to scrape down the sides of the bowl to ensure no dry pockets of flour remain. Increase the speed to medium-high and mix until a smooth, shiny dough forms and pulls away from the sides of the bowl, 10 to 12 minutes. Add the raisins and cinnamon and mix until combined, another 2 minutes. Remove the dough hook from the bowl and remove the bowl from the mixer.

Ferment: Cover the bowl with a tea towel or linen and let the dough ferment at room temperature for 2 hours. Fold the dough after 1 hour, then re-cover the bowl and let the dough rest for the remaining hour.

Shape: Turn out the dough onto a lightly floured work surface. Divide the dough in half, then divide each half into three pieces. The six pieces should weigh about 325 grams each, and you'll use three of them per loaf. Roll each piece into a rope about 16 inches long. (For guidance on how to roll out dough, check out the baguette shaping section on page 49.)

To braid, place three ropes vertically in front of you, with the top of each rope overlapping. Press firmly on the ropes where they overlap to seal. Pick up the rope on the right and place it between the other two ropes. Next, pick up the leftmost rope and place it between the other two ropes. Repeat this process of alternating the right- and leftmost ropes to the center until the ropes are completely braided. Press the ends of the ropes to seal at the bottom, tucking them slightly underneath the loaf. Repeat with the remaining three pieces to form a second braided loaf. If you'd prefer not to bake both loaves now, you can stash one in the fridge and bake it the following day. Place the loaves on a parchment-lined baking sheet.

Proof: Cover the loaves with a tea towel or linen and set in a warm area to proof for 1 to 2 hours, until doubled in size and very light and airy. You can test this by gently pressing the dough with your finger—the indentation should fill itself within 30 seconds. If it fills in under 10 seconds, it's underproofed. Give it 15 minutes at a time before checking again. If it doesn't fill in at all, it's over-proofed. If it's overproofed, you're just gonna have to roll with it—there's no going back. It'll still taste good, I promise!

Bake: Preheat the oven to 350°F. In a small bowl, whisk the egg and water. Brush the loaves with the egg wash and bake for 35 minutes, or until deep golden brown. Let cool before serving.

Rye English Muffins

Alright, now let's get into that sourdough starter. These English muffins are our jumping-off point because we'll just be focusing on letting the dough ferment and that's pretty much it—no kneading, no shaping the dough, none of that. Only punching out the muffins with a ring cutter and throwing 'em on the griddle. We'll talk about the timing of the fermentation too, because the move is to make the dough the night before you want to bake, keep the dough in the fridge overnight, then bake off the muffins in the morning when you want 'em fresh and warm. You can go indulgent and use these as the base for classic eggs Benedict, or keep it simple with butter and jam.

Makes 12 muffins

Ingredient	Weight	Volume	Baker's %
Total flour			100.00%
>>Bread flour	1138g	8¾ cups	79.69%
>>Rye flour	290g	2½ cups	20.31%
Water	861g	3⅔ cups	60.29%
Active sourdough starter	260g	1¼ cups	18.21%
Fine sea salt	38g	2 tablespoons	2.66%
Caraway seed (optional)	11g	1 tablespoon	0.77%
Dried shallot or onion flakes (optional)	11g	1 tablespoon	0.77%
Unsalted butter, for greasing			

First mix: Calculate your water temperature if desired (see page 310) or use warm (80°F) water.

In a large bowl, add the bread flour, water, rye flour, and sourdough starter. Mix by hand until all of the flour has been absorbed, 3 to 4 minutes. Cover with a tea towel or linen and let the dough rest for 30 minutes.

Second mix: Sprinkle the salt evenly over the dough and incorporate it by squeezing it in with your hand while folding the dough over itself. Continue for 2 to 3 minutes; the dough should feel much stronger once the salt is added. Add the caraway and/or shallot flakes, if using, and squeeze and fold until they are evenly dispersed, another 1 to 2 minutes.

Ferment: Cover the bowl with a tea towel or linen and let the dough ferment at room temperature for 4 hours. During this time, fold the dough after 45 minutes, 1½ hours, 2 hours 15 minutes, and 3 hours, re-covering the bowl each time. Let the dough rest for the remaining hour. The dough is properly fermented when it's light, airy, and about doubled in size.

Proof: Lay a tea towel or linen over a baking sheet and dust it heavily with flour. Place the dough on the towel and dust the dough with more flour. Press the dough and stretch it to the size of the pan. Cover with another towel or linen and refrigerate overnight.

Cook: On a griddle or in a large skillet over medium heat, melt about a tablespoon of butter. Use a 4-inch ring mold to punch out muffins from the refrigerated dough. (You can also choose to cut the muffins as squares to eliminate any scrap waste.) Working in batches, place the rounds on the griddle and cook for 3 to 5 minutes, until golden. Flip the muffins and cook for another 3 to 5 minutes. The muffins should rise significantly while they are cooking. They are done when they are golden on both sides and remain fluffy when you press on them. Let cool slightly before serving.

If you have leftovers, you can freeze them. Just thaw and toast.

Rye Focaccia

You could make this bread in a completely naturally leavened way, but using a preferment means that you don't have to fully rely on your starter for fermentation. And more reliable fermentation means that your focaccia will be nice and light, which it generally likes to be.

For this build, you have a couple flavor options, both of which are assertive enough to stand up to the robustness of the rye. First is a combination of sunchokes, blue cheese, and rosemary—a powerhouse trio. In my opinion, you're going to want some cheese in any focaccia you make (I'm from Wisconsin, so don't try to convince me otherwise), and in this case it's a funky blue that pairs really well with the floral, fruity, spicy thing that rye has going on. Add the earthy sunchokes and rosemary and you have a fantastic late-fall, early-winter offering. Second up is goat cheese and giardiniera, a spicy Italian relish with pickled vegetables in oil. Goat cheese and rye is a winning combo as well. You can play around with the cheeses that you use here, but you gotta go bold.

Serves about 8 (Makes 1 half-sheet tray)

For the Preferment:

Ingredient	Weight	Volume	Baker's %
Total flour			100.00%
>>Bread flour	60g	⅓ cup + 2 tablespoons	100.00%
Water	60g	¼ cup	100.00%
Active dry yeast	1g	¼ teaspoon	0.50%

For the Levain:

Ingredient	Weight	Volume	Baker's %
Total flour			100.00%
>>Bread flour	70g	½ cup	100.00%
Water	45g	3 tablespoons	64.29%
Active sourdough starter	10g	1 tablespoon	14.29%

Continued

For the Bread:

Ingredient	Weight	Volume	Baker's %
Total flour			100.00%
>>Bread flour	315g	2⅓ cups + 2 tablespoons	60.00%
>>Rye flour	210g	1¾ cups + 2 tablespoons	40.00%
Water 1	365g	1½ cups	69.52%
Fine sea salt	20g	1 tablespoon + ¾ teaspoon	3.81%
Water 2	50g	½ cup	9.52%
Extra-virgin olive oil, for the pan			

Make the preferment: Make this the evening before you bake. In a small bowl, add the flour, warm (80°) water, and yeast. Mix by hand until completely combined, about 2 minutes. Cover with a tea towel or linen and ferment at room temperature for 12 hours.

Make the levain: The same evening, make the levain. In a small bowl, combine the flour, warm (80°F) water, and sourdough starter. Mix by hand until completely combined, about 2 minutes. Cover with a tea towel or linen and let ferment at room temperature for 12 hours.

First mix: Calculate your water temperature if desired (see page 310) or use warm (80°F) water. In a large bowl, add the preferment, levain, bread flour, rye flour, and water 1. Mix by hand until all of the flour has been absorbed, 3 to 4 minutes. Cover and let rest for 30 minutes at room temperature (ideally 72° to 75°F).

Second mix: Sprinkle the salt evenly over the dough and incorporate it by squeezing it in with your hand while folding the dough over itself. Continue for 2 to 3 minutes; the dough should feel much stronger once the salt is added. Add water 2 and continue squeezing and folding until the water is completely absorbed and the dough coheres as one solid mass again, 3 to 4 minutes.

Ferment: Cover the bowl with a tea towel or linen and let the dough ferment at room temperature for 2½ hours. During this time, fold the dough after 45 minutes and again at 1½ hours, re-covering the bowl each time. Let the dough rest for the final hour. The dough is properly fermented when it's light, airy, and about doubled in size.

Proof: Line a baking sheet with parchment. Pour about ½ cup olive oil on the parchment and spread it evenly with your hand to coat the pan. Turn out the dough onto the pan and stretch the dough to roughly the size of the pan. If it doesn't want to stretch and contracts back on itself, let it rest for about 10 minutes before trying again. Then cover the dough with a tea towel or linen and let it rise for 30 to 40 minutes, until light and airy.

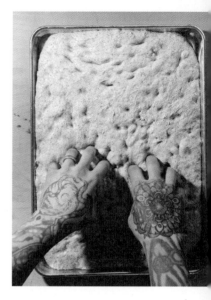

Bake: Preheat the oven to 425°F.

Pour another generous amount of oil, about ¼ cup, over the top of the dough. Using your fingertips, press dimples all over the dough. Top the focaccia if desired (see the riffs below, but plain is also phenomenal!), and bake for 25 to 30 minutes, until golden brown. Allow to cool slightly before serving, but I do encourage you to enjoy this bread warm from the oven.

RIFFS

Sunchoke, Blue Cheese, and Rosemary

2 cups very thinly shaved sunchokes (for best results, use a mandoline)
2 rosemary sprigs, needles stripped and chopped
Extra-virgin olive oil, as needed
Fine sea salt and freshly ground black pepper, to taste
½ cup crumbled blue cheese, or to taste

In a large bowl, combine the sunchokes and rosemary with enough olive oil to coat. Sprinkle with salt and pepper and give a toss. Scatter the blue cheese over the proofed dough—as much as you're into. Remember, a little goes a long way. Top with an even layer of the sunchokes. Bake according to the instructions above.

Giardiniera and Goat Cheese

1 cup crumbled fresh chèvre
1 cup store-bought or homemade giardiniera

Scatter the cheese over the proofed dough. Disperse the giardiniera, including its oil, over the dough. Bake according to the instructions above.

Buckwheat Banana Bread

I wanted to include this recipe because (1) everyone loves banana bread and (2) it's something you can make with the portion of your sourdough starter that you discard when you're feeding it. Incorporating the discards into a quick bread is a great way to add some structure and flavor while also making it healthier for you. For this banana bread, I went with buckwheat because I like how it plays off the sweetness of the bananas. You could embellish it with chocolate chips, though that's not my road of choice because I like to keep it simple. And in my opinion, you should never add nuts to your banana bread. Do it if you want, just don't tell me about it. Serve in thick slices with too much butter on top.

Note: This recipe calls for vanilla paste, which you can find in the baking aisle of your grocery store or online. You can sub vanilla extract, but the paste will give you a much richer, more spot-on vanilla flavor.

Makes one 9-by-5-inch loaf

Ingredient	Weight	Volume	Baker's %
Total flour			100.00%
>>All-purpose flour, plus more for dusting	180g	1 cup + ⅓ cup	70.59%
>>Buckwheat flour	75g	½ cup	29.41%
Unsalted butter, softened, plus more for greasing	120g	½ cup	47.06%
Granulated sugar	115g	½ cup	45.10%
Dark brown sugar	115g	½ cup, packed	45.10%
Large egg	55g	1 whole	21.57%
Ripe bananas	350g	1 cup	137.25%
Active sourdough starter	320g	1 cup	125.49%
Vanilla bean paste or extract (see note)	10g	2 tablespoons	3.92%
Fine sea salt	8g	2 teaspoons	3.14%
Baking powder	5g	1 teaspoon	1.96%
Baking soda	3g	½ teaspoon	1.18%

Preheat the oven to 350°F. Rub the inside of a 9-by-5-inch loaf pan with a layer of butter, followed by a dusting of flour, coating all sides.

In the bowl of a stand mixer fitted with the paddle attachment, add the butter, granulated sugar, and brown sugar. Beat on high speed for about 5 minutes, until light and fluffy. Reduce the speed to low, add the egg, and mix for another minute, until the egg is fully incorporated. Add the bananas and continue beating on low speed for 2 minutes. Add the sourdough starter, all-purpose flour, buckwheat flour, vanilla, salt, baking powder, and baking soda and mix for another minute, until all of the ingredients are combined and no dry flour remains.

Transfer the batter to the prepared pan. Knock the pan on the counter a few times to ensure there are no air pockets.

Bake for 30 to 40 minutes, until a cake tester or toothpick comes out clean. Allow the loaf to cool in the pan for 10 minutes, then transfer it to a wire cooling rack to cool for another hour before serving.

Buckwheat Brownies

Buckwheat and chocolate go incredibly well together, each lending the other a deep richness. To further perk up the buckwheat, though, I add ground cardamom, which is a floral, almost minty, but still earthy baking spice. You'll notice that the recipe calls for blending buckwheat flour with all-purpose, which is to help maintain the signature-brownie dense structure. That said, you can go all buckwheat to make these gluten-free; they'll just be a bit more on the crumbly side.

Makes 20 (3½ x 3-inch) brownies

Ingredient	Weight	Volume	Baker's %
Total flour			100.00%
>>Buckwheat flour	200g	1¾ cups	58.82%
>>All-purpose flour	140g	1 cup + 2 tablespoons	41.18%
Cooking spray, for greasing			
Sugar	860g	4¼ cups	252.94%
Baking powder	4g	1 teaspoon	1.18%
Ground cardamom	4g	1½ teaspoons	1.18%
Bittersweet chocolate (60 to 70%)	340g	2⅓ cups	100.00%
Unsalted butter	340g	1½ cups	100.00%
Large eggs	440g	8 whole	129.41%
Vanilla bean paste or extract (see note on page 86)	10g	1 tablespoon	2.94%

Preheat the oven to 325°F. Coat a half-sheet tray with cooking spray, line with parchment, and spray the parchment.

In a medium bowl, add the sugar, buckwheat flour, all-purpose flour, baking powder, and cardamom. Whisk briefly to combine.

Pour about an inch of water into a medium saucepan. Set a larger, heat-safe bowl over the pot and bring the water to a boil over medium-high heat. Reduce the heat to low and add the chocolate and butter to the bowl. Melt the chocolate and butter together, stirring occasionally.

Remove the bowl from the pot and let the chocolate mixture cool slightly. Whisk in the eggs and vanilla, beating until thoroughly combined.

Continued

Add a third of the flour mixture to the chocolate mixture. Use a spatula to scoop up from underneath the batter and fold it up over the flour to combine. Rotate the bowl as you go and make sure the flour is completely incorporated. Repeat this with the remaining thirds of the flour mixture.

Pour the batter into the prepared pan. Bake for about 30 minutes, until the tops are crackly but do not spring back like a cake does when pressed. In my opinion, brownies are best just slightly underbaked and fudgy. Let cool before slicing and serving.

Heritage Cornbread

Cornbread is one of those feel-good breads—it's easy and it's reminiscent of a time when home cooking prevailed. And it's almost always served with equally comforting foods like pulled pork, chili, or Thanksgiving turkey—anything with gravy, sauce, or ample melted butter that the cornbread can sop up. This also happens to be the first recipe in this book where you're working with the soaker method, or soaking your grain (or corn) before including it in the dough so it softens and also begins to ferment naturally.

Corn itself is distinctly American, and it grows very well in the Midwest. Some folks, like my farmer friends Marty and Will Travis, have been gifted the seeds of heritage cornmeals by indigenous communities (in this case, the Iroquois Nation). The distinct flavor of these varieties—from their farm and others—makes this otherwise simple canvas that much more interesting. Any heritage cornmeal will work (see page 38). A fire-roasted cornmeal is particularly tasty, like Spence's Iroquois white, with the smoky flavor permeating the sweet bread. Or it's a fun recipe to make with colored cornmeal like Bloody Butcher or Blue Hopi, as the distinct color of the corn makes it very obvious that this is not just any ordinary cornbread. If you're feeling indulgent, spread a pat of butter over the warm loaf or muffins and drizzle with a little honey before serving.

Note: While I like using a coarse cornmeal for this recipe, fine cornmeal can be used if you prefer. Coarse will give you more texture, while finer will be a softer, smoother crumb. How do you decide? Do what the professionals do: Get a bunch of different varieties and textures and try them all in a side-by-side sampling. Or just take good notes and try a new variety the next time you make this recipe.

Makes one 8 ½-inch round, 1 dozen standard muffins, or 6 jumbo muffins

For the Soaker:

Ingredient	Weight	Volume	Baker's %
Total flour			100.00%
>>Heritage cornmeal	80g	½ cup	100.00%
Buttermilk	335g	1⅓ cups	418.00%

Continued

For the Cornbread:

Ingredient	Weight	Volume	Baker's %
Total flour			100.00%
>>All-purpose flour	80g	⅔ cup	66.67%
>>Spelt flour	40g	⅓ cup	33.33%
Dark brown sugar	30g	2 tablespoons + 1 teaspoon, packed	25.00%
Raw sugar	30g	2 tablespoons + 1 teaspoon	25.00%
Baking powder	14g	1 tablespoon + 1 teaspoon	11.67%
Fine sea salt	4g	1 heaping teaspoon	3.33%
Baking soda	1g	¼ teaspoon	0.83%
Large eggs	110g	2 whole	91.67%
Honey	35g	2 tablespoons	29.16%
Unsalted butter, melted, plus more for greasing	25g	2 tablespoons	20.83%

Make the soaker: The day before you bake, make the soaker. In a medium bowl, add the buttermilk and cornmeal and mix by hand until thoroughly combined. Cover with a tea towel or linen and let the mixture sit at room temperature for 12 to 24 hours.

Make the cornbread: Preheat the oven to 400°F. Grease a cast-iron or other heavy-bottomed skillet (or muffin tin, if you're making muffins) with butter and set in the oven to preheat.

In a large bowl, add the all-purpose flour, spelt flour, brown sugar, raw sugar, baking powder, salt, and baking soda. Whisk to combine thoroughly. Add the eggs, honey, melted butter, and the soaker and whisk until all of the dry ingredients have been absorbed.

Carefully remove the preheated pan or muffin tin from the oven and pour the batter in. Bake for about 20 minutes for a loaf or 10 to 15 minutes for muffins (depending on their size), or until golden brown. If the pan is preheated properly, the bottom should be just slightly more caramelized than the top. I like serving this cornbread by inverting the pan onto a serving platter so the more caramelized side faces up. Serve warm.

Cornmeal Whoopie Pies

This recipe came about sort of by accident—I wanted to try cooking the cornmeal before adding it to a cookie. Sure enough, just like in bread, the pre-gelatinization of the starches made for a soft, tender, not-quite-cake, not-quite-cookie result that was perfect for a whoopie pie. I like pairing these with a lime zest–flecked marshmallow filling. Bonus points for torching the marshmallow before you finish assembling the pies.

Makes 10 whoopie pies

For the Cookies:

Ingredient	Weight	Volume	Baker's %
Total flour			100.00%
>>All-purpose flour	175g	1⅓ cups + 1 tablespoon	100.00%
Cooking spray, for greasing			
Fine-ground cornmeal	120g	¾ cup	100.00%
Water	360g	1½ cups	300.00%
Baking powder	4g	1 teaspoon	2.29%
Baking soda	2g	½ teaspoon	1.14%
Fine sea salt	2g	⅓ teaspoon	1.14%
Unsalted butter	115g	½ cup	65.71%
Granulated sugar	75g	⅓ cup + 1 tablespoon	42.86%
Dark brown sugar	70g	⅓ cup packed	40.00%
Honey	16g	2¼ teaspoons	9.14%
Large egg	55g	1 whole	31.43%
Vanilla bean paste or extract (see note on page 86)	8g	1 teaspoon	4.57%

For the Marshmallow Filling:

Ingredient	Weight	Volume	Baker's %
Cold water	56g	¼ cup	147.37%
Powdered gelatin	7g	1 packet (2½ teaspoons)	18.42%
Large egg white	38g	1 each	100.00%
Granulated sugar	220g	1 cup	578.95%
Water	100g	⅓ cup plus 2 tablespoons	263.00%
Honey	20g	1 tablespoon	52.63%
Fine sea salt	2g	⅛ teaspoon	5.26%
Grated lime zest	1g	1 lime	2.63%

Continued

Make the cookies: Preheat the oven to 375°F. Coat a baking sheet with cooking spray, line with parchment, and spray the parchment.

In a medium saucepan over medium-high heat, add the cornmeal and water and stir with a wooden spoon to combine. Stir often to prevent scorching as you bring the mixture to a boil. Reduce the heat to low and cook until the porridge is very thick, 3 to 4 minutes after it comes to a boil. Spread the mixture over a baking sheet or plate to help it cool completely.

In a medium bowl, add the flour, baking powder, baking soda, and salt and whisk to combine.

In the bowl of a stand mixer fitted with the paddle attachment, add the butter, granulated sugar, brown sugar, and honey. Beat on high for 5 minutes to cream the butter and sugars until light and fluffy. Turn off the mixer and scrape down the sides of the bowl with a spatula. Turn the mixer to low speed and add the egg and vanilla, allowing them to fully incorporate, about 2 minutes. Add the cooked cornmeal and mix until the consistency becomes very even, about 2 more minutes. Add the flour mixture and mix until just combined and no dry flour remains, 1 to 2 minutes.

Using a 1-ounce scoop or 2-tablespoon measure to portion the cookie dough, space 10 cookies evenly on the prepared baking sheet. Press down on the tops of the cookies to flatten them into roughly ⅓-inch-thick disks. Bake until the edges are golden brown and the center is firm to the touch, 12 to 15 minutes. Repeat with the remaining dough to bake 10 more cookies. Let cool before filling.

Make the filling: In a small bowl, combine the cold water and gelatin and let sit for 15 minutes to bloom.

In the bowl of a stand mixer fitted with the whisk attachment, add the egg white and whip on high speed until it is just past firm peaks and starting to break down, about 5 minutes. It will start to look grainy and broken, like curdling a custard.

In a small saucepan over high heat, add the sugar, water, and honey. Cook until the mixture reaches 238°F; this should take about 5 minutes. If you watch the mixture, you will see the bubbles start off very small when boiling. They will turn into larger bubbles when the mixture is reaching the proper temperature.

Turn the mixer to medium speed and drizzle the hot sugar mixture into the whipped white. Add the bloomed gelatin, increase the mixer speed to high, and allow the mixture to whip until the bowl is cool to the touch, 15 to 20 minutes. Once cool, whisk in the salt and lime zest.

Assemble the cookies: Transfer the filling to a piping bag fitted with a round tip or a large zip-top plastic bag with one corner snipped off. Invert half of the cookies so the flat side faces up. Pipe a thick layer of filling onto the center of the cookie, leaving about ¼ inch of space around the outside of the cookie. Place the other half of the cookies on top of the filling, flat-side down, creating a sandwich. Press on the pie lightly to evenly spread the filling to the sides of the cookies. If you're feeling adventurous, you can torch the top of the filling until it caramelizes before adding the second cookie. Let the assembled whoopie pies cool for 1 hour at room temperature before enjoying.

Oat Galette with Seasonal Fruit

When I'm choosing a whole grain for a recipe, I'm looking to play up its strengths—flavor, definitely, but also its natural textural tendencies. Oat flour soaks up a ton of moisture while also being low in gluten, so it's great if you're using it in pastry applications—especially the dough for this free-form pie—because you want that to be a little on the dry side, yielding a flaky and tender rust with nice, rich flavor.

You can make this galette with pretty much any filling you're into, but I recommend rolling with softish seasonal fruit—your berries in early summer, your stone fruit in late summer (not apples). You can also combine fruits—I like a mix of berries, or stone fruit combos like peaches and nectarines. And while I use Grand Marnier for added liquid here, you can use another liquor (bourbon with peaches would work well) or orange juice in the same ratio. Dealer's choice.

Note: This recipe makes enough filling for one pie but enough dough for two pies. You could tuck half of the dough into a pie shell and do a double-crust pie or lattice topping, or you could stash the other half in the freezer so you'll be ready the next time a galette hankering strikes.

Makes 1 (10-inch) pie (see note)

For the Pie Dough:

Ingredient	Weight	Volume	Baker's %
Total flour			100.00%
>>All-purpose flour	175g	1⅓ cups + 1 tablespoon	63.64%
>>Oat flour	100g	¾ cup + 2 tablespoons	36.36%
Granulated sugar	25g	2 tablespoons	9.09%
Fine sea salt	4g	⅔ teaspoon	1.45%
Cold unsalted butter	225g	1 cup	81.82%
Ice water	100g	⅓ cup	36.36%
Raw sugar, for sprinkling			

Continued

For the Filling:

Ingredient	Weight	Volume	Baker's %
Softish seasonal fruit, cut into ½-inch pieces if needed	380g	2½ cups	100.00%
Granulated sugar	85g	¼ cup + 3 tablespoons	21.57%
Grand Marnier	55g	3½ tablespoons	15.03%
Cornstarch	4g	1 tablespoon	0.92%
Fine sea salt	2g	¼ teaspoon	0.39%

For the Egg Wash:

Ingredient	Volume
Large egg	1 whole
Water	1 tablespoon

Make the dough: In a large mixing bowl, add the all-purpose flour, oat flour, sugar, and salt. Whisk briefly to combine and place in the freezer for 1 hour. If your bowl won't fit in your freezer, transfer the mixture to a vessel that will. The idea is to drop the temperature of your dry ingredients so that when you cut in the butter, it won't melt, thus ensuring the flakiness of the pastry.

Cut the cold butter into marble-size pieces and toss the butter into the cold flour mixture. Using a rubbing motion between your thumb and forefingers, pinch each piece of butter in the flour. You are trying to coat the butter nicely with the flour, which will create flaky layers in the pie dough. Add the ice water a few tablespoons at a time and toss to combine. The dough should be quite shaggy and firm. If it doesn't come together as a dough, add another few tablespoons of water. Divide the dough in half and wrap each piece in plastic. Refrigerate for 1 hour. (If you're planning to freeze one piece of dough for future use, pop it in the freezer now and use it within 3 months.)

Make the filling: In a medium bowl, add the fruit, sugar, Grand Marnier, cornstarch, and salt and toss to combine. Reserve until ready to fill the galettes. The filling can be covered and refrigerated for up to a day before using.

Make the galette: Preheat the oven to 350°F. Line a baking sheet with parchment paper.

On a floured surface, roll the dough to about ⅛ inch thick and about 12 inches in diameter. Place the dough on the prepared baking sheet. Scoop half of the filling onto the center of the dough, leaving about 2 inches of dough without filling around the edge of the pie. Starting with one side of the dough, fold pieces of the dough over, encasing the filling. There should be a circle of exposed fruit in the center of the pie. Refrigerate for 30 minutes. (You can also prepare this as a regular pie in a pie tin, and use the second piece of dough to make a double-crusted fruit pie.)

In a small bowl, whisk together the egg and water. Brush the dough with the egg wash and sprinkle with the raw sugar. Bake for 30 to 40 minutes, until the crust is golden brown and the filling is bubbling. Serve warm.

Oat Doughnuts

I much prefer a yeasted doughnut to a cake doughnut (shocking, right?). These are soft and buttery and can be filled with your choice of fillings like cream, jam, or a bright citrus curd like the one I've included here. (Store-bought is fine, too.) Or, go with no filling and toss the freshly fried doughnuts in a cinnamon-sugar blend.

Note: When making a citrus curd, I like doing a blend of citrus fruits, in this case equal parts lemon, orange, and lime. You could choose just one type, if you prefer.

Makes 12 doughnuts

For the Doughnuts:

Ingredient	Weight	Volume	Baker's %
Total flour			100.00%
>>All-purpose flour	400g	3 cups + 1 tablespoon	66.67%
>>Oat flour	200g	1¾ cups	33.33%
Whole milk, at room temperature	375g	1½ cups	62.50%
Large eggs	110g	2 whole	18.33%
Sugar, plus more for finishing	95g	½ cup	15.83%
Unsalted butter	70g	⅓ cup	11.67%
Active sourdough starter	65g	⅓ cup	10.83%
Fine sea salt	6g	1 teaspoon	1.00%
Active dry yeast	5g	1 teaspoon	0.83%
Cooking spray, for greasing			
Rice bran oil or vegetable oil, for frying			

For the Citrus Curd (optional):

Ingredient	Weight	Volume	Baker's %
Sugar	400g	2 cups	100.00%
Large egg yolks	200g	10 each	50.00%
Large eggs	110g	2 whole	27.50%
Grated citrus zest (I use equal parts lemon, orange, and lime.)	10g	2 tablespoons	2.50%
Citrus juice (I use equal parts lemon, orange, and lime.)	300g	1¼ cups	75.00%
Unsalted butter	250g	1 cup + 2 tablespoons	62.50%
Fine sea salt	1g	¼ teaspoon	0.25%

Make the dough: In the bowl of a stand mixer fitted with the dough hook attachment, add the all-purpose flour, oat flour, milk, eggs, sugar, butter, sourdough starter, salt, and yeast. Mix on low speed for 4 minutes, or until no dry pockets of flour remain. Increase the speed to medium-high and mix until the dough is smooth, shiny and strong, 10 to 12 minutes. Remove the dough hook from the bowl and remove the bowl from the mixer.

Ferment: Cover the bowl with a tea towel or linen and let the dough ferment at room temperature for 2 hours, folding it after 1 hour. The dough is ready when it has doubled in size. While the dough is proofing, cut out 4-by-7-inch rectangles of parchment paper for your doughnuts to proof on. Spray each rectangle with cooking spray.

Portion: Turn out the dough onto a lightly floured work surface. Roll it into a ¼-inch-thick rectangle. Cut the dough into 3-by-6-inch rectangles and place each on one of the prepared pieces of parchment; set all the pieces on a baking sheet. Cover the whole sheet loosely with plastic and proof for 30 minutes at room temperature, then refrigerate overnight.

Make the curd (if using): In a medium saucepan, add the sugar, egg yolks, whole eggs, and citrus zest. Whisk until smooth. Add the citrus juice and whisk again until smooth. Place the pan over medium-low heat, stirring with a spatula to prevent scorching. Cook until the curd reaches 150°F, then add the butter. Continue stirring until the mixture has thickened substantially and reaches 190°F.

Place a fine-mesh sieve over a medium bowl and strain the curd mixture. Stir in the salt. Cover the bowl and refrigerate until ready to use, up to 1 week.

Fry the doughnuts: In a large, deep, heavy-bottomed pot over medium-high heat, heat at least 3 inches of oil to 350°F. Set a wire cooling rack over a baking sheet nearby.

Pick up each doughnut by slipping your hand under the parchment paper. Gently invert the doughnut and peel off the parchment from the bottom of the dough as you release it into the oil. Fry each doughnut for about 5 minutes per side, until golden and significantly puffed. Using tongs, carefully transfer the

Continued

doughnut to the cooling rack to drain. Repeat with the remaining pieces and let cool. I also recommend letting your oil cool and storing it in the refrigerator because it'll still be good for another two or three fry sessions.

If you're filling the doughnuts, transfer the citrus curd to a piping bag fitted with a round tip or a large zip-top plastic bag with a corner snipped off. Pierce the side of each doughnut and squeeze about ¼ cup of curd into each doughnut. Toss each doughnut in sugar before serving.

Sorghum Blondies

Blondies are the dense, chewy, best slightly underdone baked good that have been coming out of grandmothers' ovens since, well, forever. They're easy to make, don't take too long to throw together, and can be loaded with ice cream as a special treat. I made this version with sorghum to accentuate their inherent butteriness, with sorghum syrup and brown butter to deepen the flavor even more. I also like to make these with caramelized white chocolate chips (aka Valrhona Dulcey chips), but you can also use regular white chocolate chips or butterscotch chips.

Makes 12 (3-inch square) blondies

Ingredient	Weight	Volume	Baker's %
Total flour			100.00%
>>Sorghum flour	220g	1½ cups	66.66%
>>Whole-wheat pastry flour	110g	1 cup	33.33%
Cooking spray, for greasing			
Baking soda	6g	1 teaspoon	1.81%
Fine sea salt	6g	1 teaspoon	1.81%
Ground ginger	2.5g	1 teaspoon	0.75%
Unsalted butter	225g	1 cup	68.18%
Sorghum syrup	170g	½ cup	51.51%
Dark brown sugar	155g	1½ cups, packed	46.97%
Large eggs, room temperature	110g	2 each	33.33%
Vanilla bean paste or extract (see note on page 86)	5g	1 teaspoon	1.51%
Valrhona Dulcey chips, white chocolate chips, or butterscotch chips	125g	¾ cup	37.87%

Place a rack in the center of the oven and preheat to 350°F. Coat a 9-by-13-inch pan with cooking spray, line with parchment, and spray the parchment.

In a medium bowl, add the sorghum flour, whole-wheat pastry flour, baking soda, salt, and ginger. Mix by hand to thoroughly combine.

In a small saucepan over medium heat, add the butter. Cook for 10 minutes, until the butter gets very foamy and smells nutty and the milk solids start to brown.

Continued

Set a few layers of cheesecloth over a fine-mesh strainer and place the strainer over a large mixing bowl. Strain the brown butter through the cheesecloth to remove the milk solids.

Let the brown butter cool slightly. Add the sorghum syrup and brown sugar and whisk to combine. Add the eggs one at a time, whisking after each one to incorporate completely. Add the vanilla and whisk again. Add the flour mixture and whisk until no dry flour is left. Fold in the Dulcey chips.

Pour the batter into the prepared pan, spreading it evenly with a spatula. Note that this batter will be slightly thicker than regular brownie batter.

Bake for 35 to 40 minutes. The blondies will puff and look fairly airy in the oven. They are done when the top feels dry but the center isn't quite set and still jiggles slightly if moved.

Let the blondies cool in the pan for 10 minutes. Use the sides of the parchment to lift and transfer the blondies to a wire cooling rack. Cool for 1 hour before cutting and serving.

Spelt and Apple Muffins

What can I say? This is just a nice muffin. It gets a subtle earthiness from the spelt, tartness from baking apples, and sweetness from apple cider to balance both those out. Consider this a basic fruit-liquid-muffin ratio that you can play with, swapping in things like berries for the apples and milk for the cider. You'll notice that there are egg yolks called for in addition to whole eggs. This means more fat and less protein, which also means a more tender muffin.

Makes 12 muffins

Ingredient	Weight	Volume	Baker's %
Total flour			100.00%
>>Spelt flour	300g	3 cups	68.97%
>>All-purpose flour	135g	1 cup + 1 tablespoon	31.03%
Cooking spray, for greasing			
Baking powder	25g	2 tablespoons	5.75%
Rolled oats, plus more for topping	12g	¼ cup	2.76%
Fine sea salt	10g	2 teaspoons	2.30%
Whole milk	200g	¾ cup	45.98%
Apple cider	100g	½ cup	22.99%
Honey	50g	2½ tablespoons	11.49%
Sugar	230g	1 cup	52.87%
Unsalted butter	145g	⅔ cup	33.33%
Large egg yolks	70g	4 each	16.09%
Large egg	55g	1 whole	12.64%
Granny Smith or similar baking apples, peeled, cored, and cut into ½-inch pieces	200g	2 to 3 each	45.98%

Preheat the oven to 350°F. Spray a muffin tin with cooking spray. (Alternatively, you can use paper or silicone liners.)

In a medium bowl, add the spelt flour, all-purpose flour, baking powder, oats, and salt. Whisk briefly to combine.

In a small bowl, add the milk, apple cider, and honey. Whisk to combine.

In the bowl of a stand mixer fitted with the paddle attachment, add the sugar and butter. On high speed, cream the sugar and butter together for

Continued

3 minutes, or until light and fluffy. Reduce the speed to low and add the egg yolks and whole egg one at a time, mixing until each is incorporated before adding the next. Add about a third of the flour mixture and mix until incorporated, followed by about half of the milk mixture. Repeat with another third of the flour mixture and the remaining milk mixture. Add the remaining flour mixture and mix until incorporated and no dry ingredients remain. Add the apples and mix until they are evenly dispersed.

Scoop the batter into the prepared muffin tins and top each muffin with a sprinkle of rolled oats. Bake for 20 to 25 minutes, until a cake tester comes out clean. Let cool slightly before serving.

Spiced Rye Cookies

Rye's spicy, floral flavor pairs really well with the smoky molasses and warm baking spices in this recipe. Just be sure to keep an eye on these—between the dark dough and quick bake time, it's easy to take these a little too far. They will also be soft and bubbly when first coming out of the oven, but will crisp as they cool.

Makes about 60 cookies

Ingredient	Weight	Volume	Baker's %
Total flour			100.00%
>>Rye flour	42g	⅓ cup	100.00%
Dark brown sugar	105g	½ cup, loosely packed	250.00%
Unsalted butter	85g	6 tablespoons	202.38%
Molasses	30g	2 tablespoons	71.43%
Fresh lemon juice	8g	1 tablespoon	19.05%
Ground ginger	2g	½ teaspoon	4.76%
Ground cinnamon	1g	½ teaspoon	2.38%
Ground nutmeg	1g	¼ teaspoon	2.38%
Fine sea salt	1g	¼ teaspoon	2.38%

Preheat the oven to 350°F. Line a baking sheet with parchment paper.

In a small saucepan over medium-high heat, add the brown sugar, butter, molasses, and lemon juice and bring to a boil. Boil the mixture for 1 minute, then remove the pan from the heat. Add the rye flour, ginger, cinnamon, nutmeg, and salt and whisk until smooth. Let the dough cool to room temperature.

Using a ½-teaspoon measure or small spoon, portion out pieces of dough and roll them into balls. Space the balls 4 inches apart on the prepared baking sheet. They will spread significantly and become lacey. Bake for about 7 minutes, until the cookies are flat and golden. Transfer the parchment with the cookies to a wire cooling rack. Repeat with the remaining cookie dough, adding a new sheet of parchment each time. Let the cookies cool for at least 5 minutes before serving. Once cool, store in an airtight container at room temperature for about a week.

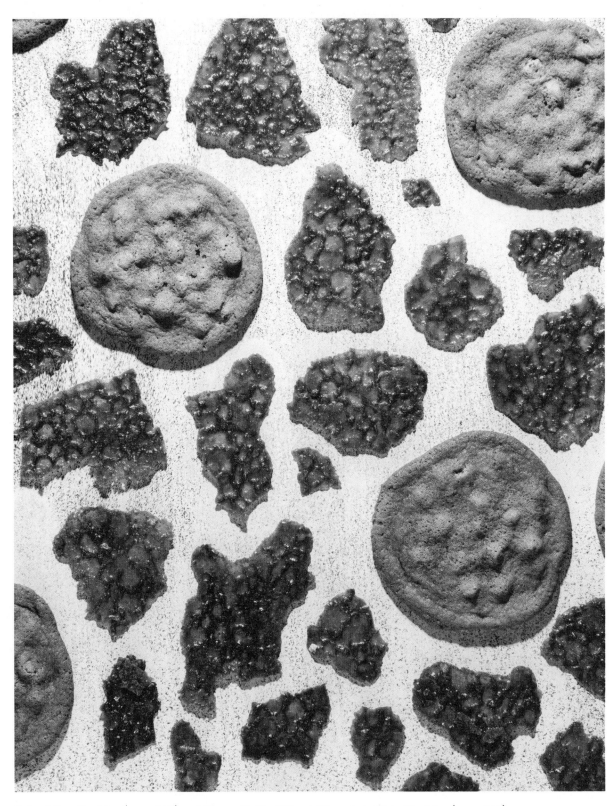

Spiced Rye Cookies (page 107) and Brown Butter Wheat Chocolate Chip Cookies (page 109)

Brown Butter Wheat Chocolate Chip Cookies

This is essentially your classic Nestlé Toll House chocolate chip cookie. I think we can all agree that a chocolate chip cookie warm from the oven is one of the most comforting foods ever, like a hug from everyone who has ever loved you wrapped up in one bite. And when you go the extra mile to find farm-fresh eggs, good butter, and whole-wheat pastry flour, it's the perfect example of how better ingredients make a better product. Then this recipe becomes one of those super special, super recognizable treats presented in a whole new mind-blowing way. I highly recommend you do what my wife and I do in our house: Portion out the cookie dough, freeze it, then bake a couple from frozen anytime you want a warm, fresh-from-the-oven cookie. (Which, frankly, is the only correct way to eat a cookie.)

Makes 24 cookies

Ingredient	Weight	Volume	Baker's %
Total flour			100.00%
>>Whole-wheat pastry flour	250g	2¼ cups	100.00%
Unsalted butter	225g	1 cup	90.00%
Granulated sugar	150g	¾ cup	60.00%
Dark brown sugar	145g	¾ cup packed	58.00%
Large eggs	110g	2 whole	44.00%
Buttermilk	30g	2 tablespoons	12.00%
Vanilla bean paste or extract (see note on page 86)	10g	2 teaspoons	4.00%
Fine sea salt	6g	1 teaspoon	2.40%
Baking soda	4g	1 teaspoon	1.40%
Semisweet chocolate chips	340g	2 cups	136.00%

Preheat the oven to 375°F. Line a baking sheet with parchment paper.

In a small saucepan over medium heat, melt the butter. Continue heating the butter until the solids have browned and it smells robust and nutty, about 10 minutes. Strain through a fine-mesh strainer or cheesecloth to remove the browned solids. Transfer the browned butter to a small bowl to cool.

Continued

In the bowl of a stand mixer fitted with the paddle attachment, combine the cooled browned butter, granulated sugar, and brown sugar. Beat on high speed to cream the butter and sugars together until they're light and fluffy, about 5 minutes. Turn the mixer off and scrape down the sides of the bowl with a spatula. Turn the mixer on to low and add the eggs one at a time, waiting for the first one to incorporate before adding the second. With the mixer running, carefully add the buttermilk and vanilla and mix for about 2 more minutes, until incorporated.

In a medium bowl, add the flour, salt, and baking soda and whisk briefly to combine. With the mixer on low speed, slowly add the dry ingredients to the butter and egg mixture and mix until just combined, 1 to 2 minutes. Add the chocolate chips and mix until they're evenly dispersed, just another minute or so.

Portion the cookie dough into balls roughly the size of golf balls, or about a 2-ounce scoop. Place 6 cookies on the prepared baking sheet, evenly spaced. Bake until the edges are golden brown and the center is just set, 12 to 15 minutes. Transfer the cookies to a wire cooling rack. Repeat with the remaining dough, adding a new sheet of parchment each time. Let the cookies cool for at least 5 minutes before serving. Once cool, store in an airtight container at room temperature for up to 5 days.

Baking from frozen: To bake frozen portioned cookies, bake in a 375°F oven for 16 minutes.

Honey Wheat Graham Cracker S'Mores

Every summer, Marty Travis and I host Bread Camp at Spence Farm, a two-day intensive workshop for bakers and chefs who want to learn more about incorporating local grains into their program. We unplug, talk, bake, cook over fire, and rough it under the rural Illinois stars. And what better after-class treat than a round of s'mores around a campfire—especially with homemade graham crackers that showcase the perfect union between whole wheat and honey. I also like to make my own honey marshmallows, which I encourage you to do if you're willing to go the extra mile, but store-bought will do just fine. All that's left after that is grabbing a bar of good chocolate and getting to roasting.

Note: If you want to make these ahead, cut the marshmallows and crackers and store them in airtight containers at room temperature until ready to assemble.

Makes 8 sandwiches

For the Honey Marshmallows (optional):

Ingredient	Weight	Volume	Baker's %
Cold water	118g	½ cup	15.70%
Powdered gelatin	55g	6 tablespoons	7.33%
Water	600g	2½ cups	80.00%
Granulated sugar	750g	3¾ cups	100.00%
Honey	300g	1 cup	40.00%
Fine sea salt	10g	1½ teaspoons	1.33%
Large egg whites	270g	9 each	36.00%
Cooking spray, for greasing			
Cornstarch, for dusting			
Powdered sugar, for dusting			

Continued

For the Graham Crackers:

Ingredient	Weight	Volume	Baker's %
Total flour			100.00%
>>Whole-wheat flour	450g	4 cups	80.36%
>>Oat flour	110g	1 cup	19.64%
Sugar	100g	½ cup	17.86%
Fine sea salt	20g	1 tablespoon + ½ teaspoon	3.57%
Baking powder	6g	1⅓ teaspoons	1.07%
Baking soda	4g	1 teaspoon	0.71%
Cold unsalted butter	170g	¾ cup	30.36%
Honey	130g	⅓ cup	23.21%
Water	90g	⅓ cup	16.07%
Vanilla bean paste or extract (see note on page 86)	10g	1 tablespoon + ½ teaspoon	1.79%

Make the marshmallows: In a small bowl, combine the cold water and gelatin and let sit for 15 minutes to bloom.

In a medium saucepan over medium heat, add the water, granulated sugar, honey, and salt. Heat the mixture to 230°F, then reduce the heat to low. Let this continue cooking while you whip the egg whites.

In the bowl of a stand mixer fitted with the whisk attachment, add the egg whites and whip on medium speed until medium peaks form, 3 to 4 minutes. With the mixer still running, continue heating the sugar until it reaches 250°F. Add the bloomed gelatin to the hot sugar, stir to combine, and remove from the heat.

Increase the mixer speed to medium-high and slowly drizzle in the hot sugar and gelatin mixture. Continue mixing until the bowl is completely cool to the touch, 15 to 20 minutes.

Line a baking sheet with parchment and spray well with cooking spray. Dust heavily with an equal mixture of powdered sugar and cornstarch. Pour the cooled marshmallow mixture onto the prepared baking sheet and spread evenly. Dust the surface heavily with more cornstarch and powdered sugar and let the marshmallow rest at room temperature for 24 hours. Cut into 3-inch squares, the same size as your crackers.

Make the graham crackers: In the bowl of a food processor, add the whole-wheat flour, oat flour, sugar, salt, baking powder, and baking soda and pulse until the mixture is the texture of wet sand. Add the honey, water, and vanilla. Pulse until a dough forms, 10 to 15 pulses.

Turn out the dough onto a work surface and press it into a 9-inch square. Wrap the dough in plastic wrap and refrigerate for at least 2 hours or up to overnight.

Preheat the oven to 325°F. Line a baking sheet with parchment paper.

Roll the dough to ¼-inch thickness and place on the prepared pan. Prick with a fork all over, then use a knife to score the dough into 3-inch square crackers. Bake for 16 minutes, or until golden brown and slightly darker on the edges. The dough will still be soft to the touch when hot. Let the dough cool completely before breaking it into crackers. At this point you could also save the crackers for another day by storing them in an airtight container at room temperature.

Assemble: Get your best bar of chocolate and a marshmallow roasting stick, build a fire, and make s'mores.

Whole-Wheat Biscuits

I've been making these for years and pretty much always have a bag of 'em in my freezer to bake off whenever I'm in the mood for fresh-out-of-the-oven biscuits. I've found that the secret is to first acidulate the cream with a little vinegar, which makes it nice and thick and a little tangy. Then I use a rolling and folding method for the dough that's similar to how you'd make croissants, so you end up with even more buttery, flaky layers.

Makes 12 large biscuits

Ingredient	Weight	Volume	Baker's %
Total flour			100.00%
>>All-purpose flour	575g	4⅓ cups + 1 tablespoon	57.50%
>>Whole-wheat flour	425g	3¾ cups	42.50%
Heavy cream	1000g	4¼ cups	100.00%
Apple cider vinegar	125g	½ cup	12.50%
Granulated sugar	60g	¼ cup + 2 teaspoons	6.00%
Baking powder	60g	4½ tablespoons	6.00%
Fine sea salt	17g	1 tablespoon	1.70%
Baking soda	4g	1 teaspoon + ¼ teaspoon	0.40%
Cold unsalted butter	500g	2¼ cups	50.00%
Raw sugar, for dusting			

In a medium bowl, add the cream and cider vinegar and whisk to combine. Refrigerate for at least 30 minutes or overnight.

Preheat the oven to 400°F. Line a baking sheet with parchment paper.

In a large bowl, add the all-purpose flour, wheat flour, sugar, baking powder, salt, and baking soda and whisk to combine. (If you're acidulating the cream overnight, you can also do this step the night before and keep the dry ingredient mixture in the freezer.)

Cut the cold butter into marble-size pieces and toss them into the flour mixture. Using your thumb and forefingers, pinch each piece of butter in the flour with a rubbing motion. You are trying to coat the butter nicely with the flour, which will create flaky layers in the biscuits.

Remove the cream and vinegar mixture from the fridge (it should be thick) and reserve ½ cup of the mixture. Add the remaining 4¼ cups to the flour and butter mixture and stir to combine. The dough should be quite shaggy and firm, but if it doesn't come together as a dough, add another ¼ cup of the reserved cream mixture, reserving the remaining ¼ cup.

Turn out the dough onto a floured surface and dust the top of the dough with flour as well. Roll the dough to ½-inch thickness. Book fold (see page 275) and roll to ½-inch thickness. Repeat with another book fold and roll to ¾-inch thickness. Cut the dough into 3-inch squares and place them on the prepared baking sheet.

Brush the tops of the biscuits with the reserved cream mixture and dust with raw sugar. Bake for 20 to 25 minutes, until golden brown. Cool slightly and serve.

Whole-Wheat Crumpets

These fluffy, doughy little guys are like the snack that you never knew you wanted. It's an easy batter to make, and the crumpets can be cooked free-form in a skillet. Or you can use a ring mold in the pan, which helps keep the crumpets uniform and also gets a little more height on them, which means more nooks and crannies for your butter and jam.

Makes about 18 small crumpets

Ingredient	Weight	Volume	Baker's %
Total flour			100.00%
>>Whole-wheat flour	720g	4¾ cups	100.00%
Water	1010g	4¼ cups	140.28%
Fine sea salt	29g	1 tablespoon + 2 teaspoons	4.03%
Sugar	25g	2 tablespoons	3.47%
Extra-virgin olive oil	12g	1 tablespoon	1.67%
Active dry yeast	6g	1½ teaspoons	0.83%
Baking soda	1g	⅓ teaspoon	0.14%
Unsalted butter, for cooking			
Cooking spray, for greasing			

In a large bowl, add the water, flour, salt, sugar, olive oil, and yeast. Mix by hand to combine thoroughly, about 2 minutes. Cover with a tea towel or linen and set aside at room temperature to ferment for 4 hours.

Sprinkle the baking soda over the top of the batter and stir with a wooden spoon or spatula to thoroughly combine, 2 to 3 minutes. Cover the bowl again and let the batter rise for 30 minutes at room temperature. At this point you can either cook the crumpets or refrigerate the batter overnight.

In a medium nonstick pan over low heat, melt 1 tablespoon butter. Place ring molds in the size of your choice into the pan and spray the inside of the molds with cooking spray. Scoop enough batter into each mold to reach a third of the way up the sides. Cook until the crumpets are golden brown on one side and completely cooked through to the top. Remove the crumpets from the pan and repeat with the remaining batter, adding more butter to the pan as necessary.

You can also make free-form crumpets by scooping a few tablespoons of batter straight into the preheated and buttered pan. They'll look much more rustic and get a bit wider rather than tall, but they'll still be enjoyable. Serve warm.

Whole-Wheat Sponge Cake with Honey Buttercream

No matter what I'm cooking or baking, I want what I'm making to taste like what it's made out of—I want the ingredients to shine through for what they are. So for this cake, I want it to taste like butter and eggs and honey and wheat (or whatever grain I'm using—oats would work here too). The same goes for the honey buttercream, which is nothing more than honey, sugar, and eggs. Because of that, you'll want to use a lighter variety of honey, like light amber or orange blossom, not something dark and funky like avocado or buckwheat. And, by the way, the buttercream is just as good smeared on biscuits.

Makes 1 (8-inch) cake

For the Cake:

Ingredient	Weight	Volume	Baker's %
Total flour			100.00%
>>Whole-wheat pastry flour	100g	¾ cup + 2 tablespoons	100.00%
Cooking spray, for greasing			
Unsalted butter	60g	3 tablespoons	45.00%
Granulated sugar	130g	⅔ cup	130.00%
Large eggs	220g	4 whole	220.00%
Fine sea salt	1g	⅛ teaspoon	1.00%

For the Honey Buttercream:

Ingredient	Weight	Volume	Baker's %
Large egg yolks	90g	5 each	29.03%
Honey, preferably orange blossom	310g	1 cup	100.00%
Unsalted butter, softened	300g	1⅓ cups	96.77%
Fine sea salt		to taste	

Continued

Whole Wheat Sponge Cake with Honey Buttercream (page 117) and Spiced Rye Cookies (page 107)

Make the cake: Preheat the oven to 350°F. Cut a piece of parchment paper to fit in an 8-inch cake pan. Spray the pan with cooking spray, line with the parchment, and spray the parchment.

Make clarified butter by adding the butter to a medium pot over low heat. Once the butter melts, allow it to gently simmer until all of the buttermilk has evaporated and the milk solids have solidified and sunk to the bottom of the pot but have not browned, about 6 minutes. Set aside.

In a medium bowl, add the flour and 2 tablespoons of the sugar. Whisk to combine.

In the bowl of a stand mixer fitted with the whisk attachment, combine the remaining sugar, eggs, and salt and beat on high speed for 5 minutes. The mixture should be light-colored and tripled in volume.

Add a third of the flour mixture to the egg mixture and fold to combine with a spatula. Repeat with the remaining flour mixture, adding and folding in thirds. Add one-quarter of the batter to the clarified butter and fold to combine. Pour the butter-batter mixture into the remaining batter and fold just until blended.

Pour the batter into the prepared cake pan. Bake until golden brown, 30 to 35 minutes. Let the cake cool in the pan for 5 minutes, then transfer to a wire cooling rack to cool completely before frosting.

Make the buttercream: In the bowl of a stand mixer fitted with the whisk attachment, add the egg yolks and whip on high speed for 5 minutes, until the yolks take on a ribbony appearance.

While the yolks whip, add the honey to a small saucepan over medium-high heat. Heat the honey until it reaches 240°F. When the yolks have reached the ribbon stage, with the mixer running, slowly pour the hot honey into the yolks. Continue mixing until the mixing bowl is cool to the touch, 10 to 15 minutes. Begin adding the softened butter a pinch at a time, continuing to whip and incorporate the butter as you go. Season to taste with salt.

Frost the cooled cake generously with the buttercream and enjoy.

CHAPTER 2

Golden Loaves to Unlimited Devotion

Farmhouse Sourdough *125*

Malted Rye *127*

Peach and Cashew Loaf *130*

Apple and Peanut Loaf *133*

Millet Porridge and Cherry Loaf *135*

Buckwheat and Thyme Loaf *138*

Carolina Gold *141*

Chile Polenta Loaf *144*

Seeded Pumpernickel *149*

Multigrain Baguette *152*

Multigrain Sourdough *156*

Farmer's Favorite *159*

Honey-Oat Porridge Loaf *162*

Honey and Sprouted Wheat Loaf *166*

Marbled Rye *169*

Roasted Garlic and Mashed Potato Ciabatta *173*

Ryebatta *176*

Sorghum and Rosemary Ciabatta *179*

Spelt, Cumin, and Walnut Ring Loaf *181*

Toasted Sesame Loaf *185*

The title for this chapter is no accident—these are the recipes that are meant to hook ya. I promise that if you give them a shot, you'll be forever devoted to naturally leavened sourdough bread and baking with whole grains. It's the type of bread that could just as easily come out of Publican Quality Bread—thoughtful loaves that are purposeful in their method, focus on the quality of fermentation, let the ingredients speak for themselves, and use all the techniques at our disposal to make what is, in my opinion, the best bread.

Since the point of this book is to learn skills that we can build on, you'll see familiar steps from the previous chapter, like making a preferment and combining it with a sourdough starter, and cooking grain into a porridge before incorporating it into the dough. Now we're just putting them together to add up to a bread that you can make your own, along with a few more handy skills like controlling water and dough temperature; toasting grains before cooking them; adding dried fruit, nuts, and whole grains as "inclusions"; and employing the soaker and autolyse methods.

The soaker method is where you're taking whole grains and soaking them before including them in the dough. We do this so the grains don't stay too firm when you bake them, and also so the grains start to ferment naturally, which adds more flavor. We call for cracked grain in a number of these recipes; this is just the whole grain cracked into relatively large pieces. Sometimes this can be harder to find than whole wheat or rye berries, so you've got a few options. You can get the whole grain and crack them yourself with a home mill (I recommend the Mockmill brand), you can put the grain between pieces of parchment paper and roll over them with a rolling pin, or you can break the grain in a mortar and pestle. Or feel free to substitute whole-grain flour for cracked grain in all of these recipes. It won't be quite the same, but it will do just fine.

The autolyse method is a short rest after combining the flour and water for your dough. It more fully hydrates your flour (which is particularly beneficial when you're working with whole grains because it softens the bran), starts to develop gluten bonds, slows fermentation (leading to more flavor development), and creates more extensible dough (meaning easier shaping, greater loaf volume, and better crumb structure).

This chapter will also get into shaping, scoring, and baking techniques in your home oven that mimic the traditional hearth. That said, while there will be a few two-day builds here, there won't be a recipe that requires more than mixing and resting on day 1 and shaping and baking on day 2.

Farmhouse Sourdough

This is your basic country sourdough—though as for why it's a country sourdough versus a city sourdough or just a sourdough, I don't know. Since we buy our grains from farms, we call ours a farmhouse sourdough. It's a great starting-off point for making naturally fermented breads and is a super versatile workhorse loaf that's great for sandwiches or as table bread.

Note: I don't use the soaker method only with whole grains. In the bakery, a trick I like to use for building even more flavor is including a soaker for sourdough breads, too. It's not mandatory here, but I invite you to play around with it. Just combine the whole-wheat and rye flours and and an equal amount of water by weight and set it aside at room temperature the day before you want to bake. Then add it to the recipe when you go to mix it the next day. Make sure to reduce the water 1 weight used in the final mix by the amount you used to make the soaker!

Makes 2 (900-gram) loaves

Ingredient	Weight	Volume	Baker's %
Total flour			100.00%
>>Bread flour	630g	4¾ cups + 2 tablespoons	70.00%
>>Whole-wheat flour	135g	¾ cups + 2 tablespoons	15.00%
>>Rye flour	135g	1 cup + 2 tablespoons	15.00%
Water 1	630g	2⅔ cups	70.00%
Active sourdough starter	180g	1 cup	20.00%
Fine sea salt	20g	1 tablespoon	2.22%
Water 2	60g	¼ cup	6.67%
Semolina or fine cornmeal, for dusting			

First mix: Calculate your water temperature if desired (see page 310) or use warm (80°F) water.

In a large bowl, add the bread flour, water 1, sourdough starter, wheat flour, and rye flour. Mix by hand until all of the flour has been absorbed, 3 to 4 minutes. Cover with a tea towel or linen and let the dough rest for 30 minutes.

Second mix: Sprinkle the salt evenly over the dough and incorporate it by squeezing it in with your hand while folding the dough over itself.

Continued

Continue for 2 to 3 minutes; the dough should feel much stronger once the salt is added. Add water 2 and continue squeezing and folding until the water is completely absorbed and the dough coheres as one solid mass again, 3 to 4 minutes.

Ferment: Cover the bowl with a tea towel or linen and let the dough ferment at room temperature for 4 hours. During this time, fold the dough after 45 minutes, 1½ hours, 2 hours 15 minutes, and 3 hours, re-covering the bowl each time. Let the dough rest for the remaining hour. The dough is properly fermented when it's light, airy, and about doubled in size.

Shape: Turn out the dough onto a lightly floured work surface and divide it in half; each half should weigh about 900 grams. Pre-shape the dough (see page 50), cover with a tea towel or linen, and let it rest for 20 minutes.

Shape the dough as rounds (page 53) or batards (see page 52). Place the loaves in proofing baskets dusted with flour, seam-side up.

Proof: Cover the loaves with a tea towel or linen and proof for 1 to 1½ hours at room temperature. You can check for proper proofing by lightly flouring the top of the loaf, then pressing on the dough. You should be able to feel air in the dough, but your fingerprint should not remain in the dough for longer than 30 seconds. Once proofed, refrigerate the shaped loaves in their baskets overnight.

Bake: Preheat the oven to 475°F with a Challenger pan, cast-iron Dutch oven, or La Cloche baker on the middle rack.

Take out one of the loaves from the refrigerator. Dust a small amount of semolina or fine cornmeal on the loaf and gently transfer it from the basket to the work surface. Score as desired (see page 53), drop it into the preheated pot, place the lid on top, and return the pot to the oven. Bake for 20 minutes with the lid on.

Carefully remove the lid, lifting it away from you to avoid the steam. Bake for another 20 minutes, or until the crust is golden brown. Transfer the bread to a wire cooling rack. Cool for as long as you can resist the temptation, ideally 2 to 3 hours.

To bake the second loaf, return the pot to the oven. Once the pot is hot, remove the loaf from the fridge and bake. Alternatively, if you'd prefer fresh bread again tomorrow, keep the shaped loaf in its basket in the refrigerator and bake the following day.

Malted Rye

All right, we're moving on and up—this is the recipe where we officially start using the soaker method in a hearth bread. Here, you're taking rye malt, toasting it until it's incredibly fragrant, breaking it up, and soaking it in water before adding it to your final mix. By doing this, you're not only going to amplify the sweet, caramelized flavor of the grain, but you'll also get a deep, rich brown color to your loaf. So where other bakers may add cocoa powder, molasses, or coffee grounds to their rye bread to achieve those characteristics, you'll just be using the grain itself. This is a nice, dense loaf with a tight crumb that goes extremely well with more pungent cheeses like Gouda, and makes a damn good patty melt.

Note: You can usually find malted rye at a brewer's store. You could also substitute barley or malted wheat in the same quantity. I use a home mill to crack my grains, but you could use a mortar and pestle, or spread the grains on a baking sheet and crush them with a pot or rolling pin. This recipe also calls for cracked toasted rye malt. So first you'll need to buy rye malt, which is sold by many of the online retailers mentioned on page 35. Spread it out on a baking sheet and toast it in the oven at 325°F for 15 minutes, until it's fragrant. Lastly, roll over it with rolling pin to crack the grain.

Makes two (900-gram) loaves

For the Soaker:

Ingredient	Weight	Volume	Baker's %
Total flour			100.00%
>>Cracked toasted rye malt (see note)	150g	1 cup	85.71%
>>Rye flour	25g	3½ tablespoons	14.29%
Water	215g	1 cup	122.86%

For the Bread:

Ingredient	Weight	Volume	Baker's %
Total flour			100.00%
>>Bread flour	710g	5½ cups	100.00%
Water 1	420g	1¾ cups	59.15%
Active sourdough starter	195g	1 cup	27.46%
Fine sea salt	20g	1 tablespoon + ½ teaspoon	2.82%
Water 2	75g	⅓ cup	10.56%
Semolina or fine cornmeal, for dusting			

Continued

Make the soaker: Make this the evening before you bake. In a medium bowl, add the water, rye malt, and rye flour and mix by hand. Cover and let the mixture sit at room temperature for 12 hours.

First mix: Calculate your water temperature if desired (see page 310) or use warm (80°F) water.

In a large bowl, add the bread flour, water 1, and sourdough starter. Mix by hand until all of the flour has been absorbed, 3 to 4 minutes. Cover with a tea towel or linen and let the dough rest for 30 minutes.

Second mix: Sprinkle the salt evenly over the dough and incorporate it by squeezing it in with your hand while folding the dough over itself. Continue for 2 to 3 minutes; the dough should feel much stronger once the salt is added. Add water 2 and continue squeezing and folding until the water is completely absorbed and the dough coheres as one solid mass again, 3 to 4 minutes. Add the soaker and squeeze and fold until it is evenly dispersed, another 1 to 2 minutes.

Ferment: Cover the bowl with a tea towel or linen and let the dough ferment at room temperature for 4 hours. During this time, fold the dough after 45 minutes, 1½ hours, 2 hours 15 minutes, and 3 hours, re-covering the bowl each time. Let the dough rest for the remaining hour. The dough is properly fermented when it's light, airy, and about doubled in size.

Shape: Turn out the dough onto a lightly floured work surface and divide it in half; each half should weigh about 900 grams. Pre-shape each piece (see page 50), cover with a tea towel or linen, and let them rest for 20 minutes.

Shape the dough tightly as rounds (page 53) or batards (see page 52). Place the loaves in proofing baskets dusted with flour, seam-side up.

Proof: Cover the loaves with a tea towel or linen and proof for 1 to 1½ hours at room temperature. You can check for proper proofing by lightly flouring the top of the loaves, then pressing on the dough. You should be able to feel air in the dough, but your fingerprint should not remain in the dough for longer than 30 seconds. Once proofed, refrigerate the shaped loaves in their baskets overnight.

Bake: Preheat the oven to 475°F with a Challenger pan, cast-iron Dutch oven, or La Cloche baker on the middle rack.

Take one of the loaves from the refrigerator. Dust a small amount of semolina or fine cornmeal on the loaf and gently transfer it from the basket to the work surface. Score as desired (see page 53), drop it into the preheated pot, place the lid on top, and return the pot to the oven. Bake for 20 minutes with the lid on.

Carefully remove the lid, lifting it away from you to avoid the steam. Bake for another 20 minutes, or until the desired crust color is achieved. I go for dark brown bordering on singed with this one. Transfer the bread to a wire cooling rack. Cool for as long as you can resist the temptation, ideally 2 to 3 hours.

To bake the second loaf, return the pot to the oven. Once the pot is hot, remove the loaf from the fridge and bake. Alternatively, if you'd prefer fresh bread again tomorrow, keep the shaped loaf in its basket in the refrigerator and bake the following day.

Peach and Cashew Loaf

A lesson in simplicity: Take a straight mix of bread flour and wheat flour, pair it with honey, and throw in dried fruit and nuts (aka inclusions). I went with peaches and cashews because I love them together, but this is pretty much a blank canvas for you to realize your fruit-nut visions on. Fig and hazelnut would also be excellent, for example.

Note: You don't need to rehydrate the dried fruit before adding it to the dough, but you could plump it up with a little water, juice, or liqueur. Amaretto, an almond liqueur, is particularly nice with stone fruit because almonds are technically part of the stone fruit family. It doesn't read like almond so much as it just makes the fruit taste more like itself.

Makes 2 (900-gram) loaves

Ingredient	Weight	Volume	Baker's %
Total flour			100.00%
>>Bread flour	615g	4¾ cups	79.87%
>>Whole-wheat flour	155g	1 cup	20.13%
Water	550g	2⅓ cups	71.43%
Active sourdough starter	180g	1 cup	23.38%
Honey	70g	¼ cup	9.09%
Fine sea salt	17g	1 tablespoon	2.21%
Toasted cashews	165g	1⅓ cups	21.43%
Dried peaches, diced	45g	1 cup	5.84%
Semolina or fine cornmeal, for dusting			

First mix: Calculate your water temperature if desired (see page 310) or use warm (80°F) water.

In a large bowl, add the bread flour, water, sourdough starter, wheat flour, and honey. Mix by hand until all of the flour has been absorbed, 3 to 4 minutes. Cover with a tea towel or linen and let the mixture rest for 30 minutes.

Second mix: Sprinkle the salt evenly over the dough and incorporate it by squeezing it in with your hand while folding the dough over itself. Continue for 2 to 3 minutes; the dough should feel much stronger once the salt is added. Add the cashews and peaches and squeeze and fold until they are evenly dispersed, another 1 to 2 minutes.

Ferment: Cover the bowl with a tea towel or linen and let the dough ferment at room temperature for 4 hours. During this time, fold the dough after 45 minutes, 1½ hours, 2 hours 15 minutes, and 3 hours, re-covering the bowl each time. Let the dough rest for the remaining hour. The dough is properly fermented when it's light, airy, and about doubled in size.

Shape: Turn out the dough onto a lightly floured work surface and divide it in half; each half should weigh about 900 grams. Pre-shape each piece (see page 50), cover with a tea towel or linen, and let them rest for 20 minutes.

Shape the dough as rounds (page 53) or batards (see page 52). Place the loaves in proofing baskets dusted with flour, seam-side up.

Proof: Cover the loaves with a tea towel or linen and proof for 1 to 1½ hours at room temperature. You can check for proper proofing by lightly flouring the top of the loaves, then pressing on the dough. You should be able to feel air in the dough, but your fingerprint should not remain in the dough for longer than 30 seconds. Once proofed, refrigerate the shaped loaves in their baskets overnight.

Bake: Preheat the oven to 475°F with a Challenger pan, cast-iron Dutch oven, or La Cloche baker on the middle rack.

Take out one of the loaves from the refrigerator. Dust a small amount of semolina or fine cornmeal on the loaf and gently transfer it from the basket to the work surface. Score as desired (see page 53), drop it into the preheated pot, place the lid on top, and return the pot to the oven. Bake for 20 minutes with the lid on.

Carefully remove the lid, lifting it away from you to avoid the steam. Bake for another 20 minutes, or until the desired crust color is achieved; I prefer golden brown. Transfer the bread to a wire cooling rack. Cool for as long as you can resist the temptation, ideally 2 to 3 hours.

To bake the second loaf, return the pot to the oven. Once the pot is hot, remove the loaf from the fridge and bake. Alternatively, if you'd prefer fresh bread again tomorrow, keep the shaped loaf in its basket in the refrigerator and bake the following day.

Apple and Peanut Loaf

This loaf is inspired by my favorite snack growing up: apples and peanut butter. Although I usually consider crunchy peanut butter about as good as a kick in the shins, the toasted whole peanuts in this loaf give it a satisfying texture in contrast to the soft bread. Thick slabs make for excellent cinnamon toast, or eat the freshly baked bread with a generous amount of butter slathered on top. If you have any leftovers, use it for bread pudding.

Makes 2 (900-gram) loaves

Ingredient	Weight	Volume	Baker's %
Total flour			100.00%
>>Bread flour	670g	5 cups + 2 tablespoons	88.16%
>>Whole-wheat flour	90g	⅔ cup	11.84%
Water 1	500g	2 cups + 2 tablespoons	65.79%
Active sourdough starter	270g	1¼ cups	35.53%
Honey	100g	⅓ cup	13.16%
Fine sea salt	16g	1 tablespoon	2.11%
Water 2	60g	¼ cup	7.89%
Dried apples, diced	100g	1 cup	13.16%
Peanuts, toasted	100g	⅔ cup	13.16%
Semolina or fine cornmeal, for dusting			

First mix: Calculate your water temperature if desired (see page 310) or use warm (80°F) water.

In a large bowl, add the bread flour, water 1, sourdough starter, honey, and wheat flour. Mix by hand until all of the flour has been absorbed, 3 to 4 minutes. Cover with a tea towel or linen and let the mixture rest for 30 minutes.

Second mix: Sprinkle the salt evenly over the dough and incorporate it by squeezing it in with your hand while folding the dough over itself. Continue for 2 to 3 minutes; the dough should feel much stronger once the salt is added. Add water 2 and continue squeezing and folding until the water is completely absorbed and the dough coheres as one solid mass again, 3 to 4 minutes. Add the apples and peanuts and squeeze and fold until they are evenly dispersed, another 1 to 2 minutes.

Continued

Ferment: Cover the bowl with a tea towel or linen and let the dough ferment at room temperature for 4 hours. During this time, fold the dough after 45 minutes, 1½ hours, 2 hours 15 minutes, and 3 hours, re-covering the bowl each time. Let the dough rest for the remaining hour. The dough is properly fermented when it's light, airy, and about doubled in size.

Shape: Turn out the dough onto a lightly floured work surface and divide it in half; each half should weigh about 900 grams. Pre-shape each piece (see page 50), cover with a tea towel or linen, and let them rest for 20 minutes.

Shape the dough as rounds (page 53) or batards (see page 52). Place the loaves in proofing baskets dusted with flour, seam-side up.

Proof: Cover the loaves with a tea towel or linen and proof for 1 to 1½ hours at room temperature. You can check for proper proofing by lightly flouring the top of the loaves, then pressing on the dough. You should be able to feel air in the dough, but your fingerprint should not remain in the dough for longer than 30 seconds. Once proofed, refrigerate the shaped loaves in their baskets overnight for a minimum of 12 hours, or up to 36 hours.

Bake: Preheat the oven to 475°F with a Challenger pan, cast-iron Dutch oven, or La Cloche baker on the middle rack.

Take out one of the loaves from the refrigerator. Dust a small amount of semolina or fine cornmeal on the loaf and gently transfer it from the basket to the work surface. Score as desired (see page 53), drop it into the preheated pot, place the lid on top, and return the pot to the oven. Bake for 20 minutes with the lid on.

Carefully remove the lid, lifting it away from you to avoid the steam. Bake for another 20 minutes, or until the desired crust color is achieved. Transfer the bread to a wire cooling rack. Cool for as long as you can resist the temptation, ideally 2 to 3 hours.

To bake the second loaf, return the pot to the oven. Once the pot is hot, remove the loaf from the fridge and bake. Alternatively, if you'd prefer fresh bread again tomorrow, keep the shaped loaf in its basket in the refrigerator and bake the following day.

Millet Porridge and Cherry Loaf

Tossing some grains on a baking sheet and throwing them in the oven to toast until deeply fragrant isn't difficult, but it goes a long way as an extra step in the bread-making process. With millet in particular, toasting the grain before cooking it into a porridge adds a subtle toasted-grain flavor that gets sweetened with honey and chopped dried cherries. Think granola bar, but soft.

Makes 2 (900-gram) loaves

For the Millet Porridge:

Ingredient	Weight	Volume	Baker's %
Total flour			100.00%
>>Millet, toasted in a dry pan or in the oven until fragrant	135g	1 cup	100.00%
Water	405g	1¾ cups	300.00%
Fine sea salt	3g	½ teaspoon	2.22%

For the Bread:

Ingredient	Weight	Volume	Baker's %
Total flour			100.00%
>>Bread flour	640g	5 cups	100.00%
Water 1	425g	1¾ cups	66.41%
Active sourdough starter	210g	1 cup	32.81%
Honey	50g	2 tablespoons + 1 teaspoon	7.81%
Fine sea salt	15g	1 tablespoon	2.34%
Water 2	95g	⅓ cup	14.84%
Dried cherries	95g	1 cup	14.84%
Semolina or fine cornmeal, for dusting			

Make the porridge: In a medium saucepan, add the water, millet, and salt and stir to combine. Cook over medium heat, stirring frequently to prevent scorching, and bring to a boil. Reduce the heat to low and simmer for 3 to 4 minutes, until the porridge is very thick. Spread the porridge out on a baking sheet to help it cool to room temperature.

Continued

First mix: Calculate your water temperature if desired (see page 310) or use warm (80°F) water.

In a large bowl, add the bread flour, water 1, sourdough starter, and honey. Mix by hand until all of the flour has been absorbed, 3 to 4 minutes. Cover with a tea towel or linen and let rest for 30 minutes.

Second mix: Sprinkle the salt evenly over the dough and incorporate it by squeezing it in with your hand while folding the dough over itself. Continue for 2 to 3 minutes; the dough should feel much stronger once the salt is added. Add water 2 and continue squeezing and folding until the water is completely absorbed and the dough coheres as one solid mass again, 3 to 4 minutes. Repeat with the porridge, squeezing to combine until all is dispersed evenly. Add the cherries and squeeze and fold until they are evenly dispersed, another 1 to 2 minutes.

Ferment: Cover the bowl with a tea towel or linen and let the dough ferment at room temperature for 4 hours. During this time, fold the dough after 45 minutes, 1½ hours, 2 hours 15 minutes, and 3 hours, re-covering the bowl each time. Let the dough rest for the remaining hour. The dough is properly fermented when it's light, airy, and about doubled in size.

Shape: Turn out the dough onto a lightly floured work surface and divide it in half; each half should weigh about 900 grams. Pre-shape each piece (see page 50), cover with a tea towel or linen, and let them rest for 20 minutes.

Shape the dough as rounds (page 53) or batards (see page 52). Place the loaves in proofing baskets dusted with flour, seam-side up.

Proof: Cover the loaves with a tea towel or linen and proof for 1 to 1½ hours at room temperature. You can check for proper proofing by lightly flouring the top of the loaves, then pressing on the dough. You should be able to feel air in the dough, but your fingerprint should not remain in the dough for longer than 30 seconds. Once proofed, refrigerate the shaped loaves in their baskets overnight.

Bake: Preheat the oven to 475°F with a Challenger pan, cast-iron pot, or La Cloche baker on the middle rack.

Take out one of the loaves from the refrigerator. Dust a small amount of semolina or fine cornmeal on the loaf and gently transfer it from the basket to the work surface. Score as desired (see page 53), drop it into the preheated pot, place the lid on top, and return the pot to the oven. Bake for 20 minutes with the lid on.

Carefully remove the lid, lifting it away from you to avoid the steam. Bake for another 20 minutes, or until the desired crust color is achieved. Transfer the bread to a wire cooling rack. Cool for as long as you can resist the temptation, ideally 2 to 3 hours.

To bake the second loaf, return the pot to the oven. Once the pot is hot, remove the loaf from the fridge and bake. Alternatively, if you'd prefer fresh bread again tomorrow, keep the shaped loaf in its basket in the refrigerator and bake the following day.

Buckwheat and Thyme Loaf

Buckwheat flour is at the center of this recipe, so I like to fortify its unique earthy flavor. Thyme makes an appearance here, as does buckwheat honey, which, unlike its more floral counterparts, is just about as barnyard-y as the plant that the bees extract the nectar from. It's the kind of pairing that I love to showcase in breads because it's like capturing a living moment in the growing cycle. The overall effect is a robust loaf that's great in fall and winter for sopping up your soups and braises.

Note: Feel free to use another grain, like wheat, instead of buckwheat and switch to a more subtle honey like clover or orange blossom.

Makes 2 (900-gram) loaves

Ingredient	Weight	Volume	Baker's %
Total flour			100.00%
>>Bread flour	710g	5½ cups	79.78%
>>Buckwheat flour	180g	1½ cups	20.22%
Water 1	580g	2½ cups	65.17%
Active sourdough starter	180g	¾ cup	20.22%
Buckwheat honey	70g	3 tablespoons + 1 teaspoon	7.87%
Fine sea salt	18g	1 tablespoon	2.02%
Water 2	60g	¼ cup	6.74%
Fresh thyme leaves	15g	¼ cup	1.69%
Semolina or fine cornmeal, for dusting			

First mix: Calculate your water temperature if desired (see page 310) or use warm (80°F) water.

In a large bowl, add the bread flour, water 1, buckwheat flour, sourdough starter, and honey. Mix by hand until all of the flour has been absorbed, 3 to 4 minutes. Cover with a tea towel or linen and let rest for 30 minutes.

Second mix: Sprinkle the salt evenly over the dough and incorporate it by squeezing it in with your hand while folding the dough over itself. Continue for 2 to 3 minutes; the dough should feel much stronger once the salt is added. Add water 2 and continue squeezing and folding until the water is completely absorbed and the dough coheres as one solid mass again, 3 to 4 minutes.

Add the thyme leaves and squeeze and fold until they are evenly dispersed, another 1 to 2 minutes.

Ferment: Cover the bowl with a tea towel or linen and let the dough ferment at room temperature for 4 hours. During this time, fold the dough after 45 minutes, 1½ hours, 2 hours 15 minutes, and 3 hours, re-covering the bowl each time. Let the dough rest for the remaining hour. The dough is properly fermented when it's light, airy, and about doubled in size.

Shape: Turn out the dough onto a lightly floured work surface and divide it in half; each half should weigh about 900 grams. Pre-shape each piece (see page 50), cover with a tea towel or linen, and let them rest for 20 minutes.

Shape the dough as rounds (page 53) or batards (see page 52). Place the loaves in proofing baskets dusted with flour, seam-side up.

Proof: Cover the loaves with a tea towel or linen and proof for 1 to 1½ hours at room temperature. You can check for proper proofing by lightly flouring the top of the loaves, then pressing on the dough. You should be able to feel air in the dough, but your fingerprint should not remain in the dough for longer than 30 seconds. Once proofed, refrigerate the shaped loaves in their baskets overnight.

Bake: Preheat the oven to 475°F with a Challenger pan, cast-iron Dutch oven, or La Cloche baker on the middle rack.

Take out one of the loaves from the refrigerator. Dust a small amount of semolina or fine cornmeal on the loaf and gently transfer it from the basket to the work surface. Score as desired (see page 53), drop it into the preheated pot, place the lid on top, and return the pot to the oven. Bake for 20 minutes with the lid on.

Carefully remove the lid, lifting it away from you to avoid the steam. Bake for another 20 minutes, or until the desired crust color is achieved. Transfer the bread to a wire cooling rack. Cool for as long as you can resist the temptation, ideally 2 to 3 hours.

To bake the second loaf, return the pot to the oven. Once the pot is hot, remove the loaf from the fridge and bake. Alternatively, if you'd prefer fresh bread again tomorrow, keep the shaped loaf in its basket in the refrigerator and bake the following day, or up to 2 to 3 days later.

Carolina Gold

I first made this white-bread-but-not-white-bread for Sean Brock when he was in Chicago hosting a dinner at Blackbird. Being a steward of Southern foodways and ingredients, he had me source Carolina Gold rice, which has a rich and buttery flavor profile and pairs perfectly with super Southern benne seeds, a milder sesame seed. I incorporated a little bit of wheat and spelt flour to whole-grain it up a bit and the result is a soft, custardy table bread that's great for cutting thick and spreading with butter or toasting or grilling as the base of a tartine, open-face sandwich, or with some nice olive oil, heirloom tomato, and salt.

Note: You can easily sub in regular natural or white sesame seeds for the benne seeds. You can also use regular bread flour, gram for gram, instead of wheat and spelt.

Makes 2 (900-gram) loaves

For the Rice Porridge:

Ingredient	Weight	Volume	Baker's %
Total flour			100.00%
>>Carolina Gold rice or other medium-grain rice	55g	⅓ cup	100.00%
Water	110g	½ cup	200.00%
Fine sea salt	1g	pinch	1.82%

For the Bread Mix:

Ingredient	Weight	Volume	Baker's %
Total flour			100.00%
>>Bread flour	295g	2¼ cups	74.68%
>>Whole-wheat flour	50g	⅓ cup	12.66%
>>Spelt flour	50g	⅓ cup	12.66%
Water	310g	1⅓ cups	78.48%
Active sourdough starter	70g	⅓ cup	17.72%
Fine sea salt	8g	1½ teaspoons	2.03%
Benne seeds or sesame seeds	34g	⅓ cup	8.61%
Semolina or fine cornmeal, for dusting			

Continued

Make the porridge: In a medium saucepan over medium-high heat, add the water, rice, and salt and stir with a wooden spoon to combine. Bring to a boil, stirring often to prevent scorching. Boil for 1 minute, cover, and reduce the heat to low. Simmer for 13 minutes. Leaving the lid on, remove the pan from the heat and let the rice steam for an additional 5 minutes. Spread the porridge out on a baking sheet to help it cool to room temperature.

First mix: Calculate your water temperature if desired (see page 310) or use warm (80°F) water.

In a large bowl, add the water, bread flour, wheat flour, spelt flour, and sourdough starter. Mix by hand until all of the flour has been absorbed, 3 to 4 minutes. Cover with a tea towel or linen and let the mixture rest for 30 minutes.

Second mix: Sprinkle the salt evenly over the dough and incorporate it by squeezing it in with your hand while folding the dough over itself. Continue for 2 to 3 minutes; the dough should feel much stronger once the salt is added. Add the sesame seeds and the porridge and continue squeezing and folding until the porridge is completely absorbed and the dough coheres as one solid mass again, 3 to 4 minutes.

Ferment: Cover the bowl with a tea towel or linen and let the dough ferment at room temperature for 4 hours. During this time, fold the dough after 45 minutes, 1½ hours, 2 hours 15 minutes, and 3 hours, re-covering the bowl each time. Let the dough rest for the remaining hour. The dough is properly fermented when it's light, airy, and about doubled in size.

Shape: Turn out the dough onto a lightly floured work surface and divide it in half; each half should weigh about 900 grams. Pre-shape each piece (see page 50), cover with a tea towel or linen, and let them rest for 20 minutes.

Shape the dough as rounds (page 53) or batards (see page 52). Place the loaves in proofing baskets dusted with flour, seam-side up.

Proof: Cover the loaves with a tea towel or linen and proof for 1 to 1½ hours at room temperature. You can check for proper proofing by lightly flouring the top of the loaves, then pressing on the dough. You should be able to feel air in the dough, but your fingerprint should not remain in the dough for longer than 30 seconds. Once proofed, refrigerate the shaped loaves in their baskets overnight.

Bake: Preheat the oven to 475°F with a Challenger pan, cast-iron Dutch oven, or La Cloche baker on the middle rack.

Take out one of the loaves from the refrigerator. Dust a small amount of semolina flour or fine cornmeal on the loaf and gently transfer it from the basket to the work surface. Score as desired (page 53), drop it into the preheated pot, place the lid on top, and return the pot to the oven. Bake for 20 minutes with the lid on.

Carefully remove the lid, lifting it away from you to avoid the steam. Bake for another 20 minutes, or until the desired crust color is achieved. Transfer the bread to a wire cooling rack. Cool for as long as you can resist the temptation, ideally 2 to 3 hours.

To bake the second loaf, return the pot to the oven. Once the pot is hot, remove the loaf from the fridge and bake. Alternatively, if you'd prefer fresh bread again tomorrow, keep the shaped loaf in its basket in the refrigerator and bake the following day.

Chile Polenta Loaf

When I think about cooking with corn, I think about the American South-west—so that's exactly where this loaf's flavor profile comes from. I use a nice heritage cornmeal from Marty, but it's also fun to use a (more widely available) tri-color cornmeal like Bloody Butcher. Between the purple, white, and red shades of corn and the flecks of chiles, it's like seeing fire-works when you slice the bread open. For this recipe, I call for using different varieties of chiles because you're going to get a more well-rounded flavor profile. The guajillos have an almost sweet, raisiny flavor; the moritas are deeply smoky; and the anchos are smoky with a hit of spice. I'm into serving this bread with Tex-Mex flavors like table salsa or queso fundido (especially if you're grilling your slices beforehand), though it also lends itself really well to avocado toast.

Makes 2 (900-gram) loaves

For the Polenta:

Ingredient	Weight	Volume	Baker's %
Total flour			100.00%
>>Heritage cornmeal	150g	1 cup	100.00%
Water	440g	1½ cups	293.33%
Fine sea salt	3g	½ teaspoon	2.00%

For the Bread Mix:

Ingredient	Weight	Volume	Baker's %
Total flour			100.00%
>>Bread flour	780g	6 cups	100.00%
Water	544g	2⅓ cups	69.74%
Active sourdough starter	225g	1 cup	28.85%
Fine sea salt	15g	2½ teaspoons	1.92%
Toasted pepitas	85g	½ cup	10.90%
Ground ancho chiles	3g	1 teaspoon	0.38%
Ground morita chiles	3g	1 teaspoon	0.38%
Ground guajillo chiles	3g	1 teaspoon	0.38%
Semolina or fine cornmeal, for dusting			

Continued

Make the polenta: In a medium saucepan over medium-high heat, add the water, cornmeal, and salt and stir with a wooden spoon to combine. Bring to a boil, stirring often to prevent scorching. Reduce the heat and simmer the polenta until very thick, 3 to 4 minutes. Spread the polenta out on a baking sheet to help it cool to room temperature.

First mix: Calculate your water temperature if desired (see page 310) or use warm (80°F) water.

In a large bowl, add the bread flour, water, and sourdough starter. Mix by hand until all of the flour has been absorbed, 3 to 4 minutes. Cover with a tea towel or linen and let the dough rest for 30 minutes.

Second mix: Sprinkle the salt evenly over the dough and incorporate it by squeezing it in with your hand while folding the dough over itself. Continue for 4 to 5 minutes to let the dough develop strength; you should see the dough become smoother and more shiny. Add the toasted pepitas, chiles, and polenta and continue squeezing and folding until the polenta is completely absorbed and the dough coheres as one solid mass again, 3 to 4 minutes.

Ferment: Cover the bowl with a tea towel or linen and let the dough ferment at room temperature for 4 hours. During this time, fold the dough after 45 minutes, 1½ hours, 2 hours 15 minutes, and 3 hours, re-covering the bowl each time. Let the dough rest for the remaining hour. The dough is properly fermented when it's light, airy, and about doubled in size.

Shape: Turn out the dough onto a lightly floured work surface and divide it in half; each half should weigh about 900 grams. Pre-shape each piece (see page 50), cover with a tea towel or linen, and let them rest for 20 minutes.

Shape the dough as rounds (page 53) or batards (see page 52). Place the loaves in proofing baskets dusted with flour, seam-side up.

Proof: Cover the loaves with a tea towel or linen and proof for 1 to 1½ hours at room temperature. You can check for proper proofing by lightly flouring the top of the loaves, then pressing on the dough. You should be able to feel air in the dough, but your fingerprint should not remain in the dough for longer than 30 seconds. Once proofed, refrigerate the shaped loaves in their baskets overnight.

Bake: Preheat the oven to 475°F with a Challenger pan, cast-iron Dutch oven, or La Cloche baker on the middle rack.

Take out one of the loaves from the refrigerator. Dust a small amount of semolina or fine cornmeal on the loaf and gently transfer it from the basket to the work surface. Score as desired (see page 53), drop it into the preheated pot, place the lid on top, and return the pot to the oven. Bake for 20 minutes with the lid on.

Carefully remove the lid, lifting it away from you to avoid the steam. Bake for another 20 minutes, or until the desired crust color is achieved. Transfer the bread to a wire cooling rack. Cool for as long as you can resist the temptation, ideally 2 to 3 hours.

To bake the second loaf, return the pot to the oven. Once the pot is hot, remove the loaf from the fridge and bake. Alternatively, if you'd prefer fresh bread again tomorrow, keep the shaped loaf in its basket in the refrigerator and bake the following day.

Seeded Pumpernickel

There are two types of pumpernickel: You got your European style that's 100 percent rye, very dense, and baked until it's caramelized all the way through. Then there's the American style, which is what you'll find at the grocery store. It's more like a light, fluffy, traditional sandwich loaf. And that's what this recipe is a take on. (We'll revisit that European style on page 233 with Volkornbrot.)

We use a soaker here because part of the appeal of this loaf—aside from its deep rye and molasses flavor—is a mix of seeds: sunflower, sesame, and charnushka (or nigella), which is sort of halfway between an onion and a caraway seed in flavor. It's a distinctly savory note that permeates the whole loaf and really elevates things. We get a lot of "Wow, I didn't know bread could taste like that!" with this one. It's a dark, crusty, sweet, mildly musty loaf that will do fine gracing your table with just some butter or, better yet, topped with some thinly sliced prosciutto or spicy coppa, or smoked salmon with dill and cream cheese.

Note: The seed mix for this recipe is enough to make more than one recipe's worth, but it will store for months if kept in an airtight container. Also, you could make this bread with rye flour instead of cracked rye, if you can't find it. Use the same weight for your final mix.

Makes 2 (900-gram) loaves

For the Seed Mix:

Ingredient	Weight	Volume	Baker's %
Flax seeds	220g	1½ cups	28.58%
Sunflower seeds	125g	1 cup	28.58%
Sesame seeds	195g	1½ cups	28.58%
Charnushka seeds	75g	¼ cup	14.29%

For the Soaker:

Ingredient	Weight	Volume	Baker's %
Total flour			100.00%
>>Seed mix	117g	¾ cup	52.00%
>>Cracked rye	72g	½ cup	32.00%
>>Rye flour	36g	⅓ cup	16.00%
Warm water	225g	1 cup	100.00%

Continued

For the Bread:

Ingredient	Weight	Volume	Baker's %
Total flour			100.00%
>>Bread flour	650g	5 cups	100.00%
Water 1	325g	1⅓ cups	50.00%
Active sourdough starter	147g	¾ cup	22.61%
Molasses	90g	⅓ cup	13.85%
Fine sea salt	30g	2 tablespoons	5%
Water 2	110g	½ cup	16.92%
Semolina or fine cornmeal, for dusting			

Make the seed mix: Make this the evening before the first mix. In a medium bowl, add the flax seeds, sunflower seeds, sesame seeds, and charnushka seeds and mix by hand until thoroughly combined. Store in an airtight container at room temperature. This will make enough for eight or so batches of bread.

Make the soaker: The same evening, make the soaker. In a small bowl, add the seed mix, cracked rye, rye flour, and water. Mix briefly to combine, cover with a tea towel or linen, and let it sit at room temperature for 12 hours.

First mix: Calculate your water temperature if desired (see page 310) or use warm (80°F) water.

In a large bowl, add the bread flour, water 1, sourdough starter, and molasses. Mix by hand until all of the flour has been absorbed, 3 to 4 minutes. Cover with a tea towel or linen and let the mixture rest for 30 minutes.

Second mix: Sprinkle the salt evenly over the dough and incorporate it by squeezing it in with your hand while folding the dough over itself. Continue for 2 to 3 minutes; the dough should feel much stronger once the salt is added. Add water 2 and continue squeezing and folding until the water is completely absorbed and the dough coheres as one solid mass again, 3 to 4 minutes. Add the soaker and squeeze and fold until it is evenly incorporated, another 1 to 2 minutes.

Ferment: Cover the bowl with a tea towel or linen and let the dough ferment at room temperature for 4 hours. During this time, fold the dough after 45 minutes,

1½ hours, 2 hours 15 minutes, and 3 hours, re-covering the bowl each time. Let the dough rest for the remaining hour. The dough is properly fermented when it's light, airy, and about doubled in size.

Shape: Turn out the dough onto a lightly floured work surface and divide it in half; each half should weigh about 900 grams. Pre-shape each piece (see page 50), cover with a tea towel or linen, and let them rest for 20 minutes.

Shape the dough as rounds (page 53) or batards (see page 52). Place the loaves in proofing baskets dusted with flour, seam-side up.

Proof: Cover the loaves with a tea towel or linen and proof for 1 to 1½ hours at room temperature. You can check for proper proofing by lightly flouring the top of the loaves, then pressing on the dough. You should be able to feel air in the dough, but your fingerprint should not remain in the dough for longer than 30 seconds. Once proofed, refrigerate the shaped loaves in their baskets overnight.

Bake: Preheat the oven to 475°F with a Challenger pan, cast-iron Dutch oven, or La Cloche baker on the middle rack.

Take out one of the loaves from the refrigerator. Dust a small amount of semolina or fine cornmeal on the loaf and gently transfer it from the basket to the work surface. Score as desired (page 53), drop it into the preheated pot, place the lid on top, and return the pot to the oven. Bake for 20 minutes with the lid on.

Carefully remove the lid, lifting it away from you to avoid the steam. Bake for another 20 minutes, or until the desired crust color is achieved. Transfer the bread to a wire cooling rack. Cool for as long as you can resist the temptation, ideally 2 to 3 hours.

To bake the second loaf, return the pot to the oven. Once the pot is hot, remove the loaf from the fridge and bake. Alternatively, if you'd prefer fresh bread again tomorrow, keep the shaped loaf in its basket in the refrigerator and bake the following day.

Multigrain Baguette

A crackly, warm, aromatic, fresh-from-the-oven baguette enjoyed with too much butter is one of life's great rewards. To make sure you get a light, fluffy interior and thin exterior crust, you're going to add a little bit of commercial yeast to your preferment. If you went completely sourdough-leavened, all the gases that are expelled during fermentation would get up under the surface of the bread, making for a thicker crust, which you don't want. A yeast-reinforced preferment also means that you get to mix, shape, and bake in the same day.

Note: You can turn this into a hearth loaf by mixing and shaping on day 1, refrigerating it overnight, and baking on day 2. What you'll end up with is very similar to the Multigrain Sourdough (page 156), which is essentially the same dough but is sweetened with honey. The multigrain seed mix will make enough for multiple batches of bread. Stored in a cool dry place, the seed mix will keep for many months. It's the same seed mix used in the Multigrain Sourdough (page 156).

Makes 4 (200-gram) baguettes

For the Multigrain Seed Mix:

Ingredient	Weight	Volume	Baker's %
Rolled oats	150g	1½ cups	21.50%
Flax seeds	115g	¾ cup	19.00%
Millet	115g	½ cup	18.50%
Cracked wheat (see note on page 40)	100g	½ cup	17.00%
Sesame seeds	120g	¾ cup	16.00%
Poppy seeds	40g	¼ cup	7.00%

For the Preferment:

Ingredient	Weight	Volume	Baker's %
Total flour			100.00%
>>Bread flour	60g	½ cup	100.00%
Water	60g	¼ cup	100.00%
Active dry yeast	0.3g	pinch	

For the Soaker:

Ingredient	Weight	Volume	Baker's %
Seed mix	65g	⅓ cup	100.00%
Water	65g	¼ cup + 1 teaspoon	100.00%

Continued

For the Bread:

Ingredient	Weight	Volume	Baker's %
Total flour			100.00%
>>Bread flour	195g	1½ cups	81.25%
>>Whole-wheat flour	30g	¼ cup	12.50%
>>Rye flour	15g	2 tablespoons	6.25%
Water 1	150g	⅔ cup	62.50%
Active sourdough starter	100g	½ cup	41.67%
Fine sea salt	10g	1½ teaspoons	4.17%
Water 2	15g	1 tablespoon	6.25%
Toasted pepitas	25g	3 tablespoons	10.42%
Sunflower seeds	25g	3 tablespoons	10.42%

Make the seed mix: In a large bowl, add the oats, flax seeds, millet, cracked wheat, sesame seeds, and poppy seeds. Mix with a spoon until combined. Store in an airtight container at room temperature.

Make the preferment: Make this the evening before you bake. In a medium bowl, add the bread flour, water, and yeast. Mix by hand until a homogeneous batter forms, about 2 minutes. Cover with a tea towel or linen and let the mixture sit at room temperature for 12 hours.

Make the soaker: The same evening, make the soaker. In a small bowl, add the seed mix and water. Mix briefly to combine, cover with a tea towel or linen, and let the mixture sit at room temperature for 12 hours.

First mix: Calculate your water temperature if desired (see page 310) or use warm (80°F) water.

In a large bowl, add the bread flour, water 1, sourdough starter, wheat flour, rye flour, and preferment. Mix by hand until all of the flour has been absorbed, 3 to 4 minutes. Cover with a tea towel or linen and let the dough rest for 30 minutes.

Second mix: Sprinkle the salt evenly over the dough and incorporate it by squeezing it in with your hand while folding the dough over itself. Continue for 2 to 3 minutes; the dough should feel much stronger once the salt is added. Add water 2 and continue squeezing and folding until the water is completely absorbed and the dough coheres as one solid mass again, 3 to 4 minutes. Add the soaker, toasted pepitas, and sunflower seeds, and squeeze and fold until everything is evenly dispersed, another 1 to 2 minutes.

Ferment: Cover the bowl with a tea towel or linen and let the dough ferment at room temperature for 2 hours. During this time, fold the dough after 45 minutes and again at 1½ hours. The dough is properly fermented when it's light, airy, and about doubled in size.

Shape: Turn out the dough onto a lightly floured work surface and divide the dough in quarters; each quarter should weigh about 400 grams. Pre-shape each piece (see page 50), cover with a tea towel or linen, and let them rest for 20 minutes.

Shape the dough as baguettes (see page 49). Place the shaped loaves in a proofing linen dusted with flour, seam-side down.

Proof: Cover the loaves with a tea towel or linen and proof for 1 to 1½ hours at room temperature. You can check for proper proofing by lightly flouring the top of the loaves, then pressing on the dough. You should be able to feel air in the dough, but your fingerprint should not remain in the dough for longer than 30 seconds.

Bake: Preheat the oven to 500°F with a Challenger pan, cast-iron Dutch oven, or La Cloche baker on the middle rack.

Once hot, remove the pan from the oven. Using a baguette board, cutting board, serving board, or an appropriately long piece of wood that's roughly ½ inch thick and 4 inches long, transfer one loaf seam-side up onto the board and then seam-side down onto the preheated pan base. Score as desired (page 53), place the lid on the pot, and return the pot to the oven. Bake for 10 minutes with the lid on. Remove the lid, being careful to lift the lid away from you to avoid the steam, and bake for another 10 minutes, or until the desired crust color is achieved. Transfer the bread to a wire cooling rack.

Refrigerate the remaining loaves in the linen until ready to bake, up to 2 days.

Multigrain Sourdough

This was one of the first breads we developed at Publican Quality Bread, and it's been a top seller since day 1. It's similar to the **Multigrain Baguette** (page 152), except you'll be going a little wetter with the dough to make it in a hearth loaf style, where it is naturally fermented and supported by a proofing basket. The other big difference is that this bread doesn't call for yeast. Now that we're looking for that thicker exterior crust, going with all-natural leavening is the route we'll take. The result is a honey-fortified, heavy-on-the-grains loaf that's a solid bread for building sandwiches, sopping up soup, or throwing on the grill.

Note: This bread is pretty forgiving, so you could swap out some of the rye flour for more whole-wheat. If you're having trouble getting a light loaf here, you can make the preferment from the Multigrain Baguette (page 152) and add it to this recipe. It will help the dough ferment much more predictably and quickly. You'll just shorten your fermentation time by a couple hours and then proceed as usual.

Makes 2 (900-gram) loaves

For the Soaker:

Ingredient	Weight	Volume	Baker's %
Total flour			100.00%
>>Multigrain Seed Mix (page 152)	115g	¾ cup	100.00%
Water	115g	½ cup	100.00%

For the Bread:

Ingredient	Weight	Volume	Baker's %
Total flour			100.00%
>>Bread flour	550g	4¼ cups	85.27%
>>Whole-wheat flour	65g	⅓ cup + 2 tablespoons	10.08%
>>Rye flour	30g	¼ cup	4.65%
Water 1	415g	1¾ cups	64.34%
Active sourdough starter	175g	1 cup	27.13%
Honey	85g	¼ cup	13.18%
Fine sea salt	15g	1 tablespoon	2.33%
Water 2	90g	⅓ cup	13.95%
Toasted pepitas	70g	½ cup	10.85%
Sunflower seeds	70g	½ cup	10.85%
Semolina or fine cornmeal, for dusting			

Make the soaker: Make this the evening before you bake. In a small bowl, add the seed mix and water. Mix briefly to combine, cover, and let sit at room temperature for 12 hours.

First mix: Calculate your water temperature if desired (see page 310) or use warm (80°F) water.

In a large bowl, add the bread flour, water 1, sourdough starter, wheat flour, rye flour, and honey. Mix by hand until all of the flour has been absorbed, 3 to 4 minutes. Cover with a tea towel or linen and let the dough rest for 30 minutes.

Second mix: Sprinkle the salt evenly over the dough and incorporate it by squeezing it in with your hand while folding the dough over itself. Continue for 2 to 3 minutes; the dough should feel much stronger once the salt is added. Add water 2 and continue squeezing and folding until the water is completely absorbed and the dough coheres as one solid mass again, 3 to 4 minutes. Add the soaker, toasted pepitas, and sunflower seeds and squeeze and fold until they are evenly dispersed, another 1 to 2 minutes.

Ferment: Cover the bowl with a tea towel or linen and let the dough ferment at room temperature for 4 hours. During this time, fold the dough after 45 minutes, 1½ hours, 2 hours 15 minutes, and 3 hours, re-covering the bowl each time. Let the dough rest for the remaining hour. The dough is properly fermented when it's light, airy, and about doubled in size.

Shape: Turn out the dough onto a lightly floured work surface and divide it in half; each half should weigh about 900 grams. Pre-shape each piece (see page 50), cover with a tea towel or linen, and let them rest for 20 minutes.

Shape the dough as rounds (page 53) or batards (see page 52). Place the loaves in proofing baskets dusted with flour, seam-side up.

Proof: Cover the loaves with a tea towel or linen and proof for 1 to 1½ hours at room temperature. You can check for proper proofing by lightly flouring the top of the loaves, then pressing on the dough. You should be able to feel air in the dough, but your fingerprint should not remain in the dough for longer than 30 seconds. Once proofed, refrigerate the shaped loaves in their baskets overnight.

Continued

Bake: Preheat the oven to 475°F with a Challenger pan, cast-iron Dutch oven, or La Cloche baker on the middle rack.

Take out one of the loaves from the refrigerator. Dust a small amount of semolina or fine cornmeal on the loaf and gently transfer it from the basket to the work surface. Score as desired (page 53), drop it into the preheated pot, place the lid on top, and return the pot to the oven. Bake for 20 minutes with the lid on.

Carefully remove the lid, lifting it away from you to avoid the steam. Bake for another 20 minutes, or until the desired crust color is achieved. Transfer the bread to a wire cooling rack. Cool for as long as you can resist the temptation, ideally 2 to 3 hours.

To bake the second loaf, return the pot to the oven. Once the pot is hot, remove the loaf from the fridge and bake. Alternatively, if you'd prefer fresh bread again tomorrow, keep the shaped loaf in its basket in the refrigerator and bake the following day.

Farmer's Favorite

There's a farmer in the Spence Farm cooperative named Jane, and she would occasionally make her deliveries to the bakery with Marty. One day, she came up to me and asked if I could make her a bread with fennel, anise, and poppy seed—a flavor combination that reminded her of growing up. I love making farmers happy, so I said, "Yes, Jane, I will." I ended up incorporating the seeds both inside the bread and coated on the outside after the bake, so you get two totally different flavors out of them. The final product is a perfumed, aromatic, slightly sweet honey-fortified loaf that makes great table bread.

Note: I highly recommend going the extra mile to locate charnushka seeds instead of their more common cousin, nigella. They add a ton of flavor to this bread.

Makes 2 (900-gram) loaves

For the Bread:

Ingredient	Weight	Volume	Baker's %
Total flour			100.00%
>>Bread flour	560g	4⅓ cups	70.00%
>>Whole-wheat flour	160g	1 cup + 1 tablespoon	20.00%
>>Rye flour	80g	¾ cup	10.00%
Water 1	560g	2⅓ cups	70.00%
Active sourdough starter	180g	¾ cup	22.50%
Honey	45g	2 tablespoons	5.63%
Fine sea salt	18g	1 tablespoon	2.25%
Water 2	100g	⅓ cup	12.50%
Poppy seeds	50g	⅓ cup	6.25%
Fennel seeds	16g	2 tablespoons	4.00%
Anise seeds	8g	1 tablespoon	2.00%
Semolina or fine cornmeal, for dusting			

For the Seed Mix Garnish:

Ingredient	Weight	Volume	Baker's %
Sesame seeds	150g	2 cups	100.00%
Flax seeds	150g	2 cups	100.00%
Sunflower seeds	150g	2 cups	100.00%
Charnushka or nigella seeds (see note)	60g	1 cup	40.00%

Continued

First mix: Calculate your water temperature if desired (see page 310) or use warm (80°F) water.

In a large bowl, add water 1, the bread flour, wheat flour, rye flour, sourdough starter, and honey. Mix by hand until all of the flour has been absorbed, 3 to 4 minutes. Cover with a tea towel or linen and let the mixture rest for 30 minutes.

Second mix: Sprinkle the salt evenly over the dough and incorporate it by squeezing it in with your hand while folding the dough over itself. Continue for 2 to 3 minutes; the dough should feel much stronger once the salt is added. Add water 2 and continue squeezing and folding until the water is completely absorbed and the dough coheres as one solid mass again, 3 to 4 minutes. Add the poppy seeds, fennel seeds, and anise seeds and squeeze and fold until they are evenly dispersed, another 1 to 2 minutes.

Ferment: Cover with a tea towel or linen and let the dough ferment at room temperature for 4 hours. During this time, fold the dough after 45 minutes, 1½ hours, 2 hours 15 minutes, and 3 hours, re-covering the bowl each time. Let the dough rest for the remaining hour. The dough is properly fermented when it's light, airy, and about doubled in size.

Make the seed mix garnish: In a small bowl, combine the sesame, flax, sunflower, and charnushka seeds. Mix briefly to combine.

Shape: Turn out the dough onto a lightly floured work surface and divide it in half; each half should weigh about 900 grams. Pre-shape each piece (see page 50), cover with a tea towel or linen, and let them rest for 20 minutes.

Shape the dough as rounds (page 53) or batards (see page 52) and roll them in the seed mix. Place the loaves in a proofing basket dusted with flour, seam-side up.

Proof: Cover the loaves with a tea towel or linen and proof for 1 to 1½ hours at room temperature. You can check for proper proofing by lightly flouring the top of the loaves, then pressing on the dough. You should be able to feel air in the dough, but your fingerprint should not remain in the dough for longer than 30 seconds. Once proofed, refrigerate the shaped loaves in their baskets overnight.

Bake: Preheat the oven to 475°F with a Challenger pan, cast-iron Dutch oven, or La Cloche baker on the middle rack.

Take out one of the loaves from the refrigerator. Dust a small amount of semolina or fine cornmeal on the loaf and gently transfer it from the basket to the work surface. Score as desired (page 53), drop it into the preheated pot, place the lid on top, and return the pot to the oven. Bake for 20 minutes with the lid on.

Carefully remove the lid, lifting it away from you to avoid the steam. Bake for another 20 minutes, or until the desired crust color is achieved. Transfer the bread to a wire cooling rack. Cool for as long as you can resist the temptation, ideally 2 to 3 hours.

To bake the second loaf, return the pot to the oven. Once the pot is hot, remove the loaf from the fridge and bake. Alternatively, if you'd prefer fresh bread again tomorrow, keep the shaped loaf in its basket in the refrigerator and bake the following day.

Honey-Oat Porridge Loaf

This is one of my absolute favorites that I take home from the bakery all the time. Because it's a porridge bread, it has a very soft interior, thin crust, and open crumb; and even though it's got that sweet, nutty, buttery thing going on from the oats and honey, it's truly an all-purpose bread. I've had more than one person tell me that it makes the best grilled cheese. I love it slathered in butter and honey. Just be sure to cut it a little bit thicker given how soft it is.

Note: This dough's going to be a little bit wetter than you may be used to, so it may be a little bit more difficult to shape. But no worries; it just means you're doing something right.

Makes 2 (900-gram) loaves

For the Levain:

Ingredient	Weight	Volume	Baker's %
Total flour			100.00%
>>Bread flour	155g	1¼ cups	100.00%
Water	100g	½ cup	64.52%
Active sourdough starter	15g	1 tablespoon	9.68%

For the Porridge:

Ingredient	Weight	Volume	Baker's %
Total flour			100.00%
>>Rolled oats	130g	1¾ cups	100.00%
Water	400g	1¾ cups	307.69%
Fine sea salt	3g	½ teaspoon	2.31%

For the Bread:

Ingredient	Weight	Volume	Baker's %
Total flour			100.00%
>>Bread flour	660g	5 cups	100.00%
Water 1	500g	2 cups	75.76%
Honey	50g	2 tablespoons + 1 teaspoon	7.58%
Fine sea salt	15g	1 tablespoon	2.27%
Water 2	40g	2 tablespoons + 2 teaspoons	6.06%
Semolina or fine cornmeal, for dusting			

Make the levain: Make this the evening before you bake. In a large bowl, add the bread flour, water, and sourdough starter. Mix by hand for 3 to 4 minutes, until a solid dough forms with no dry pockets of flour. Be sure to use a bowl with plenty of headroom; this dough will about triple in volume. Cover with a tea towel or linen and let the mixture ferment in a cool area (65° to 70°F) for 8 to 10 hours or overnight.

Make the porridge: The following morning—or an hour before you mix the final dough—make the porridge. In a medium saucepan over medium heat, add the water, oats, and salt and stir to combine. Bring the mixture to a boil, stirring frequently to prevent scorching. Reduce the heat to low and simmer for 3 to 4 minutes, until the porridge is very thick. (Low and slow is the way to go here.) Spread the porridge out on a baking sheet to help it cool to room temperature.

First mix: Calculate your water temperature if desired (see page 310) or use warm (80°F) water.

In a large bowl, add the mature levain, bread flour, water 1, and honey. Mix by hand until all of the flour has been absorbed, 3 to 4 minutes. Cover with a tea towel or linen and let the mixture rest for 30 minutes.

Second mix: Sprinkle the salt evenly over the dough and incorporate it by squeezing it in with your hand while folding the dough over itself. Continue for 2 to 3 minutes; the dough should feel much stronger once the salt is added. Add water 2 and continue squeezing and folding until the water is completely absorbed and the dough coheres as one solid mass again, 3 to 4 minutes. Add the porridge and squeeze and fold until it is evenly dispersed, another 1 to 2 minutes.

Ferment: Cover the bowl with a tea towel or linen and let the dough ferment at room temperature for 4 hours. During this time, fold the dough after 45 minutes, 1½ hours, 2 hours 15 minutes, and 3 hours, re-covering the bowl each time. Let the dough rest for the remaining hour. The dough is properly fermented when it's light, airy, and about doubled in size.

Shape: Turn out the dough onto a lightly floured work surface and divide it in half; each half should weigh about 900 grams. Pre-shape each piece (see page 50), cover with a tea towel or linen, and let them rest for 20 minutes.

Continued

Shape the dough as rounds (page 53) or batards (see page 52). Place the loaves in proofing baskets dusted with flour, seam-side up.

Proof: Cover the loaves with a tea towel or linen and proof for 1 to 1½ hours at room temperature. You can check for proper proofing by lightly flouring the top of the loaves, then pressing on the dough. You should be able to feel air in the dough, but your fingerprint should not remain in the dough for longer than 30 seconds. Once proofed, refrigerate the shaped loaves in their baskets overnight.

Bake: Preheat the oven to 475°F with a Challenger pan, cast-iron Dutch oven, or La Cloche baker on the middle rack.

Take out one of the loaves from the refrigerator. Dust a small amount of semolina or fine cornmeal on the loaf and gently transfer it from the basket to the work surface. Score as desired (page 53), drop it into the preheated pot, place the lid on top, and return the pot to the oven. Bake for 20 minutes with the lid on.

Carefully remove the lid, lifting it away from you to avoid the steam. Bake for another 20 minutes, or until the desired crust color is achieved. Transfer the bread to a wire cooling rack. Cool for as long as you can resist the temptation, ideally 2 to 3 hours.

To bake the second loaf, return the pot to the oven. Once the pot is hot, remove the loaf from the fridge and bake. Alternatively, if you'd prefer fresh bread again tomorrow, keep the shaped loaf in its basket in the refrigerator and bake the following day.

Honey and Sprouted Wheat Loaf

"How do you feel about sprouted flour?" I get that question a lot, namely because sprouting has gotten a lot of attention as something that's nutritious and good for you. And that's 100 percent true. But when you're talking about making bread out of flour that's already sprouted, that's when I change my tune. When you sprout a grain, you're breaking down the complex sugars, making them easier to digest—which is exactly what happens during natural fermentation. So if you're doing it beforehand in your flour, then you're not going to end up with a quality hearth loaf dough that has any structure.

But where the sprouting process can work for your bread is when you incorporate the whole sprouted grains themselves as an inclusion, which is what we do here. You're going to sprout the wheat berries first, then fold them in as you would a seed or a nut. That way you get the benefits of sprouted grain, but without altering your flour's fermentation process and the integrity of your dough. In the end, you get a healthful, slightly sweet loaf that's rounded out with natural nuttiness. It's the kind of bread that's pretty much made for breakfast toast.

Makes 2 (900-gram) loaves

Ingredient	Weight	Volume	Baker's %
Total flour			100.00%
>>Bread flour	615g	4¾ cups	80.39%
>>Whole-wheat flour	150g	1 cup	19.61%
Water 1	530g	2¼ cups	69.28%
Active sourdough starter	180g	1 cup	23.53%
Honey	90g	¼ cup	11.76%
Fine sea salt	16g	1 tablespoon	2.09%
Water 2	40g	2 tablespoons + 2 teaspoons	5.23%
Sprouted wheat berries	150g	1 cup	19.61%
Semolina or fine cornmeal, for dusting			

Sprout the wheat berries: In a large bowl, submerge the wheat berries in water and soak overnight. Drain off the water and place the berries between damp paper towels in a warm area for 24 to 48 hours. You should see a little seed "tail" form, which is the sprout. They are ready to use when the tail is the same length as the grain.

First mix: Calculate your water temperature if desired (see page 310) or use warm (80°F) water.

In a large bowl, add the bread flour, water 1, sourdough starter, wheat flour, and honey. Mix by hand until all of the flour has been absorbed, 3 to 4 minutes. Cover with a tea towel or linen and let the mixture rest for 30 minutes.

Second mix: Sprinkle the salt evenly over the dough and incorporate it by squeezing it in with your hand while folding the dough over itself. Continue for 2 to 3 minutes; the dough should feel much stronger once the salt is added. Add water 2 and continue squeezing and folding until the water is completely absorbed and the dough coheres as one solid mass again, 3 to 4 minutes. Add the sprouted wheat berries and squeeze and fold until they are evenly dispersed, another 1 to 2 minutes.

Ferment: Cover with a tea towel or linen and let the dough ferment at room temperature for 4 hours. During this time, fold the dough after 45 minutes, 1½ hours, 2 hours 15 minutes, and 3 hours, re-covering the bowl each time. Let the dough rest for the remaining hour. The dough is properly fermented when it's light, airy, and about doubled in size.

Shape: Turn out the dough onto a lightly floured work surface and divide it in half; each half should weigh about 900 grams. Pre-shape each piece (see page 50), cover with a tea towel or linen, and let them rest for 20 minutes.

Shape the dough as rounds (page 53) or batards (see page 52). Place the loaves in proofing baskets dusted with flour, seam-side up.

Proof: Cover the loaves with a tea towel or linen and proof for 1 to 1½ hours at room temperature. You can check for proper proofing by lightly flouring the top of the loaves, then pressing on the dough. You should be able to feel air

Continued

in the dough, but your fingerprint should not remain in the dough for longer than 30 seconds. Once proofed, refrigerate the shaped loaves in their baskets overnight.

Bake: Preheat the oven to 475°F with a Challenger pan, cast-iron Dutch oven, or La Cloche baker on the middle rack.

Take out one of the loaves from the refrigerator. Dust a small amount of semolina or fine cornmeal on the loaf and gently transfer it from the basket to the counter. Score as desired (page 53), drop it into the preheated pot, place the lid on top, and return the pot to the oven. Bake for 20 minutes with the lid on.

Carefully remove the lid, lifting it away from you to avoid the steam. Bake for another 20 minutes, or until the desired crust color is achieved. Transfer the bread to a wire cooling rack. Cool for as long as you can resist the temptation, ideally 2 to 3 hours.

To bake the second loaf, return the pot to the oven. Once the pot is hot, remove the loaf from the fridge and bake. Alternatively, if you'd prefer fresh bread again tomorrow, keep the shaped loaf in its basket in the refrigerator and bake the following day.

Marbled Rye

Normally when you see a marbled rye sandwich bread—the kind everyone knows comes with a proper pastrami sandwich—what the baker has done is roll ropes of light dough and dark dough, wrapped those ropes together, and then coiled them before proofing and baking. For our purposes, that technique won't work because this is a hearth bread dough, so we're going to use hearth bread techniques with two different doughs that will get layered and proofed together. Both are heavy on rye flour and both will be fermented, but one will get a color contrast from cocoa powder, so as you fold the dough, you'll get an organic psychedelic effect.

Note: Each of the steps outlined in this recipe is for *both the light and dark doughs*.

Makes 2 (900-gram) loaves

For the Light Dough:

Ingredient	Weight	Volume	Baker's %
Total flour			100.00%
>>Bread flour	325g	2½ cups	74.71%
>>Rye flour	110g	¾ cup + 2 tablespoons	25.29%
Water 1	345g	1½ cups	79.31%
Active sourdough starter	90g	½ cup	20.69%
Fine sea salt	11g	2 teaspoons	2.53%
Water 2	20g	1 tablespoon + 1 teaspoon	4.60%

For the Dark Dough:

Ingredient	Weight	Volume	Baker's %
Total flour			100.00%
>>Bread flour	300g	2⅓ cups	68.97%
>>Rye flour	110g	¾ cup + 2 tablespoons	25.29%
Water 1	345g	1½ cups	79.31%
Active sourdough starter	90g	½ cup	20.69%
Cocoa powder	25g	2 tablespoons + 2 teaspoons	5.75%
Fine sea salt	11g	2 teaspoons	2.53%
Water 2	20g	1 tablespoon + 1 teaspoon	4.60%
Semolina or fine cornmeal, for dusting			

Continued

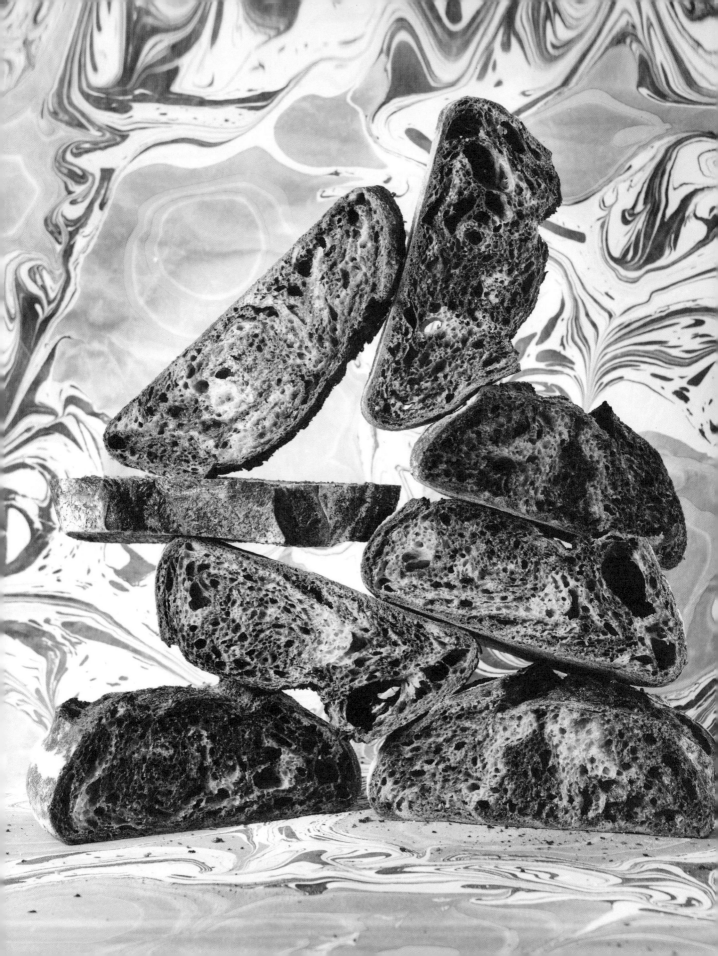

First mix: For both the light and the dark doughs, calculate your water temperature if desired (see page 310) or use warm (80°F) water.

In a large bowl for each dough, add water 1, the bread flour, rye flour, sourdough starter, and the cocoa powder for the dark dough. Mix by hand until all of the flour has been absorbed, 3 to 4 minutes. Cover both bowls with a tea towel or linen and let the mixture rest for 30 minutes.

Second mix: Sprinkle the salt evenly over both doughs and incorporate it by squeezing it in with your hand while folding the dough over itself. Continue for 2 to 3 minutes; the dough should feel much stronger once the salt is added. Add water 2 to each dough and continue squeezing and folding until the water is completely absorbed and the dough coheres as one solid mass again, 3 to 4 minutes. Divide each dough into two pieces and place in alternating layers in a bowl. No need to get fancy, just toss 'em in there.

Ferment: Cover with a tea towel or linen and let the dough ferment at room temperature for 3 hours. During this time, fold the dough after 45 minutes and again at 1½ hours, re-covering the bowl each time. Take care while stretching and folding to accentuate the different colors in the dough, trying to get them to overlap. The dough is properly fermented when it's light, airy, and about doubled in size.

Shape: Turn out the dough onto a lightly floured work surface and divide it in half; each half should weigh about 900 grams. Pre-shape each piece (see page 50), cover with a tea towel or linen, and let them rest for 20 minutes.

Shape the dough as rounds (page 53) or batards (see page 52). Place the loaves in proofing baskets dusted with flour, seam-side up.

Proof: Cover the loaves with a tea towel or linen and proof for 1 to 1½ hours at room temperature. You can check for proper proofing by lightly flouring the top of the loaves, then pressing on the dough. You should be able to feel air in the dough, but your fingerprint should not remain in the dough for longer than 30 seconds. Once proofed, refrigerate the shaped loaves in their baskets overnight.

Bake: Preheat the oven to 475°F with a Challenger pan, cast-iron Dutch oven, or La Cloche baker on the middle rack.

Take out one of the loaves from the refrigerator. Dust a small amount of semolina or fine cornmeal on the loaf and gently transfer it from the basket to the work surface. Score as desired (page 53), drop it into the preheated pot, place the lid on top, and return the pot to the oven. Bake for 20 minutes with the lid on.

Carefully remove the lid, lifting it away from you to avoid the steam. Bake for another 20 minutes, or until the desired crust color is achieved. Transfer the bread to a wire cooling rack. Cool for as long as you can resist the temptation, ideally 2 to 3 hours.

To bake the second loaf, return the pot to the oven. Once the pot is hot, remove the loaf from the fridge and bake. Alternatively, if you'd prefer fresh bread again tomorrow, keep the shaped loaf in its basket in the refrigerator and bake the following day.

Roasted Garlic and Mashed Potato Ciabatta

This bread has a light, open, and airy crumb with the flavor profile of mashed potatoes—what's not to love? Especially because I can't remember the last time I made mashed potatoes and didn't have some leftovers, which is the perfect excuse to make this bread. It's mixed, shaped, and baked in the same day and is another great example of how using a starter and yeast in tandem is going to give different qualities to your bake and your bread.

Makes 2 (750-gram) loaves

Note: I call for making plain mashed potatoes, but if you have leftovers from a recipe that included butter or cream, it's fine to use them here.

Ingredient	Weight	Volume	Baker's %
Total flour			100.00%
>>Bread flour	590g	4½ cups	100.00%
Head of garlic		1 whole	
Extra-virgin olive oil, for drizzling			
Water	413g	1⅔ cups	70.00%
Active sourdough starter	400g	2 cups	67.80%
Yukon Gold potatoes		2 large	
Fine sea salt	18g	1 tablespoon	3.05%
Active dry yeast	7g	1½ teaspoons	1.19%

Roast the garlic: Preheat the oven to 400°F.

Trim the top off the head of garlic, about ¼ inch. Lightly drizzle the garlic with olive oil and wrap the head in aluminum foil. Place in a small baking pan and roast for 40 minutes, or until very soft. When cool enough to handle, squeeze the garlic out of its skins. Set aside.

First mix: While the garlic is roasting, proceed with your first mix: Calculate your water temperature if desired (see page 310) or use warm (80°F) water.

In the bowl of a stand mixer fitted with the paddle attachment, add the bread flour, water, and sourdough starter. Mix on low speed until all of the flour has been absorbed, 2 to 3 minutes. Cover the bowl and let rest for 30 minutes.

Continued

Make the mashed potatoes: While the garlic is roasting and your first mix is resting, make the mashed potatoes. Peel and cut the potatoes into ½-inch pieces and add them to a pot with just enough cold water to cover. Bring the water to a boil, reduce the heat to a simmer, and cook until the potatoes are tender, about 15 minutes. Drain and mash, using either a fork, a masher, or a food mill.

Second mix: To the first mix, add ¼ cup of the mashed potatoes, 2 table-spoons of the roasted garlic (or according to the old cook's adage: If some is good, more is better), the salt, and yeast and mix on low speed until thoroughly combined. Increase the speed to medium and mix until the dough pulls completely away from the sides of the bowl and begins to climb up the paddle. The dough should look shiny and be very strong. Remove the paddle from the bowl and remove the bowl from the mixer.

Ferment: Cover the bowl with a tea towel or linen and let the dough ferment at room temperature for 3 hours. During this time, fold the dough every 30 minutes, for a total of 4 times, re-covering the bowl each time and letting the dough rest for the final hour. The dough is properly fermented when it's light, airy, and about doubled in size.

Shape: Turn out the dough onto a lightly floured work surface and divide it in half; each half should weigh about 750 grams. Pre-shape each piece (see page 50), cover with a tea towel or linen, and let them rest for 30 minutes. Once proofed, shape each piece of dough into a square. Fold the bottom of the square to the top third, then the top to the middle. Flip the dough over so it's seam-side down and let it rest for 45 minutes to 1 hour.

Bake: Preheat the oven to 500°F with a Challenger pan, cast-iron Dutch oven, or La Cloche baker on the middle rack.

Once hot, remove the pan from the oven. Gently scoop each loaf from the counter and place in the pan. (If you can't fit them both in your pan side by side, bake off one at a time.) It's OK if the loaf stretches out and elongates a bit. Place the lid back on the pot, return the pot to the oven, and bake for 15 minutes.

Carefully remove the lid, lifting it away from you to avoid the steam. Bake for another 15 minutes, or until the desired crust color is achieved. Transfer the bread to a wire cooling rack. Cool for as long as you can resist the temptation, ideally 2 to 3 hours.

Ryebatta

Now we're just taking the Roasted Garlic and Mashed Potato Ciabatta recipe (page 173), adding a whole grain by way of rye flour, and then naturally leavening it, which helps break down the grain and draw out its naturally spicy, floral flavor. The dough also gets laced with olive oil, which makes for a soft, rich bread. It's a pretty wet dough, but that's what you want with ciabatta because water is what gives you a nice, light texture.

Makes 2 (750-gram) loaves

Ingredient	Weight	Volume	Baker's %
Total flour			100.00%
>>Bread flour	545g	4¼ cups	73.65%
>>Rye flour	195g	1⅔ cups	26.35%
Water	580g	2½ cups	78.38%
Active sourdough starter	155g	¾ cup	20.95%
Extra-virgin olive oil	50g	¼ cup	6.76%
Fine sea salt	15g	1 tablespoon	2.03%

First mix: Calculate your water temperature if desired (see page 310) or use warm (80°F) water.

In the bowl of a stand mixer fitted with the paddle attachment, add the water, bread flour, rye flour, and sourdough starter. Mix on low speed until all of the flour has been absorbed, 2 to 3 minutes. Cover and let rest for 30 minutes.

Second mix: Pour the olive oil and sprinkle the salt evenly over the dough and mix on low speed until thoroughly combined. Increase the speed to medium and mix until the dough pulls completely away from the sides of the bowl and begins to climb up the paddle. The dough should look very shiny and be very strong. Remove the paddle from the dough and remove the bowl from the mixer.

Ferment: Cover the bowl with a tea towel or linen and let the dough ferment at room temperature for 3 hours. During this time, fold the dough every 30 minutes, for a total of 4 times, re-covering the bowl each time and letting the dough rest for the final hour. The dough is properly fermented when it's light, airy, and about doubled in size.

Shape: Turn out the dough onto a lightly floured work surface and divide it in half; each half should weigh about 750 grams. Pre-shape each piece (see page 50), cover with a tea towel or linen, and let them rest for 30 minutes. Once proofed, shape each piece of dough into a 5-inch square. Fold the bottom of the square to the top third, then the top to the middle. Flip the dough over so it's seam-side down and let it rest for 45 minutes to 1 hour.

Bake: Preheat the oven to 500°F with a Challenger pan, cast-iron Dutch oven, or La Cloche baker on the middle rack.

Once hot, take the pan out of the oven. Gently scoop each loaf from the counter and place into the pan. (If you can't fit them both in your pan side by side, bake off one at a time.) It's OK if the loaf stretches out and elongates a bit. Place the lid back on the pot, return the pot to the oven, and bake for 15 minutes.

Carefully remove the lid, lifting it away from you to avoid the steam. Bake for another 15 minutes, or until the desired crust color is achieved. Transfer the bread to a wire cooling rack. Cool for as long as you can resist the temptation, ideally 2 to 3 hours.

Sorghum and Rosemary Ciabatta

Another great ciabatta for your arsenal: Sorghum flour and olive oil give the bread a buttery richness, while rosemary infuses the loaf with a woodsy perfume.

Note: I know one of the cook's mantras is "If some is good, more is better," but when it comes to adding fresh herbs to bread, exercise restraint. It's easy for the oils from the herbs to overwhelm the loaf. Start with what's here and if you still want to add more next time, go for it.

Makes 2 (750-gram) loaves

For the Sorghum Porridge:

Ingredient	Weight	Volume	Baker's %
Total flour			100.00%
>>Sorghum flour	75g	¾ cup	100.00%
Water	225g	1 cup	300.00%
Fine sea salt	1g	⅛ teaspoon	1.33%

For the Bread:

Ingredient	Weight	Volume	Baker's %
Total flour			100.00%
>>Bread flour	570g	4⅓ cups	100.00%
Water 1	400g	1¾ cups	70.18%
Active sourdough starter	150g	¾ cup	26.32%
Extra-virgin olive oil	30g	2 tablespoons + 1 teaspoon	5.26%
Fine sea salt	18g	1 teaspoon	3.16%
Water 2	30g	2 teaspoons	5.26%
Chopped fresh rosemary leaves	5g	1 teaspoon	0.88%

Make the porridge: In a medium saucepan, add the water, sorghum flour, and salt and stir to combine. Cook over medium heat, stirring frequently to prevent scorching, and bring to a boil. Reduce the heat to low and simmer for 3 to 4 minutes, until the porridge is very thick. Spread the porridge out on a baking sheet to help it cool to room temperature.

First mix: Calculate your water temperature if desired (see page 310) or use warm (80°F) water.

Continued

In the bowl of a stand mixer fitted with the paddle attachment, add the bread flour, water 1, and sourdough starter. Mix on low speed until all of the flour has been absorbed, 2 to 3 minutes. Cover and let rest for 30 minutes.

Second mix: Add the olive oil and salt and mix on low speed until thoroughly combined. Increase the speed to medium and mix until the dough pulls completely away from the sides of the bowl and begins to climb up the paddle. The dough should look shiny and be very strong. Reduce the speed back down to low and slowly drizzle in water 2. Mix again until the dough coheres as one solid mass, 1 to 2 minutes. Add the rosemary and mix until it has been incorporated, about 1 more minute. Remove the paddle from the bowl and remove the bowl from the mixer.

Ferment: Cover the bowl with a tea towel or linen and let the dough ferment at room temperature for 3 hours. During this time, fold the dough every 30 minutes, for a total of 4 times, re-covering the bowl each time and letting the dough rest for the final hour. The dough is properly fermented when it's light, airy, and about doubled in size.

Shape: Turn out the dough onto a lightly floured work surface and divide it in half; each half should weigh about 750 grams. Pre-shape each piece (see page 50), cover with a tea towel or linen, and let them rest for 30 minutes. Once proofed, shape each piece of dough into a square. Fold the bottom of the square to the top third, then the top to the middle. Flip the dough over so it's seam-side down and let it rest for 45 minutes to 1 hour.

Bake: Preheat the oven to 500°F with a Challenger pan, cast-iron Dutch oven, or La Cloche baker on the middle rack.

Once hot, take the pan out of the oven. Gently scoop each loaf from the counter and place into the pan. (If you can't fit them both in your pan side by side, bake off one at a time.) It's OK if the loaf stretches out and elongates a bit. Place the lid back on the pot, return the pot to the oven, and bake for 15 minutes.

Carefully remove the lid, lifting it away from you to avoid the steam. Bake for another 15 minutes, or until the desired crust color is achieved. Transfer the bread to a wire cooling rack. Cool for as long as you can resist the temptation, ideally 2 to 3 hours.

Spelt, Cumin, and Walnut Ring Loaf

This is another one of those great mix-and-match Mr. Potato Head breads where you can plug in different flours and inclusions at a 1:1 ratio. At the foundation, I wanted to show off spelt's versatility and the unique flavor of a cumin seed inclusion. But you could go with rye and caraway seeds or sorghum and coriander—get interesting with it. This is a decorative ring loaf made for a party. I highly recommend making a flavor-appropriate dip or spread, plunking it in the middle of the ring (I recommend beet muhammara).

Note: When using walnuts in bread, it's likely going to turn your crumb slightly purple. There's nothing wrong with your bread, it just has to do with the chemicals the walnuts give off while baking. So don't worry about it and just enjoy the color.

Makes 2 (900-gram) loaves

Ingredient	Weight	Volume	Baker's %
Total flour			100.00%
>>Bread flour	545g	4¼ cups	69.87%
>>Spelt flour	235g	2 cups	30.13%
Water 1	500g	2 cups	64.10%
Active sourdough starter	180g	¾ cup	23.08%
Molasses	60g	3 tablespoons	7.69%
Fine sea salt	17g	1 tablespoon	2.18%
Water 2	90g	½ cup	11.54%
Chopped walnuts, or halves if you like larger pieces	155g	1⅓ cups	19.87%
Cumin seed	16g	2 tablespoons	2.05%
Semolina or fine cornmeal, for dusting			

First mix: Calculate your water temperature if desired (see page 310) or use warm (80°F) water.

In a large bowl, add the bread flour, water 1, spelt flour, sourdough starter, and molasses. Mix by hand until all of the flour has been absorbed, 3 to 4 minutes. Cover and let rest for 30 minutes.

Continued

Second mix: Sprinkle the salt evenly over the dough and incorporate it by squeezing it in with your hand while folding the dough over itself. Continue for 2 to 3 minutes; the dough should feel much stronger once the salt is added. Add water 2 and continue squeezing and folding until the water is completely absorbed and the dough coheres as one solid mass again, 3 to 4 minutes. Add the walnuts and cumin and squeeze and fold until they are evenly dispersed, another 1 to 2 minutes.

Ferment: Cover the bowl with a tea towel or linen and let the dough ferment at room temperature for 4 hours. During this time, fold the dough after 45 minutes, 1½ hours, 2 hours 15 minutes, and 3 hours, re-covering the bowl each time. Let the dough rest for the remaining hour. The dough is properly fermented when it's light, airy, and about doubled in size.

Shape: Turn out the dough onto a lightly floured work surface and divide it in half; each half should weigh about 900 grams. Pre-shape both pieces (see page 50). Cover the dough with a tea towel or linen and let it rest for 20 minutes. Shape each piece of dough as a ring loaf (see page 53).

Proof: Cover the loaves with a tea towel or linen and proof for 1 to 1½ hours at room temperature. You can check for proper proofing by lightly flouring the top of the loaves, then pressing on the dough. You should be able to feel air in the dough, but your fingerprint should not remain in the dough for longer than 30 seconds. Once proofed, refrigerate the shaped loaves in their baskets overnight.

Bake: Preheat the oven to 475°F with a Challenger pan, cast-iron Dutch oven, or La Cloche baker on the middle rack.

Take out one of the loaves from the refrigerator. Remove the center mold from the proofing basket. Dust a small amount of semolina or fine cornmeal on the loaf and gently transfer it from the basket to the work surface. Score as desired (page 53), drop it into the preheated pot, place the lid on top, and return the pot to the oven. Bake for 20 minutes with the lid on.

Carefully remove the lid, lifting it away from you to avoid the steam. Bake for another 20 minutes, or until the desired crust color is achieved. Transfer the bread to a wire cooling rack. Cool for as long as you can resist the temptation, ideally 2 to 3 hours.

To bake the second loaf, return the pot to the oven. Once the pot is hot, remove the loaf from the fridge and bake. Alternatively, if you'd prefer fresh bread again tomorrow, keep the shaped loaf in its basket in the refrigerator and bake the following day.

Toasted Sesame Loaf

Another one that's heavy in my rotation. Namely because I'm very fond of sesame seeds and the deep, nutty flavor they give off after they're toasted, plus the richness of olive oil and a little bit of sweetness from honey. It's a solid sandwich bread, especially if you're going Italian-style with cold cuts or porchetta.

Makes 2 (900-gram) loaves

Ingredient	Weight	Volume	Baker's %
Total flour			100.00%
>>Bread flour	660g	5 cups	80.00%
>>Whole-wheat flour	165g	1 cup + 2 tablespoons	20.00%
Water 1	530g	2¼ cups	64.24%
Active sourdough starter	180g	1 cup	21.82%
Fine sea salt	18g	1 tablespoon	2.18%
Honey	65g	¼ cup	7.88%
Extra-virgin olive oil	35g	2½ tablespoons	4.24%
Water 2	100g	½ cup	12.12%
Toasted sesame seeds, plus more for topping	50g	½ cup	6.06%
Semolina or fine cornmeal, for dusting			

First mix: Calculate your water temperature if desired (see page 310) or use warm (80°F) water.

In a large bowl, add the bread flour, water 1, sourdough starter, and wheat flour. Mix by hand until all of the flour has been absorbed, 3 to 4 minutes. Cover and let rest for 30 minutes.

Second mix: Sprinkle the salt evenly over the dough and incorporate it by squeezing it in with your hand while folding the dough over itself. Continue for 2 to 3 minutes; the dough should feel much stronger once the salt is added. Add the honey and olive oil and continue squeezing and folding until the honey and oil are completely absorbed and the dough coheres as one solid mass again. Add water 2 and repeat, squeezing and folding until the water is absorbed and the dough is uniform again. Add the sesame seeds and squeeze and fold until they are evenly dispersed, another 1 to 2 minutes.

Continued

Ferment: Cover with a tea towel or linen and let the dough ferment at room temperature for 4 hours. During this time, fold the dough after 45 minutes, 1½ hours, 2 hours 15 minutes, and 3 hours, re-covering the bowl each time. Let the dough rest for the remaining hour. The dough is properly fermented when it's light, airy, and about doubled in size.

Shape: Turn out the dough onto a lightly floured work surface and divide it in half; each half should weigh about 900 grams. Pre-shape each piece (see page 50), cover with a tea towel or linen, and let them rest for 20 minutes.

Spread out some sesame seeds on a baking sheet, enough to coat the bottom of the tray. Shape the dough as rounds (page 53) or batards (see page 52). Brush the shaped loaves lightly with water, just to dampen them. Roll the shaped loaves in the sesame seeds; the water will help them adhere to the bread. Place the loaves in proofing baskets dusted with flour, seam-side up.

Proof: Cover the loaves with a tea towel or linen and proof for 1 to 1½ hours at room temperature. You can check for proper proofing by lightly flouring the top of the loaves, then pressing on the dough. You should be able to feel air in the dough, but your fingerprint should not remain in the dough for longer than 30 seconds. Once proofed, refrigerate the shaped loaves in their baskets overnight.

Bake: Preheat the oven to 475°F with a Challenger pan, cast-iron Dutch oven, or La Cloche baker on the middle rack.

Take out one of the loaves from the refrigerator. Dust a small amount of semolina or fine cornmeal on the loaf and gently transfer it from the basket to the work surface. Score as desired (page 53), drop it into the preheated pot, place the lid on top, and return the pot to the oven. Bake for 20 minutes with the lid on.

Carefully remove the lid, lifting it away from you to avoid the steam. Bake for another 20 minutes, or until the desired crust color is achieved. Transfer the bread to a wire cooling rack. Cool for as long as you can resist the temptation, ideally 2 to 3 hours.

To bake the second loaf, return the pot to the oven. Once the pot is hot, remove the loaf from the fridge and bake. Alternatively, if you'd prefer fresh bread again tomorrow, keep the shaped loaf in its basket in the refrigerator and bake the following day.

CHAPTER 3

Fire on the Mountain

Farinata *190*

Bagels *193*

    Rye and Blueberry Bagels *196*

    Cornmeal and Jalapeño Bagels *196*

Wheat Pitas *197*

Rye Naan *199*

Whole-Grain Chile Pide Bread *201*

Whole-Wheat Pretzels *205*

Sourdough Pizza Dough *209*

    Margherita Pizzas *212*

    Celery Root and Rosemary Pizzas *213*

Wheat Neapolitan Pizza Dough *214*

    Sungold and Church Bell Pepper Pizzas *216*

    Asparagus, Spring Onion, and Fresno Pepper Pizzas *217*

Nothing compares to cooking over live fire. Something special and alchemic happens from all the intense direct heat, not to mention the smokiness and the general cool factor of playing with fire. These recipes are meant to impart techniques that are suited for live-fire cooking but don't necessarily require a wood-burning oven. In fact, you'd be fine across the board using a pizza stone or skillet set inside a grill or oven. And in some cases, just a skillet on the stove. Whatever route you go, these recipes and their cooking variations have you covered.

Farinata

Because it's not a grain, we haven't yet talked about chickpea flour. But this product—made, as you probably guessed, from ground chickpeas—should have a place on your alt-flour shelf. It's super flavorful and high in protein, and it makes for pretty great savory pancakes called farinata, a discovery first made by the Italians. Aerated with sparkling water and flavored simply with olive oil, Parm, and salt, these are light, fluffy and accommodating of pretty much any fillings you're into. I like to make mine in the style of pizza guru Chris Bianco, with charred leeks, mushrooms, or lemon slices down in the pan first, followed by the batter, so when you flip it over you end up with an attractive tarte tatin–style dish.

Makes 1 to 2 large pancakes

Ingredient	Weight	Volume	Baker's %
Total flour			100.00%
>>Chickpea flour	100g	1 cup	100.00%
Sparkling water	235g	1 cup	235.00%
Parmesan cheese	75g	¼ cup	75.00%
Extra-virgin olive oil, plus more for cooking	55g	¼ cup	55.00%
Fine sea salt	2g	small pinch	2.00%

Preheat the oven to 375°F.

In a large bowl, add the sparkling water, chickpea flour, Parmesan cheese, olive oil, and salt. Whisk thoroughly to combine.

In a large oven-safe nonstick or cast-iron pan over medium heat, heat a teaspoon or two of oil. If adding toppings (see headnote), sauté them until soft, 2 to 3 minutes. Add about 1 cup batter to the pan—enough for a layer about ¼ inch thick. Increase the heat to medium-high and cook for 3 to 4 minutes. Transfer to the oven and cook for another 5 to 6 minutes, until just golden. Remove from the pan and repeat batches with the remaining batter.

🔥 **Grilling Variation:** Preheat the grill to medium heat. Heat a grill-safe pan and add the batter as above. Cook until golden brown on one side, 3 to 4 minutes. Flip and cook for another 2 to 3 minutes on the other side or until golden. Remove from the pan and repeat.

Wood-Fired Oven Variation: Build a medium-size fire and let the oven heat for 1 to 2 hours. Heat the pan and add the batter as above. Cook next to the fire until golden brown on both sides, 3 to 4 minutes. Remove from the pan and repeat.

Bagels

At first glance, it doesn't seem completely status quo to cook bagels with live fire. But Montreal-style bagels—which are my personal preference over New York–style—are traditionally made in a wood-fired oven. I like that they're a little breadier and have a bit more chew to them, and that they're first boiled in water and honey, as opposed to baking soda or lye. The combination of the honey and high heat gives them a kind of shell that breaks open to reveal a soft, open-crumb interior thanks to sourdough leavening (my own twist). Another difference you'll notice if you've made bagels before is that this dough is slightly wetter than usual. That increased hydration will help the dough stand up to the extended exposure to intense heat. Whether you go with the sweet-tart blueberry and floral rye or Southwest-style jalapeño and cornmeal variations, plain, or with toppings like sesame seeds, poppy seeds, or an "everything" mix, fire-roasting makes for a damn good bagel.

Makes 12 (150-gram) bagels

Ingredient	Weight	Volume	Baker's %
Total flour			100.00%
>>Bread flour	820g	6⅓ cups	86.77%
>>Whole-wheat flour	125g	¾ cup plus 1 tablespoon	13.23%
Water	660g	2¾ cups	69.84%
Active sourdough starter	180g	1 cup	19.05%
Fine sea salt	20g	1 tablespoon	2.12%
Honey	340g	1 cup	35.98%
Semolina or fine cornmeal, for dusting			
Everything bagel topping mix, sesame seeds, or poppy seeds, for topping (optional)			

First mix: Calculate your water temperature if desired (see page 310) or use warm (80°F) water.

In a large bowl, combine the bread flour, water, sourdough starter, and wheat flour. Mix by hand until all of the flour has been absorbed, 3 to 4 minutes. Cover and let rest for 30 minutes.

Continued

Second mix: Sprinkle the salt evenly over the dough and incorporate it by squeezing it in with your hand while folding the dough over itself. Continue for 2 to 3 minutes; the dough should feel much stronger once the salt is added. Knead for 4 to 5 minutes, until the dough is smooth and shiny.

Ferment: Cover the bowl with a tea towel or linen and let the dough ferment at room temperature for 2½ hours. Fold the dough after 1½ hours, then re-cover the bowl and let the dough rest for the final hour. Keep the bowl covered and refrigerate overnight.

Shape and boil: Preheat the oven to 450°F with a pizza stone or the base of a Challenger pan.

In a large, wide pot over medium-high heat, add 2 quarts water and the honey and bring to a boil. Dust a baking sheet with semolina or cornmeal.

Turn out the dough onto a lightly floured work surface and divide it into twelve pieces; each piece should weigh about 150 grams. Lightly flour your hands by pressing them into the flour on the table. Take a piece of dough and pull the top edge with your fingertips, fold it about a third of the way down the dough, and press gently to seal. Repeat that again, taking the top edge and bringing it down about a third, and then another third until you've formed a cylinder.

Place the cylinder seam-side down and use the palms of your hands to roll it into a rope about 1 inch in diameter. Wrap the dough around your hand to form a loop, pressing the two ends together. Hold the top of the loop with one hand as you roll the loop's seam under your other palm against the table just to seal the bagel's shape. Place the shaped bagel on the prepared baking sheet. Repeat to shape all the bagels.

Carefully boil the bagels in batches for 1 minute per side. Don't crowd the pot as the bagels will grow slightly when boiling, and as best you can, you'll want to keep the water at a rolling boil. Transfer each bagel to a wire cooling rack and let drain.

Once the bagels are all boiled and drained, you can top them if you like. Dip the tops of the bagels in the desired topping while still damp from boiling, then place each bagel bottom-side down back on the dusted baking sheet.

Bake: Place the bagels directly on the preheated pizza stone or bakeware. Bake for 15 to 20 minutes, until the desired crust color is achieved.

🔥 **Wood-Fired Oven Variation:** Light a small fire in the back corner of your oven. Let this heat for about an hour. When ready to bake the bagels, you want a medium-low roar of a fire going from about two medium-size logs. Use a peel to load the bagels into the oven, placing them directly on the floor of the oven about a foot away from the fire itself. Bake for 6 to 7 minutes. You may need to rotate the bagels as they bake so as to not burn the backs.

🔥 **Grill Variation:** Prepare a medium amount of charcoals on a round grill. Once the coals are hot, move the coals into a ring around the perimeter of the grill and place a grill-safe pizza stone in the center of the grate. Let this heat for 15 minutes. Place the bagels directly on the stone, close the lid, and grill for 6 to 7 minutes, until baked through with good color.

Continued

Rye and Blueberry Bagels

Ingredient	Weight	Volume	Baker's %
Total flour			100.00%
>>Bread flour	820g	6⅓ cups	86.77%
>>Rye flour	125g	1 cup plus 1 tablespoon	13.23%
Water	660g	2¾ cups	69.84%
Active sourdough starter	180g	1 cup	19.05%
Salt	20g	1 tablespoon	2.12%
Dried blueberries	100g	¾ cup	10.58%

For this riff, mix as instructed above. During the second mix, after the salt has been kneaded in, add and knead in the dried blueberries until evenly dispersed. Ferment, shape, and boil as instructed, then bake as desired.

Cornmeal and Jalapeño Bagels

Ingredient	Weight	Volume	Baker's %
Total flour			100.00%
>>Bread flour	820g	6⅓ cups	86.77%
>>Cornmeal	125g	¾ cup	13.23%
Water	660g	2¾ cups	69.84%
Active sourdough starter	180g	1 cup	19.05%
Salt	20g	1 tablespoon plus 1 teaspoon	2.12%
Minced jalapeños	75g	½ cup	7.94%
Aged Gouda cheese, shredded, for topping			

For this riff, mix as instructed above. During the second mix, after the salt has been kneaded in, add and knead in the jalapeños until evenly dispersed. Ferment, shape, and boil as instructed above, then top each bagel with a small handful of Gouda cheese. Bake as desired.

Wheat Pitas

Something that really bothers me is the drab "baked" flavor that you get when you make pita bread in a regular oven. It's like the difference between a regular potato chip and a baked one—all you can think is, *Why didn't you just fucking fry this?* It's missing texture and it's definitely missing flavor. The oven also steals any of the signature suppleness that a pita really deserves. So I figured out two solutions: The first is, simply, not cooking them in the oven. Instead, I either throw them on the grill with a pizza stone or, the gold standard, I arrange a couple bricks on either side of a stovetop burner, set a grill grate in between, and toss the pita right on there. I also add yogurt to the batter, which tenderizes the bread, gives it a deeper sour flavor, and makes it very soft and tearable—which is exactly what you want for swabbing up spreads or parceling up grill-fired meats and/or vegetables.

Note: These should puff up after hitting the heat, giving you the pita-signature pocket on the inside. If yours aren't doing that, it means you're not developing strong enough gluten in the dough and you need to mix longer in the initial mix, until the dough is very strong. Also, these keep really well in the freezer if you make a bunch (which you might as well do since you're already getting your stove all messy with flour); you can just refresh them in a skillet with some (garlic-infused) butter.

Makes 12 (100-gram) pitas

Ingredient	Weight	Volume	Baker's %
Total flour			100.00%
>>Bread flour	470g	3⅔ cups	70.15%
>>Whole-wheat flour	200g	1⅓ cups	29.85%
Water	335g	1½ cups	50.00%
Plain Greek-style or whole-milk yogurt	170g	⅔ cup	25.37%
Fine sea salt	17g	1 tablespoon	2.54%
Active dry yeast	5g	1 teaspoon	0.75%

Mix the dough: Calculate your water temperature if desired (see page 310) or use warm (80°F) water.

In the bowl of a stand mixer fitted with the dough hook attachment, combine the bread flour, water, wheat flour, yogurt, salt, and yeast. Mix on low speed for about 4 minutes, or until the mixture is homogeneous. You may need

Continued

to scrape down the sides of the bowl to ensure no dry pockets of flour remain. Increase the speed to medium-high and mix until a smooth, shiny dough forms and pulls away from the sides of the bowl, 10 to 12 minutes. Remove the dough hook from the bowl and remove the bowl from the mixer.

Ferment: Cover the bowl with a tea towel or linen and let the dough ferment at room temperature for 2 hours. Fold the dough after 1 hour, then re-cover the bowl and let the dough rest for the remaining hour.

Shape: Turn out the dough onto a lightly floured work surface and divide the dough into twelve equal pieces; each piece should weigh about 100 grams. Using a pre-shaping method (see page 50) round each dough piece by hand, cover, and let rest for 30 minutes.

Use a rolling pin to roll out each piece of dough to about 6 inches in diameter and about ¼ inch thick.

Cook: Using bricks or other fireproof items, create a stand on either side of a gas burner so you can set a wire cooling rack over the top and it will sit 2 to 3 inches above a medium flame. Place a dough circle on the rack directly over the flame and cook for 2 to 3 minutes, until you see bubbles forming along the side of the dough. Flip the dough over and cook until the pita pops open, about 2 minutes more. Repeat with the remaining dough.

Grill Variation: Preheat the grill to medium heat. If using charcoal, arrange the coals in a ring around the perimeter of the grill. Place a grill-safe pizza stone in the center of the grate. Let this heat for 15 minutes. Place the pitas directly on the stone, close the lid, and grill for 6 to 7 minutes, until they pop open and are baked through with good color.

Wood-Fired Oven Variation: Light a small fire in the back corner of your oven and let this heat for about an hour. When you're ready to bake the pitas, you want a medium-low roar of a fire going from about two medium-size logs. Use a peel to load the pitas into the oven, placing them directly on the floor of the oven about a foot away from the fire itself. Bake for 3 to 4 minutes; the pitas will pop open when they're done.

Rye Naan

This Indian flatbread might be a little bit less traditional with the addition of whole grain, as well as brown butter and yogurt to tenderize the dough and deepen the flavor, but the intention is the same as the original: Make a doughy, pliable slab of bread that's smoky from live-fire cooking and the perfect complement to savory dishes eaten with your hands.

If this recipe looks somewhat familiar, it's because the technique is essentially the same as making pita (page 197). The biggest difference is that now you're naturally leavening the dough.

Makes 12 naan

Ingredient	Weight	Volume	Baker's %
Total flour			100.00%
>>Bread flour	515g	4 cups	64.78%
>>Rye flour	280g	2⅓ cups	35.22%
Unsalted butter	225g	1 cup	28.30%
Water	410g	1¾ cups	51.57%
Active sourdough starter	330g	1½ cups	41.51%
Plain Greek-style or whole-milk yogurt	120g	½ cup	15.09%
Honey	40g	2 tablespoons	5.03%
Fine sea salt	20g	1 tablespoon plus 1 teaspoon	2.52%

Brown the butter: In a medium saucepan over medium heat, melt the butter. Continue cooking until the milk solids are browned and toasted and the buttermilk has evaporated, about 10 minutes. Reserve 80 grams (¼ cup) for the dough and the rest for cooking the naan.

Mix the dough: Calculate your water temperature if desired (see page 310) or use warm (80°F) water.

In the bowl of a stand mixer fitted with the dough hook attachment, add the bread flour, water, sourdough starter, rye flour, yogurt, honey, salt, and reserved 80 grams (¼ cup) butter. Mix on low speed until everything is incorporated and homogeneous, about 4 minutes. You may need to scrape down the sides of the bowl to ensure no dry pockets of flour remain. Increase the speed

Continued

to medium-high and mix until a smooth, shiny dough forms and pulls away from the sides of the bowl, 10 to 12 minutes. Remove the dough hook from the bowl and remove the bowl from the mixer.

Ferment: Cover the bowl with a tea towel or linen and let the dough ferment at room temperature for 3 hours. Fold the dough after 1 hour, then re-cover the bowl and let the dough rest for the remaining 2 hours.

Shape: Turn out the dough onto a lightly floured work surface and divide it into twelve equal pieces; each piece should weigh about 150 grams. Pre-shape each piece (see page 50), arrange them on one or two baking sheets, and cover them with a tea towel or linen. Let them rest at room temperature for 1 hour.

Cook: Heat a large skillet over medium heat.

Dust each dough piece in flour and use a rolling pin to roll to about ¼ inch thick in an oblong shape. The dough will be about 4 inches wide and 6 or 7 inches long. Brush each piece generously with the remaining brown butter. Place the dough in the pan, buttered-side down, and cook for 3 to 4 minutes, until you see a lot of bubbles forming and a golden color on the cooked side. Flip the bread over and cook for another 2 to 3 minutes, until golden on both sides. Remove from the pan and repeat with the remaining pieces. Serve warm. You can store leftovers in a plastic bag in the pantry for up to a week. These also freeze well. To warm them back up, heat a sauté pan over medium-low heat, add some butter, and heat the naan for about 2 minutes per side.

Grill Variation: Preheat the grill to medium heat. If using charcoal, do this about 20 minutes before you're ready to cook so the coals have time to come down in temperature. Roll out the dough pieces as above and brush each piece generously with brown butter on one side. Place the dough, dry-side down, on the grate and grill for about 2 minutes, until you see a lot of bubbles forming on the top of the dough. Flip the dough and grill for another 2 to 3 minutes. Note that some charring of the dough is a good thing. Repeat with the remaining dough pieces and serve warm.

Whole-Grain Chile Pide Bread

Pide bread hails from Turkey and is a soft, light, foldable flatbread that's a great go-to for dips, spreads, or fold-up sandwiches. These are just as good piled high with roasted meats and spreads as they are kept simple, sprinkled with herbs and cheese or sprinkled with good olive oil and salt. And while pide is done best justice on the grill—especially if you're using charcoal or wood—it can also be cooked in a pan if it isn't grilling season.

Adding cracked grains here—in this case cracked wheat and rye—in addition to white flour means you get the flavor and benefits of the whole grains while still achieving the chewy, fluffy texture and internal structure you want. But if you can't find cracked wheat or rye, just substitute the same amount of whole-wheat flour and/or rye flour.

Note: Feel free to make this bread to fit your purpose: If you want to serve gyro-style wraps for lunch, use a bigger portion for a larger bread. Just be aware that larger pieces will need longer cook times, which means you'll need a lower cooking temp. If you find your bread burning on the grill before it cooks all the way through, get the bread started on the grill to get some good color, then transfer to a 350°F oven to bake the rest of the way.

In the bakery, I make the chile oil using a spice blend from Lior Lev Sercarz at La Boîte in New York called Shabazi N.38, which mimics the flavors of traditional zhoug, a spicy Yemenite condiment with green chilies, cilantro, and mint. You can buy this spice blend online, or use a store-bought version of zhoug.

Makes 10 (80-gram) pides

For the Chile Oil:

Ingredient	Weight	Volume	Baker's %
Vegetable oil or rice bran oil	200g	1 cup	100.00%
Chili powder	50g	⅓ cup	25.00%
Shabazi spice blend or zhoug	50g	⅓ cup	25.00%
Za'atar spice blend	50g	⅓ cup	25.00%

Continued

For the Bread:

Ingredient	Weight	Volume	Baker's %
Total flour			100.00%
>>Bread flour	320g	2½ cups	72.73%
>>Whole-wheat flour	60g	⅓ cup + 1 tablespoon	13.64%
>>Rye flour	60g	½ cup	13.64%
Water	300g	1¼ cups	68.18%
Active sourdough starter	80g	⅓ cup	18.18%
Fine sea salt	10g	1½ teaspoons	2.27%
Cooking spray, for greasing			

Make the chile oil: In a medium bowl, add the oil, chili powder, shabazi, and za'atar and whisk to combine. Cover and store at room temperature until ready to use.

Mix the dough: Calculate your water temperature if desired (see page 310) or use warm (80°F) water.

In a large bowl, combine the bread flour, water, sourdough starter, wheat flour, and rye flour. Mix by hand until all of the flour has been absorbed, 3 to 4 minutes. Cover and let rest for 30 minutes.

Second mix: Sprinkle the salt evenly over the dough and incorporate it by squeezing it in with your hand while folding the dough over itself. Continue for 2 to 3 minutes; the dough should feel much stronger once the salt is added. Squeeze and fold the dough for 4 or 5 minutes, until smooth and shiny.

Ferment: Cover the bowl with a tea towel or linen and let the dough ferment at room temperature for 3 hours. Fold the dough after 1½ hours, then re-cover the bowl and let the dough rest for the remaining 1½ hours.

Shape: Coat a baking sheet with cooking spray. Turn out the dough onto a lightly floured work surface and divide it into ten equal pieces; each piece should weigh about 80 grams. Using a pre-shaping method (see page 50), gently round each dough piece by hand and place on the prepared baking sheet. Cover and let the dough rest for another 45 minutes to 1 hour. The dough is ready to cook once it has about doubled in size again.

Cook: Preheat the grill to medium heat. If using charcoal, do this about 20 minutes before you're ready to cook so the coals cool down to just the right temperature. Dust each piece of dough with flour and use a rolling pin to roll to about an 8-inch diameter, or slightly more than ⅛ inch thick. Brush each piece generously with the chile oil, making sure to get a healthy amount of the spices in with the oil. Place the dough pieces on the grill, dry-side down, and cook for 2 minutes, or until you see a lot of bubbles forming on the top of the dough. Flip and cook for another 2 to 3 minutes; note that some charring of the dough and spices is a good thing.

Stovetop Variation: Preheat a large skillet over medium heat. Roll out the dough pieces and brush with chile oil as above. Place the dough, oiled-side down, in the pan and cook for 3 to 4 minutes, until you see a lot of bubbles forming and a golden color on the cooked side. Flip the bread and cook the other side for another 2 to 3 minutes, until golden on both sides. Repeat with the remaining pieces and serve warm.

Whole-Wheat Pretzels

When I think about pretzels, I think about beer. And when I think about beer, I think about toasted malt, which is exactly what I was going for when I reinvented this recipe. The first update I made was calling for malted rye that gets roasted then pulverized. It gives the pretzels a robust but subtle sweetness that's not dissimilar from what a brewer's going for when they make their beer. It's not necessarily something people can pick out when they eat these, but it adds a little special something. (If you can't find malted rye, feel free to omit.) Second, I make these with a sourdough starter and give them a second rise after shaping them. Again, not traditional, but these upgrades make for a fluffier, doughier, more flavorful product, which I think pretty much everyone wants with a pretzel, besides beer mustard and sausage.

Note: You're going to be working with lye to make a traditional bath that the pretzels get dipped into. Lye is extremely caustic, so use caution: Wear gloves and make sure your pot (as well as any other tools you introduce to the lye) are not made of aluminum, which can create a potentially explosive chemical reaction.

Makes 12 pretzels

Ingredient	Weight	Volume	Baker's %
Total flour			100.00%
>>Bread flour	530g	4 cups	79.70%
>>Whole-wheat flour	115g	¾ cup	17.29%
>>Toasted rye malt, milled (optional)	20g	3 tablespoons	3.01%
Water	280g	1 cup plus 3 tablespoons	42.11%
Active sourdough starter	120g	½ cup	18.05%
Honey	110g	⅓ cup	16.54%
Fine sea salt	18g	1 tablespoon	2.71%
Lye	200g	½ cup	
Semolina or fine cornmeal, for dusting			
Coarse salt, for finishing			

First mix: Calculate your water temperature if desired (see page 310) or use warm (80°F) water.

In a large bowl, combine the bread flour, water, sourdough starter, wheat flour, honey, and rye malt (if using). Mix by hand until all of the flour has been absorbed, 3 to 4 minutes. Cover and let rest for 30 minutes.

Continued

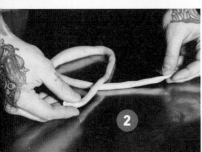

Second mix: Sprinkle the sea salt evenly over the dough and incorporate it by squeezing it in with your hand while folding the dough over itself. Continue for 2 to 3 minutes; the dough should feel much stronger once the salt is added. Knead for 4 to 5 minutes, until the dough becomes smooth and shiny.

Ferment: Cover the bowl with a tea towel or linen and let the dough ferment at room temperature for 2½ hours. Fold the dough after 1½ hours, then re-cover the bowl and let the dough rest for the remaining hour. Keep the dough covered and refrigerate overnight.

Shape: Turn out the dough onto a lightly floured work surface and divide the dough into twelve equal pieces; each piece should weigh about 100 grams. Lightly flour your hands by pressing them into the flour on the table. Take a piece of dough, pull the top edge with your fingertips, and fold it about a third of the way down the dough, then press gently to seal. Repeat that again, taking the top edge and bringing it down about a third, then another third until you've formed a cylinder.

Lightly flour your hands again, then roll each cylinder into a long rope. You'll want to keep the middle 3 to 4 inches of the rope fatter, or about 1½ inches in diameter, then allow the ends to taper as you roll the rope to about 18 inches in length.

Bring the ends of the rope toward you so the dough forms an arc in front of you. Pick up each end of the rope and cross them over so you've made a ribbon shape on the table. Continue crossing the ends over one another until you have about an inch of dough left (you'll probably get 2 to 4 loops in before that point). Bring the ends up and over the top loop of the pretzel (which should be the middle of the rope you left slightly fatter).

Bake: Preheat the oven to 450°F with a pizza stone or the base of a Challenger pan on the top rack of the oven.

Dust a baking sheet with semolina or fine cornmeal. Wearing gloves, create a lye bath by adding 10 cups of water and, carefully, the lye to a large, deep non-aluminum bowl. Working very gently to avoid splashing, whisk to combine. Using your gloved hands, dip each pretzel in the lye bath for 10 seconds, then place on the prepared sheet. Top each pretzel with coarse salt. If desired, you can also use your lame to add one score, lengthwise, to the fat part of the pretzel.

Continuing to wear gloves, place the pretzels directly on the pizza stone or bakeware in the oven. Bake for 15 to 20 minutes, until the pretzels are deep brown. They should be darker than a regular golden-brown crust.

🔥 **Grill Variation:** Preheat the grill to medium heat. If using charcoal, arrange the coals in a ring around the perimeter and place a grill-safe pizza stone in the center of the grate. Let this heat for 15 minutes. Wearing gloves, place the pretzels directly on the stone, close the lid, and grill for 6 to 7 minutes, until baked through with good color—darker than a regular golden-brown crust. Allow to cool slightly before serving, but feel free to enjoy warm.

🔥 **Wood-Fired Oven Variation:** Light a small fire in the back corner of your oven and let this heat for about an hour. When you're ready to bake the pretzels, you want a medium-low roar of a fire going from about two medium-size logs. Use a peel to load the pretzels into the oven, placing them directly on the floor of the oven about a foot away from the fire itself. Bake for 6 to 7 minutes. You may need to rotate the pretzels as they bake as to not burn the backs.

Sourdough Pizza Dough

This is my go-to pizza dough. It's sourdough leavened, super flavorful, crispy, and chewy. It doesn't get particularly thick, but the cornicione, or the edges of the dough, puff up and blister really nicely, so you get this toasted marshmallow effect happening. Cook it at high heat on the grill or in the oven, and you end up with a gorgeous pizza in minutes.

Note: This recipe yields enough dough for two pizzas. If you don't need both, you can refrigerate one piece of dough for up to 3 days.

Makes 2 (250-gram) pies

Ingredient	Weight	Volume	Baker's %
Total flour			100.00%
>>Bread flour	280g	2 cups plus 2 tablespoons	86.15%
>>Whole-wheat flour	45g	¼ cup plus 2 tablespoons	13.85%
Water 1	210g	1¼ cups plus 2 tablespoons	64.62%
Active sourdough starter	62g	⅓ cup	19.23%
Fine sea salt	9g	1 ½ teaspoons	2.77%
Water 2	17g	3 ½ teaspoons	5.38%
Cooking spray, for greasing			
Semolina or fine cornmeal, for dusting			

First mix: Calculate your water temperature if desired (see page 310) or use warm (80°F) water.

In a large bowl, combine the bread flour, water 1, sourdough starter, and wheat flour. Mix by hand until all of the flour has been absorbed, 3 to 4 minutes. The dough will be moderately sticky. Cover and let rest for 30 minutes.

Second mix: Sprinkle the salt evenly over the dough and incorporate it by squeezing it in with your hand while folding the dough over itself. Continue for 2 to 3 minutes; the dough should feel much stronger once the salt is added. Add water 2 and continue squeezing and folding until the water is completely absorbed and the dough coheres as one solid mass again, 3 to 4 minutes.

Continued

Ferment: Cover the bowl with a tea towel or linen and let the dough ferment at room temperature for 4 hours. During this time, fold the dough after 45 minutes, 1½ hours, 2 hours 15 minutes, and 3 hours, re-covering the bowl each time. Let the dough rest for the remaining hour. The dough is properly fermented when it's light, airy, and about doubled in size.

Shape: Coat a baking sheet with cooking spray. Turn out the dough onto a lightly floured work surface and divide the dough into five equal pieces; each piece should weigh about 250 grams. Using a pre-shaping method (see page 50), gently round each dough piece by hand and place it on the prepared baking sheet. Cover and let the dough rest for another 2 hours, until the pieces have doubled in size again.

Preheat the oven to 500°F with a pizza stone in the oven. Lightly dust a pizza peel (or the back of a baking sheet) with cornmeal or semolina.

Flour your work surface and dust the dough with flour. Use your pointer and middle fingertips on each hand to poke the dough so that you form a ½-inch ring around the edge of the dough. This will become your crust. Next, use all your fingertips to poke the center of the dough to flatten it. You want to poke straight down versus down and out so that you don't tear the dough.

Now you've probably seen people working their pizza dough high up in the air, but you want to be down by the table where you'll have more control. Get your hands up underneath the dough to gently stretch the center of the dough. Let gravity help you with this. The dough will start to get very thin in the middle, at which point you can gently tug on the outer edge of the dough to encourage it to keep stretching to about 10 inches in diameter. If it tears, you'll usually see a small mound of dough next to the tear—just fold that over and press to reseal. Carefully transfer the dough to the prepared peel and top as desired (see variations below).

Bake: Carefully transfer the pizza from the peel to the baking stone in the oven and bake for 15 to 20 minutes, until the crust is deep golden brown.

🔥 **Grill Variation:** Preheat the grill to medium heat. If using charcoal, arrange the coals in a ring around the perimeter. Place a grill-safe pizza stone in the center of the grate. Let this heat for 15 minutes. Place the pizza directly on the stone, close the lid, and grill for 6 to 7 minutes, until baked through with good color.

🔥 **Wood-Fired Oven Variation:** Light a small fire in the back corner of your oven and let this heat for about an hour. When you're ready to bake the pizza, you want a medium-low roar of a fire going from about two medium-size logs. Use a peel to load the first pizza into the oven, placing it directly on the floor of the oven about a foot away from the fire itself. Bake for 6 to 7 minutes, rotating the pizza about halfway through the bake to cook evenly. Repeat with the remaining pizza.

Continued

Margherita Pizzas

Super traditional: tomato sauce, mozzarella, basil, done. And by tomato sauce, I mean blended raw tomatoes, olive oil, and salt. It's one of those simple things you didn't know could be so good, especially if you're using quality ingredients.

For the Tomato Sauce:

Ingredient	Volume
Whole peeled San Marzano tomatoes	1 cup
Extra-virgin olive oil	1 tablespoon
Fine sea salt	to taste

For Each Pizza:

Ingredient	Volume
Tomato sauce	¼ cup
Fresh mozzarella cheese, torn into 1-inch pieces	¼ cup
Grated Parmesan cheese	¼ cup
Fresh basil leaves	as needed

Make the sauce: In a blender, combine the tomatoes and olive oil and blend until smooth. Season to taste with salt.

Assemble the pizzas: Using a circular motion with the back of a ladle, spread the sauce evenly over the dough. Top with the mozzarella and dust with the Parmesan. Cook as desired. Top the pizza with torn fresh basil after it comes out of the oven.

Celery Root and Rosemary Pizzas

Celery root, and other root vegetables, pretty much get me through the winter because I do my best to only eat what's coming out of the ground. And here in the Midwest, that pretty much means eating root vegetables out of cold storage after you've gone through your preserves. No hard feelings, though, because when sliced thin, celeriac gets sweet and creamy as it bakes, and is made even more unctuous by the creamy goat cheese béchamel on this pie. Then the whole thing comes alive with some fresh, pine-y rosemary.

For the Goat Cheese Sauce:

Ingredient	Volume
Heavy cream	2 cups
Fresh chèvre	2 cups
Fine sea salt	to taste

For the Celery Root:

Ingredient	Volume
Celery root, peeled	1 medium
Extra-virgin olive oil	2 tablespoons
Fine sea salt and freshly ground black pepper	to taste
Chopped fresh rosemary leaves	1 tablespoon

Make the sauce: In a blender, combine the cream and chèvre and blend until smooth. Season with salt to taste.

Roast the celery root: Preheat the oven to 400°F. Line a baking sheet with parchment.

Cut the peeled celery root in half and slice each half very thin. Then cut each slice into thirds so you have small, thin, triangle-shaped pieces. In a medium bowl, combine the celery root, olive oil, and salt and pepper and toss to coat. Spread the celery root over the prepared baking sheet and roast for 15 to 20 minutes, until golden brown and cooked through. Let cool, then toss with the chopped rosemary.

Assemble the pizzas: Using a circular motion with the back of a ladle, spread ¼ cup of the sauce evenly over the dough. Top with about ½ cup of the celery root and cook as desired.

Wheat Neapolitan Pizza Dough

This type of dough is a study in gluten formation and dough quality. Instead of getting bulk fermented before being portioned and baked, the dough gets worked until it's very, very strong with a small amount of yeast, portioned, *then* it sits to ferment for 10 to 12 hours—which is a pretty long time as far as fermentation goes. The reason being, the longer you rest gluten, the softer it gets. So you end up with a dough that's elastic, extensible, and perfect for stretching into a pie.

Note: This recipe yields enough dough for two pizzas. If you don't need that many, you can refrigerate the dough for up to 3 days.

Makes 2 (250-gram) pies

Ingredient	Weight	Volume	Baker's %
Total flour			100.00%
>>Bread flour	305g	2⅓ cups	79.22%
>>Whole-wheat flour	80g	½ cup + 1 tablespoon	20.78%
Water	227g	2 cups	59.09%
Fine sea salt	10g	1 tablespoon plus 1 teaspoon	2.60%
Active dry yeast	0.25g	pinch	0.06%
Cooking spray, for greasing			
Semolina or fine cornmeal, for dusting			

Mix the dough: Calculate your water temperature if desired (see page 310) or use warm (80°F) water.

In a large bowl, add the bread flour, water, wheat flour, salt, and yeast and mix by hand until thoroughly combined. Cover with a tea towel or linen and let rest for 30 minutes.

Turn out the dough onto a lightly floured work surface and knead for 3 to 5 minutes, until the dough becomes slightly stronger and smooth. Cover the dough and let it rest for 15 minutes, covered.

Shape and ferment: Coat a baking sheet with cooking spray. Lightly flour a work surface. Divide the dough into five equal pieces; each piece should weigh about 250 grams. Pre-shape each piece (see page 50) and place them on the prepared baking sheet. Cover with a tea towel or linen and set aside in a cool (65°F) area to ferment for 10 to 12 hours, until the dough has doubled in size.

Second shaping: Preheat the oven to 500°F with a pizza stone in the oven. Lightly dust a pizza peel (or the back of a baking sheet) with cornmeal or semolina.

Flour your work surface and dust the dough with flour. Use your pointer and middle fingertips on each hand to poke the dough so that you form a ½-inch ring around the edge of the dough. This will become your crust. Next, use all your fingertips to poke the center of the dough to flatten it. You want to poke straight down versus down and out so that you don't tear the dough.

Now you've probably seen people working their pizza dough high up in the air, but you want to be down by the table where you'll have more control. Get your hands up underneath the dough to gently stretch the center of the dough. Let gravity help you with this. The dough will start to get very thin in the middle, at which point you can gently tug on the outer edge of the dough to encourage it to keep stretching to about 10 inches in diameter. If it tears, you'll usually see a small mound of dough next to the tear—just fold that over and press to reseal.

Carefully transfer the dough to the prepared peel and top as desired (see variations below).

Bake: Carefully transfer the pizza from the peel to the baking stone in the oven and bake for 15 to 20 minutes, until the crust is deep golden brown.

Grill Variation: Preheat the grill to medium heat. If using charcoal, arrange the coals in a ring around the perimeter. Place a grill-safe pizza stone in the center of the grate. Let this heat for 15 minutes. Place the pizza directly on the stone, close the lid, and grill for 3 to 4 minutes, until baked through with good color.

Wood-Fired Oven Variation: Light a medium fire in the back corner of your oven and let this heat for about an hour. When you're ready to bake the pizza, you want a large fire going from about three good-size logs. Use a peel to load the first pizza into the oven, placing it directly on the floor of the oven about 6 inches away from the fire itself. Bake for 2 to 3 minutes, rotating the pizza about halfway through the bake to cook evenly. Repeat with the remaining pizza.

Continued

Sungold and Church Bell Pepper Neapolitan Pizzas

Church bell peppers are slightly larger than a golf ball and have three lobes on them, making them resemble a church bell. They're beautifully colored with streaks of orange going through their red-toned skin. Heat-wise, they're pretty mild, but they are incredibly fruity. I like using them alongside tangy-sweet Sungold tomatoes because they're both coming up at the same time in mid to late summer, and the combo doesn't need anything more than creamy white sauce and a blast of heat. I recommend finding a farmer who's growing a nice set of peppers and using your favorite—if it's local and seasonal, you can't go wrong.

For the White Sauce:

Ingredient	Volume
Heavy cream	1 cup
Prepared horseradish or grated fresh	2 tablespoons
Fine sea salt	to taste

For Each Pizza:

Ingredient	Volume
White sauce	2 tablespoons
Sungold tomatoes, halved	½ cup
Church bell peppers, cored and sliced thin	½ cup
Fine sea salt	to taste
Fresh oregano leaves	to taste

Make the sauce: In a medium bowl, add the cream and horseradish and whisk to combine. Season with salt to taste.

Assemble the pizzas: Using a circular motion with the back of a ladle, spread the sauce evenly over the dough. Top with the tomatoes and peppers and season with salt. Cook as desired. Top the pizza with torn oregano leaves after it comes out of the oven.

Asparagus, Spring Onion, and Fresno Pepper Pizzas

When we're getting our first hits of green with asparagus and spring onions, I'm pretty much only thinking about cooking outside again. Tossing these guys and some Fresno peppers on a pizza is a marriage made in spring heaven.

Ingredient	Volume
Asparagus, ends trimmed, cut into 1-inch pieces	4 cups
Extra-virgin olive oil	2 tablespoons
Fine sea salt and freshly ground black pepper	to taste
Tomato sauce (page 212)	1¼ cups
Spring onions, sliced thin	2½ cups
Fresno peppers, cored and sliced thin	1¼ cups

Preheat the oven to 400°F. Line a baking sheet with parchment.

In a medium bowl, combine the asparagus, olive oil, and salt and pepper and toss to coat. Transfer the asparagus to the prepared baking sheet and roast for 15 to 20 minutes, until cooked through.

Using a circular motion with the back of a ladle, spread ¼ cup of the sauce evenly over the dough. Top with about ½ cup of the roasted asparagus, ½ cup of the spring onions, ¼ cup of the Fresno peppers, and salt to taste. Cook as desired.

CHAPTER 4

Long, Strange Trip

Appam *220*

    Egg Appam *222*

Injera *223*

Puri *224*

Rghaif *226*

    Butternut Squash Filling *228*

Ensaïmada *229*

Volkornbrot *233*

Whole-Wheat Parathas *235*

    Mashed Potato Parathas *237*

Khachapuri *238*

White Wheat Tortillas *241*

As a bread baker, one of the things I love the most is constantly learning about bread heritage in places other than the United States and the parts of Europe that get the most mainstream recognition in baking (namely France and Italy). What is special about the recipes in this chapter is how they celebrate their mother culture in general—form and function go hand in hand—as well as the *agronomic* culture they come from. They are shining examples of grain use in geographical context, in addition to the vast diversity of bread-baking techniques that exist out there. These breads will expand your dough repertoire even further, as well as your comfort with working with less traditional grains. They're also an important reminder that even though I'm primarily reaching for contemporary American baking methods, there's not just one way to make bread.

Appam

Appam are fluffy, slightly sweet bowl-shaped flatbreads that hail from the Indian subcontinent. They feature both cooked and soaked rice that gets fermented overnight, along with the sweet aroma and flavor of coconut. Not unlike crepes, the cooking method takes a few tries to get right, but once mastered, it's an easy way to impress friends with your talents. Appam are traditionally used instead of utensils to scoop curries and chutneys.

Note: These are typically made with Indian varieties of medium-grain rice, such as ponni, but in the spirit of using and celebrating the grains available to you, I call for using Arborio or Valencia. Also, for a more pronounced coconutty flavor, try toasting the shredded coconut until golden brown before making the batter.

Makes about 8

Ingredient	Weight	Volume	Baker's %
Total flour			100.00%
>>Raw medium-grain rice (see note)	325g	1¾ cups	100%
Water	240g	1 cup	73.84%
Shredded unsweetened coconut, toasted	100g	1¼ cups	30.77%
Granulated sugar	5g	1 teaspoon	1.54%
Fine sea salt	4g	1 teaspoon	1.20%
Active dry yeast	1g	¼ teaspoon	0.30%

Put 275 grams (1½ cups) of the rice in a medium bowl and cover with water by a few inches. Cover and refrigerate overnight. In a small pot, combine the remaining 50 grams (¼ cup) rice with 120 grams (½ cup) water. Bring to a boil and reduce to a simmer. Cover and cook for 13 minutes, or until the rice is soft. Turn off the heat and leave the pot covered for 5 minutes. Set the rice aside to cool, then refrigerate overnight.

The following evening, drain the soaking rice and discard the water. In a blender, combine the soaked rice, cooked rice, coconut, sugar, salt, yeast, and 240 grams (1 cup) water and blend until very smooth. If you like, you can strain the batter through a fine-mesh strainer to improve the texture, but it's not necessary. The batter should be pourable and not as thick as pancake batter. If the batter is too thick, you can add a small amount of water until it is thin enough to pour.

Continued

Egg Appam (page 222)

Transfer the mixture to a large container, making sure the batter does not fill more than half the container as it will expand as it ferments. Cover and leave at room temperature overnight. The batter should grow and will be pockmarked on top when it's ready.

Heat a small nonstick saucepan over medium heat. Ladle about ½ cup of the batter into the pan and gently tilt the pan to spread the batter evenly over the bottom. Tilt again, this time at a steeper angle so you coat about an inch up the sides of the pan. It should look like a small bowl of batter in the pan. Place the pan back on the burner and set a small bowl over the top to trap the steam. Cook for 3 to 4 minutes, until the top edges of the appam pull away from the sides of the pan and the bottom is golden and crispy. Remove from the pan, repeat with the remaining batter, and serve in a stack.

RIFF

Egg Appam

There are many variations of appam, and one of my favorites is egg appam (pictured on page 221). Here, you crack an egg into the center of the batter as it cooks, resulting in a light appam with a perfectly sunny-side up egg in the center. You can then use this as the base for a more composed dish, surrounding the egg with toppings. For me, it's usually sliced avocado, chopped kimchi, shredded carrots, fresh cilantro, and toasted pumpkin seeds that I sprinkle on the egg white so the yolk is still exposed.

Injera

This spongy, soft, sour bread is traditionally made with teff, a very small grain grown in northern Africa. While there's not much to it besides flour, water, and a little salt at the end (an update I've made to the original formula), it gets its signature tang from fermenting for anywhere from 1 to 4 days, until it's really bubbly and active and ready to be cooked like a pancake. It has the perfect consistency for swabbing up sauces and stewed vegetables and meats with your hands, which is how it's traditionally served in places like Ethiopia and Eritrea.

Note: You can substitute wheat flour or buckwheat flour for the teff flour in equal amounts.

Makes about 12 (12-inch) rounds

Ingredient	Weight	Volume	Baker's %
Total flour			100.00%
>>Teff flour	600g	4 cups	100.00%
Water (80°F)	1135g	5 cups	189.17%
Fine sea salt	10g	1½ teaspoons	1.67%
Vegetable oil or rice bran oil, for the pan			

Mix the dough: In a large bowl, combine the warm water and teff flour. Mix thoroughly to combine until all of the flour has been absorbed, 2 to 3 minutes.

Ferment: Cover the bowl loosely with a tea towel or linen and let the dough ferment at room temperature for at least 24 hours and up to 4 days. The mixture will grow by about half during this time. The longer the batter ferments, the more sour your injera will become. You'll begin to smell the batter becoming pleasantly sour and see bubbles forming in the batter.

Cook: Stir the salt into the fermented batter.

Heat a large skillet over medium-high heat and coat it lightly with oil. Ladle enough batter into the hot pan to form a thin pancake when you swirl to coat the pan. (For example, for a 10-inch skillet, this would be about ¾ cup of batter; for a 12-inch skillet, 1 cup.) Cover the pan, reduce the heat to medium, and cook for 2 to 3 minutes, until you see lots of little bubbles form in the batter and the underside turns a deep golden color. Remove the injera from the pan and repeat with the remaining batter. Serve warm.

Puri

Puri is like the flavorful fried cousin of pita, who just happened to grow up on the Indian subcontinent instead of in the Middle East. Similar to pita, you're making a very strong, dry dough with wheat flour, though in this instance with the addition of sesame oil and honey for flavor and caramelization. It doesn't get leavened at all, just tossed in hot oil to puff and pocket. It's traditionally enjoyed with savory meals (especially curries), sweets (like rice pudding), or on its own as a snack.

Note: You'll notice that I don't specify water temperature in this recipe. That's because puri are not fermented.

Makes 10 puri

Ingredient	Weight	Volume	Baker's %
Total flour			100.00%
>>Whole-wheat flour	580g	3¾ cups + 2 tablespoons	96.67%
>>Semolina flour	20g	2 tablespoons	3.33%
Water	410g	1¾ cups	68.33%
Honey	45g	2 tablespoons	7.50%
Sesame oil	15g	1 tablespoon	2.50%
Fine sea salt, plus more for finishing	12g	2 teaspoons	2.00%
Vegetable oil or rice bran oil, for frying			

Mix the dough: In the bowl of a stand mixer fitted with the dough hook attachment, add the whole-wheat flour, water, honey, semolina flour, sesame oil, and salt. Mix on low speed until the mixture is homogeneous, about 4 minutes. You may need to scrape down the sides of the bowl to ensure no dry pockets of flour remain. Increase the speed to medium-high and mix until a smooth, shiny dough forms and pulls away from the sides of the bowl, 10 to 12 minutes. Cover the bowl with a tea towel or linen and let the dough rest for 15 minutes.

Shape: Turn out the dough onto a lightly floured work surface and divide it into ten equal pieces; each piece should weigh about 100 grams. Using a pre-shaping method (see page 50), gently round each dough piece by hand, cover with a tea towel or linen, and let rest at room temperature for 30 minutes.

Fry: In a large skillet over medium heat, heat about 1 inch of oil to 350°F. Line a plate or baking sheet with paper towels and place nearby.

Lightly flour a work surface and dust each dough piece with flour. Use a rolling pin to roll the dough to about ⅛ inch thick and about 5 inches in diameter. Working in batches to avoid crowding the pan, fry each piece for about 2 minutes on the first side. Carefully flip and fry the other side for a minute or two, until golden brown on both sides. Ideally, the dough will pop open and flip itself over. If your dough doesn't pop open, you'll want to develop more strength in the dough when mixing next time. Once golden brown, remove the puri from the pan and drain on the paper towels. Sprinkle with salt and let cool before serving.

Rghaif

What's cool about this Moroccan flatbread is that it features a technique that gets used all the time in fussy patisserie-style baking but in an approachable, low-key way. After starting with an enriched dough with butter, eggs, and evaporated milk, you roll it flat, brush it with butter (browned, in this case), fold it up, then brush it with more butter, continuing until you have a number of thin dough-butter layers. The most common example of this "laminated" dough in French baking is a croissant or puff pastry. But in the case of rghaif, it's a simple, flaky, doughy flatbread that's either drizzled with honey and served with tea, or folded up into a pocket, filled with mashed potatoes, and griddled. It's the perfect example of different cultures figuring out similar methods and applying them in completely different ways.

Makes 10 rghaif

Ingredient	Weight	Volume	Baker's %
Total flour			100.00%
>>All-purpose flour	250g	2 cups	50.00%
>>Whole-wheat flour	250g	1⅔ cups	50.00%
Water	150g	⅔ cup	30.00%
Brown butter (page 199), plus more for brushing	150g	⅔ cup	30.00%
Large eggs	110g	2 whole	22.00%
Evaporated milk	45g	3 tablespoons	9.00%
Granulated sugar	28g	2 tablespoons plus 1 teaspoon	5.60%
Extra-virgin olive oil, plus more for cooking	28g	2 tablespoons	5.60%
Active dry yeast	8g	1½ teaspoons	1.60%
Fine sea salt	6g	1 teaspoon	1.20%

Mix the dough: Calculate your water temperature if desired (see page 310) or use warm (80°F) water.

In the bowl of a stand mixer fitted with the dough hook attachment, add the all-purpose flour, wheat flour, water, brown butter, eggs, evaporated milk, sugar, olive oil, yeast, and salt. Mix on low speed until everything is incorporated and homogeneous, about 4 minutes. You may need to scrape down the sides of the bowl to ensure no dry pockets of flour remain. Increase the speed to medium-high and mix until a smooth, shiny dough forms and pulls away from the sides of the bowl, 10 to 12 minutes. Remove the dough hook from the bowl and remove the bowl from the mixer.

Ferment: Cover the bowl with a tea towel or linen and let the dough ferment at room temperature for 2 hours. Fold the dough after 1 hour, then re-cover the bowl and let the dough rest for the remaining hour.

Shape: Turn out the dough onto a lightly floured work surface and divide the dough into ten equal pieces; each piece should weigh about 100 grams. Using a pre-shaping method (see page 50), gently round each dough piece by hand, cover with a tea towel or linen, and let rest for 30 minutes at room temperature.

Lightly flour a work surface and dust each dough piece with flour. Roll each piece into a very thin round, at least ⅛ inch thin, but thinner if you can. Brush the piece with melted brown butter.

Cook: In a large skillet over medium heat, heat about a teaspoon of oil. Gently place the rghaif in the pan and cook for 3 to 4 minutes per side, until golden brown. Remove from the pan and enjoy warm.

Continued

Butternut Squash Filling

A sweet-savory filling alternative to enjoying rghaif plain.

Ingredient	Volume
Butternut squash	1 large
Extra-virgin olive oil	2 tablespoons
Chopped onion	1 cup
Fine sea salt	to taste
Chopped garlic	2 tablespoons
Ground cumin	2 teaspoons
Ground coriander	2 teaspoons
Chile flakes	1 teaspoon
Dried sage	1 teaspoon

Preheat the oven to 350°F. Line a baking sheet with parchment.

Cut the squash in half lengthwise and scoop out the seeds. Place the two halves cut-side down on the prepared baking sheet and roast for about 1 hour, until the squash is soft when pressed. Allow the squash to cool, then scoop out the flesh and pass it through a food mill or food processor.

In a large nonstick pan over medium heat, heat the olive oil. Add the onion, season with salt, and cook for 3 to 4 minutes, until softened. Add the garlic and cook for another 2 minutes. Add the squash puree, cumin, coriander, chile flakes, and sage and cook for about 20 minutes, until the mixture is quite thick. Check and adjust the seasoning, then transfer the mixture to a bowl to cool.

After you've rolled out the rghaif rounds and brushed them with brown butter, add about ½ cup of filling to the center of each round and use a spoon to shape the filling into a square about ¼ inch thick. Fold each side of the dough over the filling to create a packet, brushing each folded side of the dough with brown butter as you go. Repeat with the remaining pieces and cook as described above.

Ensaïmada

As a preview for what this phyllo-like, crispy-on-the-outside, soft-on-the-inside bread is all about, consider that *saïm* is Catalan for "lard." As in, "delicious." Ensaïmada is made from naturally leavened dough that's stretched really thin, rubbed with lard, rolled into a coil shape, and fermented again. You'll see folks in Mallorca, Spain, doing savory ones with chorizo, but I personally feel the best way to enjoy it is to bake the ensaïmada and then top it with powdered sugar. Or fill it with pastry cream, sprinkle with sugar, and brûlée it. It's just killer.

Note: You could use brown butter instead of lard, but the ensaïmada just won't be what it's supposed to be. Luckily nowadays you can find lard from well-raised animals in many grocery stores or online.

Makes 10

Ingredient	Weight	Volume	Baker's %
Total flour			100.00%
>>Bread flour	315g	2⅓ cups + 2 tablespoons	75.90%
>>Spelt flour	100g	¾ cup plus 2 tablespoons	24.10%
Water	190g	¾ cup	45.78%
Granulated sugar	120g	⅔ cup	28.92%
Active sourdough starter	100g	½ cup	24.10%
Vegetable oil	90g	⅓ cup	21.69%
Large egg	55g	1 whole	13.25%
Large egg yolk	15g	1 each	3.61%
Fine sea salt	5g	1 teaspoon	1.20%
Lard, as needed			
Cooking spray, for greasing			
Powdered sugar, for dusting			

Mix the dough: Calculate your water temperature if desired (see page 310) or use warm (80°F) water.

In the bowl of a stand mixer fitted with the dough hook attachment, add the bread flour, water, sugar, spelt flour, sourdough starter, oil, whole egg, egg yolk, and salt. Mix on low speed until everything is incorporated and homogeneous, about 4 minutes. You may need to scrape down the sides of the bowl

Continued

to ensure no dry pockets of flour remain. Increase the speed to medium-high and mix until a smooth, shiny dough forms and pulls away from the sides of the bowl, 10 to 12 minutes. Remove the dough hook from the bowl and remove the bowl from the mixer.

Ferment: Cover the bowl with a tea towel or linen and ferment the dough at room temperature for 4 hours. During this time, fold the dough after 1 hour and again after 2 hours, re-covering the bowl each time. Let the dough rest for the remaining 2 hours.

Shape and proof: Turn out the dough onto a lightly floured work surface and divide it into ten equal pieces; each piece should weigh about 100 grams. Pre-shape each piece (see page 50), cover with a tea towel or linen, and let them rest for 2 hours at room temperature.

Lightly oil a rolling pin and rub a small amount of oil on the work surface. Take each dough piece and roll the pin forward over the piece to create a long, thin oval. Take a small handful of the soft lard and rub it into the dough. Take the bottom left corner of the dough and gently stretch and pull the dough to get it as thin as possible. You should be able to see the countertop through the dough. Repeat this with the bottom right corner of the dough to create a very thin triangle of dough. Starting at the top, tuck and roll the dough until it forms a rope. Set this piece aside and cover while you repeat with the remaining pieces, covering as you go to prevent them from drying out. Once finished, let the pieces rest, covered, for 1 hour at room temperature.

Line two baking sheets with parchment and coat the parchment with cooking spray. Take a dough piece and stretch it as far as it will go without breaking—it should about double in length. If it does start to break, you can still use the dough, just don't stretch it any farther. Coil the dough into a spiral on the prepared baking sheet, leaving about a ½-inch gap between the rope coils. Repeat this with the remaining pieces, leaving room on the baking sheet to allow them to expand and not fuse together. Cover and let this ferment for 12 hours.

Bake: Preheat the oven to 350°F.

Bake the ensaïmadas for 10 minutes. Rotate the pans in the oven and continue baking for an additional 10 to 15 minutes, until they are golden brown. Let cool for 10 to 15 minutes, then dust generously with powdered sugar, and enjoy. Store any leftovers in an airtight container at room temp for up to 3 days.

Volkornbrot

You can't pull a recipe from northern Germany, right up there next to where the Scandinavian countries border, and not highlight rye. It's a signature of the agronomic traditions in that region—as in, rye is a common crop that grows well there, so they use a lot of rye in their culinary traditions. You don't really see 100 percent rye breads in any other part of the world. So this dark, complex, dense, chewy bread is not only a celebration of place and heritage, but also of rye itself. It's a noteworthy build because you're developing different things in the dough simultaneously. First, it's a two-stage levain, so you get a ton of sour and acid to bring out the rye flavor. Second, you're using a scald method, meaning you're boiling water and pouring it over the grain to scald, which kills bacteria and yeast on the grain and activates the sugars, essentially priming it for fermentation. Third, because rye is a very enzymatically active grain, you wrap the baked loaf in linen and let it cure overnight to let the starches settle and recrystallize. By the following morning you'll have the perfect consistency for slicing it thin and topping it with traditional horseradish cream, cured salmon, capers, and cucumbers.

Note: Heads up: you'll need a 16-by-4-by-4-inch pan for this loaf.

Makes 1 (2200-gram) loaf

For the Levain:

Ingredient	Weight	Volume	Baker's %
Total flour			100.00%
>>Rye flour 1	170g	1½ cups	49.28%
>>Rye flour 2	255g	2¼ cups	50.72%
Water	340g	1½ cups	98.55%
Active sourdough starter	20g	1½ tablespoons	5.80%

For the Scald:

Ingredient	Weight	Volume	Baker's %
Cracked rye	305g	2 cups	42.07%
Malted rye, toasted and milled	57g	⅓ cup	7.86%
Fine sea salt	18g	1 tablespoon	2.48%
Boiling water	637g	2¾ cups	87.86%

Continued

For the Final Mix:

Ingredient	Weight	Volume	Baker's %
Total flour			100.00%
>>Rye flour	200g	1¾ cups	100.00%
Flax seeds	100g	1 cup	50.00%
Sunflower seeds	100g	⅔ cup	50.00%

Make the levain: In the morning, in a medium bowl, add the water, rye flour 1, and sourdough starter and mix by hand to combine. Cover with a tea towel or linen and set aside at room temperature to ferment for 12 hours.

After 12 hours, add the rye flour 2 and mix by hand to combine thoroughly. Cover and ferment at room temperature overnight. When you add the second stage of rye flour, you should make the scald as well: In a medium bowl, add the cracked rye, malted rye, and salt. Pour the boiling water over the mixture and stir with a wooden spoon to combine, making sure all of the water is absorbed and there is no dry flour left. Cover and let sit in a warm area overnight (an oven with the pilot light on works well for this).

Final mix: In the bowl of a stand mixer fitted with the paddle attachment, add the levain, scald, and rye flour. Mix on low speed for 2 to 3 minutes, until everything is thoroughly combined. Increase the speed to medium and mix for 5 minutes. If the paste looks excessively thick, add a small amount of water until it resembles the texture of moldable, wet clay. Reduce the speed to low, add the flax and sunflower seeds, and mix for another 2 minutes to combine.

Shape: Grease and flour a 16-by-4-by-4-inch pan with rye flour. Flour a work surface with rye flour. Turn out the dough on the work surface and gently knead for 2 to 3 minutes. Shape the dough into a log by folding, rolling, and gently pressing on the dough. Roll the dough in rye flour and place it in the prepared pan. Cover and let it ferment for 2 hours in a warm area. The bread is ready to bake when it has almost doubled in size and large cracks appear in the floured surface of the dough.

Bake: Preheat the oven to 375°F.

Bake for 70 to 80 minutes, until the bread reaches an internal temperature of 200°F. Remove the loaf from the pan and immediately wrap it in a tea towel or linen. Allow it to cure overnight at room temperature before serving the next day.

Whole-Wheat Parathas

Here's another Indian subcontinent classic that's fun to make because of how versatile it is. At the most basic level, you're taking whole-wheat flour, making a dough, rolling it thin, then brushing it with oil between the layers. You can griddle it as is or go with traditional fillings like garlic mashed potatoes or cheese, rip 'n' dipper style. I've also seen a whisked egg added to the pan as the first side cooks, so when the paratha gets flipped to its second side over the egg, it fuses together for a one-stop breakfasty, snacky treat. Serve with your favorite chutneys.

Makes 8 (100-gram) parathas

Ingredient	Weight	Volume	Baker's %
Total flour			100.00%
>>Bread flour	250g	2 cups	50.00%
>>Whole-wheat flour	250g	1⅔ cups	50.00%
Whole milk	275g	1 cup plus 2 tablespoons	55.00%
Large egg	55g	1 whole	11.00%
Fine sea salt	9g	1½ teaspoons	1.80%
Sugar	8g	2 teaspoons	1.60%
Baking powder	3g	¾ teaspoon	0.60%
Vegetable oil, as needed			

Mix the dough: In the bowl of a stand mixer fitted with the dough hook attachment, add the milk, bread flour, wheat flour, egg, salt, sugar, and baking powder. Mix on low speed until the mixture is homogeneous, about 4 minutes. You may need to scrape down the sides of the bowl to ensure no dry pockets of flour remain. Increase the speed to medium-high and mix until a smooth, shiny dough forms and pulls away from the sides of the bowl, 10 to 12 minutes. Cover with a tea towel or linen and let the dough rest for 15 minutes.

Shape: Turn out the dough onto a lightly floured work surface and divide it into eight equal pieces; each piece should weigh about 100 grams. Pre-shape each piece (see page 50), cover with a tea towel or linen, and let them rest for 30 minutes.

On a floured surface, use a rolling pin to roll each dough to about a 10-inch round. It should be very thin. Lightly brush each round with oil.

Continued

Cook: In a large skillet over medium heat, heat about a teaspoon of the oil. Cook one paratha at a time for 2 to 3 minutes per side, or until golden brown. They may puff up a bit as you cook them. Repeat with the remaining parathas and serve warm.

RIFF

Mashed Potato Parathas

2 large Yukon Gold potatoes, cut into ½-inch chunks
2 tablespoons unsalted butter
2 tablespoons heavy cream
Fine sea salt, to taste

Put the potatoes in a pot and add enough cold water just to cover. Bring the water to a boil over medium-high heat and cook the potatoes until tender, about 10 minutes. Drain the potatoes, return them to the pot, and mash them with the butter and cream. Season to taste and allow the potatoes to cool before filling the parathas.

After you roll the parathas thin and brush them with oil, spoon about 2 tablespoons mashed potatoes in the center of the dough and fold the dough over the potatoes to form a half moon. Brush the exposed side of the dough with more oil, then fold the paratha into a rounded triangle. Repeat with the remaining dough pieces and mashed potatoes.

Roll each filled paratha into a thin triangle about 10 inches at the base. It's OK if some potatoes leak out the side of the dough. Cook as described above. Alternatively, you can prep these ahead of time. Place each filled paratha on a baking sheet between sheets of parchment paper brushed with oil, then refrigerate up to 1 day or freeze up to 1 week.

Khachapuri

Some breads are just meant to be a little over the top, and this **traditional Georgian dish** is one of them. You're taking an enriched dough **and fermenting it, then shaping it to accommodate a filling of cheese and eggs so you end up with** a rich, soft outside and a cheesy, eggy center.

Makes 4 khachapuris

For the Filling:

Ingredient	Volume
Crumbled feta cheese	1½ cups
Shredded low-moisture mozzarella cheese	1½ cups
Ricotta cheese	1½ cups
Large eggs	5 whole
Minced fresh garlic	2 tablespoons
Chopped fresh dill	2 tablespoons
Chopped fresh parsley	2 tablespoons
Fine sea salt	1 teaspoon

For the Dough:

Ingredient	Weight	Volume	Baker's %
Total flour			100.00%
>>Bread flour	330g	2½ cups	69.47%
>>Rye flour	145g	1¼ cups	30.53%
Water	305g	2¼ cups	64.21%
Active sourdough starter	150g	¾ cup	31.58%
Extra-virgin olive oil	20g	1½ tablespoons	4.21%
Unsalted butter, softened	20g	1½ tablespoons	4.21%
Honey	15g	2¼ teaspoons	3.16%
Fine sea salt	10g	1½ teaspoons	2.11%
Cooking spray, for greasing			

Make the filling: In a medium bowl, add the feta, mozzarella, ricotta, 1 egg, garlic, dill, parsley, and salt. Mix thoroughly until the mixture is homogeneous. Cover and refrigerate until ready to use.

Continued

Make the dough: Calculate your water temperature if desired (see page 310) or use warm (80°F) water.

In a large bowl, add the bread flour, water, sourdough starter, rye flour, olive oil, butter, honey, and salt. Mix by hand until all of the flour has been absorbed, 3 to 4 minutes. Cover and let rest for 30 minutes. Knead on a floured surface for 3 to 5 minutes, until the dough becomes slightly stronger and smooth.

Ferment: Cover the bowl with a tea towel or linen and let the dough ferment at room temperature for 3 hours. During this time, fold the dough after 1 hour and again after 2 hours, re-covering the bowl each time, then let the dough rest for the remaining hour. The dough is properly fermented when it's light, airy, and about doubled in size.

Shape and proof: Turn out the dough onto a lightly floured work surface and divide it into four equal pieces; each piece should weigh about 250 grams. Pre-shape each piece (see page 50), cover with a tea towel or linen, and let them rest for 30 minutes.

Line two baking sheets with parchment and coat with cooking spray.

Lightly flour a work surface and dust each of the dough pieces with flour. Use a rolling pin to roll the dough into a round about ¼ inch thick and roughly 8 inches in diameter. Spread ½ cup of the cheese filling over each round of dough, leaving about 1 inch of a perimeter without filling. Crack an egg over the filling and gently cover with an additional ½ cup of filling, taking care to not break the yolk. Pick up the sides of the dough and press the uncovered perimeter of the dough together to create a seam and seal in the filling. The khachapuri should take the shape of a football. Place this seam-side down on the prepared baking sheet. Place two khachapuri per baking sheet to leave room for them to expand. Cover and ferment for 1 hour.

Bake: Preheat the oven to 375°F.

Using a serrated knife, carefully slice lengthwise along the top of each khachapuri all the way through to the filling. This will allow the dough to fall open as it bakes, creating a sort of boat and revealing the filling. Bake for about 20 minutes, until the filling is melted and gooey and the dough is golden brown. Let cool slightly before serving.

White Wheat Tortillas

White Sonoran wheat hails from the Sonora region in Mexico. It is a soft wheat, but it's higher in protein than soft wheat typically is. Which, it turns out, is excellent for making tortillas. It's light as a product but has just enough protein in it to form a dough that you can roll out without tearing. Soft butter or the more traditional lard tenderizes the dough even more, which then gets rolled out as thin as you can get it and tossed into a skillet or straight onto the grill to get just a kiss of color. These tortillas are perfect for soft tacos or sandwich wraps.

Makes 10 (80-gram) tortillas

Ingredient	Weight	Volume	Baker's %
Total flour			100.00%
>>White wheat flour, such as white Sonoran	500g	3¼ cups	100.00%
Water	300g	1¼ cups	60.00%
Unsalted butter or lard	50g	3½ tablespoons	10.00%
Fine sea salt	10g	1½ teaspoons	2.00%
Active dry yeast	3g	1 teaspoon	0.60%

Mix: Calculate your water temperature if desired (see page 310) or use warm (80°F) water.

In the bowl of a stand mixer fitted with the dough hook attachment, combine the flour, water, butter, salt, and yeast and mix on low speed until the mixture is homogeneous, about 4 minutes. You may need to scrape down the sides of the bowl to ensure no dry pockets of flour remain. Increase the speed to medium-high and mix until a smooth, shiny dough forms and pulls away from the sides of the bowl, 10 to 12 minutes. Remove the dough hook from the dough and remove the bowl from the mixer.

Ferment: Cover the bowl with a tea towel or linen and ferment the dough at room temperature for 2 hours. Fold the dough after 1 hour, re-cover the bowl, and let the dough rest for the remaining hour.

Continued

Shape: Turn out the dough onto a lightly floured work surface and divide it into ten equal pieces; each piece should weigh about 80 grams. Pre-shape each piece (see page 50), cover with a tea towel or linen, and let them rest for 30 minutes to an hour at room temperature.

Dust a work surface and each dough piece with flour. Use a rolling pin to roll the dough to about ⅛ inch thick and 8 or 9 inches in diameter.

Cook: Preheat a large skillet over medium-high heat.

Add a tortilla to the pan and cook until large bubbles form on the top of the dough, 1 to 2 minutes. Flip and cook for another 1 to 2 minutes. Remove from the pan and cover with a tea towel or linen until ready to use. Repeat with the remaining tortillas, making sure to brush any excess flour out of the pan in between tortillas as the burnt flour will accumulate. These are of course best eaten warm, but you can store any leftovers in an airtight container on the counter for up to 3 days, or in the freezer for up to 1 month. Reheat the tortillas by placing them in a dry skillet over medium heat, about 2 minutes per side.

CHAPTER 5

Friends of the Devil

Whole-Grain Roman-Style Pizza Dough *247*

    Mushroom and Thyme Pizzas *248*

    Shishito and Prosciutto Pizzas *249*

Wheat Brioche *250*

Bacon-Rye Cheese Rolls *253*

Potato Fry Pockets *256*

Stollen *259*

Bee Sting Cake *263*

Buckwheat Canelés *267*

Oat Madeleines *271*

Whole-Wheat Croissants *277*

    Chocolate Croissants *279*

Cornmeal Danishes *281*

Maple Rye Kouign Amann *285*

Rye Phyllo Pies *289*

Rye Puff Pastry Galette de Rois *292*

Sorghum Shortbread Fig Tart *297*

Sourdough Pizzelles *299*

Malted Grain Ice Cream *300*

This chapter isn't a misnomer—the recipes are meant to be decadent, indulgent, and naughty. And they're also the trickiest ones in the book, with techniques that are drawn out and take time. You're going to need all the skills you've learned in the previous four chapters, and you're definitely going to need your ducks in a row. It's where you're going to find lots of preferments, soakers, and multiple-stagers with multiple builds. There are laminated butter pastries like your kouign amann, croissants, and danishes, and one of the best pizza doughs out there, which happens to take 60 hours to cold ferment. But they are also going to be some of the most delicious things you can make—on the level of what we're executing at the bakery. You can do it; you just need time, organization, and a lot of patience. I promise the reward will be sweet.

Whole-Grain Roman-Style Pizza Dough

While Sourdough Pizza Dough (page 209) is great for a relatively quick homemade pie, Roman-style pizza dough is the gold standard. It produces a light, airy, doughy crust that yields to a crisp, cracker-y bottom. Pizza perfection. The way you achieve that is by using a method that pizza whisperer Gabriele Bonci taught me and I've since adjusted. The key is using less sourdough starter than you normally would in a bread recipe but fermenting it longer—about 2 days in the fridge. So instead of mixing the dough until it toughens with gluten, it's getting that strength and structure through the low, slow fermentation period. Which contributes to the nice, doughy rise you get in the oven. Then, because Gabriele also taught me that there are fewer rules when it comes to Roman-style pizza in regards to toppings, you can really go for it here. I like to keep it simple so the ingredients can really shine. I offer two options: whole stemmed shishito peppers and salty prosciutto, or maitake mushrooms with thyme.

Makes 2 (450-gram) pies

Ingredient	Weight	Volume	Baker's %
Total flour			100.00%
>>Bread flour	305g	2⅓ cups	67.03%
>>Whole-wheat flour	150g	1 cup	32.97%
Water 1	315g	1⅓ cups	69.23%
Active sourdough starter	65g	⅓ cup	14.29%
Fine sea salt	10g	1½ teaspoons	2.20%
Water 2	50g	¼ cup	10.99%
Olive oil, plus more for the pan	9g	2 teaspoons	1.98%

First mix: Calculate your water temperature if desired (see page 310) or use warm (80°F) water.

In a large bowl, add water 1, the bread flour, wheat flour, and sourdough starter. Mix by hand until all of the flour has been absorbed, 3 to 4 minutes. Cover the bowl with a tea towel or linen and let the dough rest for 30 minutes.

Second mix: Sprinkle the salt evenly over the dough and incorporate it by squeezing it in with your hand while folding the dough over itself. Knead for 5 to 7 minutes, just long enough for the salt to be incorporated nice and evenly.

Continued

In a small bowl, whisk together water 2 and the olive oil. In three additions, slowly drizzle the mixture over the dough, squeezing it in as you go. Make sure the liquid is well incorporated before adding more.

Ferment: Cover the bowl with a tea towel or linen and let the dough ferment at room temperature for 2 hours. Fold the dough, re-cover the bowl, and refrigerate for 2 days. Fold the dough once per day.

Shape and proof: On the third day, turn out the dough onto a lightly floured work surface and divide it in half; each piece should weigh about 450 grams. Pre-shape the dough (page 50) and place each piece in a floured basket. Cover the dough with a towel or linen and let it rise for 3 hours.

Bake: Preheat the oven to 500°F with the base of a Challenger pan, cast-iron pan, or Roman-style pizza pan on the middle rack.

Add 2 tablespoons of oil to the base of the preheated pan. It may smoke because the pan's so rippin' hot, and that's fine. Stretch the dough to the size of the pan and drop it in. Top as desired, and bake as instructed below. Or, if using toppings of your choice, 15 to 20 minutes will usually get you to that golden-brown crust you're looking for.

RIFFS

Mushroom and Thyme Pizzas

Ingredient	Volume
Maitake mushrooms (or mushroom of choice), chopped or torn into bite-size pieces	1 pound
Thinly sliced shallots	½ cup
Fresh thyme leaves	¼ cup
Extra-virgin olive oil	as needed
Fine sea salt and freshly ground black pepper	to taste

In a medium bowl, combine the mushrooms, shallots, thyme, and a bit of olive oil and toss to coat. Season to taste with salt and pepper.

After the dough's been dropped into the preheated pan, drizzle more olive oil over the top. Scatter the mushroom and shallot mixture evenly across the dough and bake for 15 to 20 minutes, until the dough and mushrooms are golden brown.

Shishito and Prosciutto Pizzas

Ingredient	Volume
Shishito peppers, stemmed	1 cup
Olive oil	as needed
Fine sea salt and freshly ground black pepper	to taste
Thinly sliced prosciutto	8 ounces

In a small bowl, combine the shishitos and a bit of olive oil and toss to coat. Season with salt and pepper and toss to coat again.

After the dough's been dropped into the preheated pan, drizzle more olive oil on top of the dough. Scatter the shishitos over the dough, then drape the prosciutto over them. Bake for 15 to 20 minutes, until the dough is golden brown, the shishitos are blistered, and the ham is slightly crisp.

Wheat Brioche

Like the best things in life, brioche is worth the effort. You have to have a lot of patience with the dough because it can be kind of finicky, but the payoff is a sweet, custardy bread that you can make a sandwich loaf, rolls, or burger buns out of; fill with pastry cream, **Citrus Curd** (page 100), or ricotta; or use as the foundation for breakfast classics like sticky buns or bostock (brioche slices that have been doused in simple syrup, topped with frangipane, and baked again). And because waking up extra early to bake breakfast sucks, you can do all your fermenting and shaping the night before and bake everything off when you eventually get up.

For this build, you're starting with a biga, a type of preferment that's commonly used in Italian baking, especially for lighter, airier breads like ciabatta. It's a way to add character and flavor, in addition to getting that great texture. Plus, it lends itself to a dryer dough, meaning it won't get as tangy and instead will retain that buttery flavor we want. The real trick with brioche is keeping your butter cold but pliable, which will allow you to work the butter into the dough without it getting greasy—in case you're wondering why I have you beating the chilled chunks of butter with a rolling pin. The soft-but-cold butter gets added slowly to your final mix after it's already come together about 90 percent of the way, allowing the butter to coat the gluten strands, absorb into the dough, and give you the soft, rich texture you're looking for, whether you're shaping the dough into loaves or buns.

Makes 2 (750-gram) loaves or 15 (100-gram) buns

For the Biga:

Ingredient	Weight	Volume	Baker's %
Total flour			100.00%
>>Bread flour	75g	½ cup plus 1 tablespoon	50.00%
>>Whole-wheat flour	75g	½ cup	50.00%
Water	75g	⅓ cup	50.00%
Active dry yeast	1g	½ teaspoon	0.67%

For the Dough:

Ingredient	Weight	Volume	Baker's %
Total flour			100.00%
>>Bread flour	265g	2 cups	56.99%
>>Whole-wheat flour	200g	1⅓ cups	43.01%
Large eggs	385g	7 whole	82.80%
Honey	75g	¼ cup	16.13%
Fine sea salt	15g	2 teaspoons	3.23%
Active dry yeast	5g	1 teaspoon	1.08%
Cold unsalted butter	334g	1½ cups	71.83%

For the Egg Wash:

Ingredient	Volume
Large egg	1 whole
Water	1 tablespoon

Make the biga: In the bowl of a stand mixer fitted with the dough hook attachment, add the bread flour, wheat flour, water, and yeast. Mix on low speed for 4 minutes, or until completely combined. Cover the bowl with a tea towel or linen and set aside at room temperature to ferment for 12 hours.

Mix the dough: In the bowl of a stand mixer fitted with the dough hook attachment, add the biga, eggs, bread flour, wheat flour, honey, salt, and yeast. Mix on low speed for 4 minutes, or until thoroughly combined with no dry flour remaining. Increase the speed to medium and mix for 10 to 12 minutes, until a smooth, shiny dough forms.

While the dough is mixing, place the cold butter between two sheets of parchment paper or plastic wrap and beat with a rolling pin until pliable. You do not want to use room-temperature butter for this or the dough will become greasy instead of light and fluffy. Once the dough is strong, reduce the mixer speed to low and, with the mixer running, toss in small, flat pinches of butter. Mix until all of the butter is added and incorporated; this will take another 8 to 10 minutes on low speed. Remove the dough hook from the dough and remove the bowl from the mixer.

Continued

Ferment: Cover the bowl with a tea towel or linen and let the dough ferment at room temperature for 2 hours. Fold the dough after 1 hour, re-cover the bowl, and let the dough rest for the remaining hour. The dough is properly fermented when it's about doubled in size. Keep the bowl covered and refrigerate overnight.

Shape and proof: Turn out the dough onto a lightly floured work surface. If you're using loaf pans, divide the dough in half, with each half weighing about 750 grams. If you'd like to make buns, portion fifteen pieces at about 100 grams each. Shape the dough as sandwich loaves (see batard on page 52) or choose a pre-shaping method to form as buns (see page 50). Cover the dough with a tea towel or linen and proof for 2 to 3 hours in a warm area, until doubled in size and very light and airy.

Bake: Preheat the oven to 350°F.

In a small bowl, whisk together the egg and water. Brush the egg wash over the loaves or buns and score (see page 53). (Buns do not need to be scored unless desired.) Bake for 20 minutes for buns or 35 minutes for loaves, or until golden brown. Let cool before serving.

Bacon-Rye Cheese Rolls

Rye flour, molasses, caraway, cheese, bacon. In the dough. Pull-apart buns. Boom. If you want these for breakfast—and you know you do—shape them the day before, throw them in the fridge, and bake in the morning.

Note: This recipe uses a technique called tangzhong. This is a Chinese method of cooking your flour with liquid, which gelatinizes the starches, allowing them to swell up with water. Adding the tangzhong to your bread will help it stay very soft and retain that extra moisture for a longer period of time.

Makes 10 to 12 buns

For the Preferment:

Ingredient	Weight	Volume	Baker's %
Total flour			100.00%
>>Bread flour	100g	¾ cup	100.00%
Water	100g	⅓ cup plus 2 tablespoons	100.00%
Active dry yeast	0.5g	pinch	0.50%

For the Tangzhong:

Ingredient	Weight	Volume	Baker's %
Total flour			100.00%
>>Rye flour	90g	¾ cup	100.00%
Water	270g	1 cup plus 2 tablespoons	300.00%

For the Filling:

Ingredient	Volume
Bacon, cut into ½-inch strips	8 ounces
Sweet onions, chopped	2 large
Fine sea salt and freshly ground black pepper	to taste
Shredded fontina cheese	2 cups
Fresh thyme leaves	3 tablespoons

Continued

For the Dough:

Ingredient	Weight	Volume	Baker's %
Total flour			100.00%
>>Bread flour	480g	3¾ cups	100.00%
Whole milk	195g	¾ cup plus 2 tablespoons	40.63%
Softened lard	115g	½ cup	23.96%
Molasses	65g	¼ cup	13.54%
Fine sea salt	15g	2¼ teaspoons	3.13%
Active dry yeast	4g	1 teaspoon	0.83%
Cooking spray, for greasing			

Make the preferment: In a small bowl, add the flour, water, and yeast and mix by hand to combine, about 2 minutes. Cover the bowl with a tea towel or linen and let the mixture sit at room temperature for 12 hours.

Make the tangzhong: In a small saucepan over medium-high heat, combine the rye flour and water and cook until very thick, 2 or 3 minutes after the mixture comes to a boil. Transfer the mixture to a plate and let it cool to room temperature before mixing the dough.

Make the filling: While the tangzhong cools, make the filling. In a medium skillet over low heat, add the bacon and cook for 5 to 6 minutes, until most of the fat renders out and the bacon starts to crisp. Add the onions and season with salt and pepper. Sweat the onion and bacon mixture for 4 to 5 minutes, until the bacon is cooked through and the onions are translucent. Remove the pan from the heat and transfer the mixture to a bowl. Let it cool, then toss it with the cheese and thyme. Reserve until ready to use—covered in the fridge if you're doing this step the day before, but otherwise at room temperature.

Mix the dough: In the bowl of a stand mixer fitted with the dough hook attachment, add the preferment, the cooled tangzhong, bread flour, milk, lard, molasses, salt, and yeast. Mix on low speed for 3 to 4 minutes, until the mixture is thoroughly combined, taking care to stop the mixer and scrape underneath the dough to ensure there are no pockets of flour. Increase the speed to medium-high and mix for another 8 to 10 minutes, until a smooth, shiny dough forms. Remove the dough hook from the dough and remove the bowl from the mixer.

Ferment: Cover the bowl with a tea towel or linen and let the dough ferment for 2 hours. Fold the dough after 1 hour, re-cover the bowl, and let the dough rest for the remaining hour.

Assemble and proof: Lightly flour a work surface, turn out the dough, and lightly flour the dough. Use a rolling pin to roll the dough into a rectangle about 8 by 16 inches. The dough should be just about ¼ inch thick. Place the dough so there's a long edge closest to you. Spread the filling evenly over the surface of the dough, leaving 1 inch along the top long end of the dough uncovered by filling. Brush this strip lightly with water to help seal the dough to itself once rolled. Starting at the bottom and working toward the strip with no filling, roll the dough into a log, creating a spiral of filling. Once the dough is rolled, press the dough against that lightly moistened strip at the top to seal the log nicely.

Line a baking sheet with parchment and coat in cooking spray. Slice the log into 1½- to 2-inch-thick rolls; you should get 10 or 12. Lay the rolls flat, spiral-side up, on the prepared sheet. They should be close enough to one another that they will bake together once proofed, but not so snugly that the pan will overflow. Cover with a tea towel or linen and proof the rolls for 1 hour.

Bake: Preheat the oven to 350°F.

Bake the rolls for 20 to 25 minutes, until the cheese filling has melted and the dough is golden brown. Let cool slightly before serving.

Potato Fry Pockets

We haven't gotten to do a lot of frying, so now's your chance. These are hearty, potato-filled "alongsiders" that get a dose of wheat germ for some extra fat and sweetness and go with pretty much anything on or around them. Some stracciatella cheese or a summer ratatouille wouldn't be half bad.

Makes 9 (100-gram) breads

For the Preferment:

Ingredient	Weight	Volume	Baker's %
Total flour			100.00%
>>All-purpose flour	44g	⅓ cup	100.00%
Water	44g	¼ cup	100.00%
Active dry yeast	1g	¼ teaspoon	2.27%

For the Dough:

Ingredient	Weight	Volume	Baker's %
Total flour			100.00%
>>All-purpose flour	210g	1⅔ cups	60.69%
>>Spelt flour	136g	1¼ cups	39.31%
Russet potato	140g	1 large	40.46%
Extra-virgin olive oil, for drizzling			
Fine sea salt, plus more to taste	7g	1 teaspoon	2.02%
Water	260g	1 cup plus 1½ tablespoons	75.14%
Active sourdough starter	50g	¼ cup	14.45%
Wheat germ	13g	3 tablespoons	3.76%
Active dry yeast	1g	¼ teaspoon	0.29%
Cooking spray, for greasing			
Neutral oil, for frying			

Make the preferment: In a small bowl, add the all-purpose flour, water, and yeast and mix by hand for 2 minutes to combine thoroughly. Cover with a tea towel or linen and set aside at room temperature to ferment for 12 hours.

Make the dough: Preheat the oven to 350°F. Line a baking sheet with parchment.

Place the potato on the prepared baking sheet, drizzle with olive oil, and season with salt. Roast for 45 minutes, or until fork tender. Let the potato cool to room temperature, then roughly chop it into ¼- to ½-inch pieces.

In the bowl of a stand mixer fitted with the paddle attachment, add the pre-ferment, water, all-purpose flour, spelt flour, sourdough starter, wheat germ, salt, and yeast. Mix on low speed until thoroughly combined. Increase the speed to medium-low until the batter is smooth and shiny and starts to climb up the paddle, 3 to 5 minutes. Reduce the speed to low again, add the potato, and mix for another 30 seconds.

Ferment: Cover the bowl with a tea towel or linen and let the dough ferment at room temperature for 1 hour. Punch down the dough, then cover it and let it continue to ferment at room temperature for 30 minutes, then refrigerate for at least 3 hours or ideally overnight.

Shape: After the dough has chilled, lightly flour a work surface and dump the dough out. Gently flatten and stretch the dough into a rough square shape, then cut it into nine equal squares.

Fry the bread: In a skillet over medium-high heat, heat at least 2 inches of oil to 350°F. Line a plate or baking sheet with paper towels and set aside.

Work with one piece of dough at a time. Start by stretching it into a rough square shape. Drop it gently into the hot oil and fry for 4 to 5 minutes per side, until golden brown. Transfer the fried bread to the prepared plate or baking sheet to drain, then season with salt. Cool slightly before serving.

Stollen

My grandmother, who was born in Wisconsin and had a strong German heritage, would make this cake every Christmas, and now I've continued the tradition. Stollen is like panettone's dense German cousin, and is equally as decadent. It has a chewy, nougaty feel to it thanks to the butter bath it gets after it bakes. And it's studded with homemade marzipan perfumed with floral orange blossom water (though optional) and candied fruit (minus the neon-green candied cherries).

Makes 2 (750-gram) loaves

For the Preferment:

Ingredient	Weight	Volume	Baker's %
Total flour			100.00%
>>Bread flour	150g	1 cup plus 2 tablespoons	100.00%
Water	150g	⅔ cup	100.00%
Active dry yeast	0.5g	pinch	0.33%

For the Soaked Fruit Mix:

Ingredient	Weight	Volume
Dried cherries	140g	1 cup
Golden raisins	140g	1 cup
Store-bought or homemade candied orange peel, diced small	90g	½ cup
Store-bought or homemade candied lemon peel, diced small	90g	½ cup
Orange juice	100g	⅓ cup

For the Marzipan:

Ingredient	Weight	Volume	Baker's %
Powdered sugar	145g	1¼ cups	107.41%
Almond flour	135g	1½ cups	100.00%
Large egg white	28g	1 each	20.74%
Orange blossom water (optional)	5g	2 teaspoons	3.70%
Almond extract	4g	1 teaspoon	2.96%
Fine sea salt	2g	⅛ teaspoon	1.48%

Continued

For the Dough:

Ingredient	Weight	Volume	Baker's %
Total flour			100.00%
>>Bread flour	300g	2⅓ cups	78.95%
>>Spelt flour	80g	¾ cup	21.05%
Whole milk	170g	⅔ cup	44.74%
Granulated sugar	115g	½ cup plus 1 tablespoon	30.26%
Large egg yolks	40g	3 each	10.53%
Fine sea salt	13g	2 teaspoons	3.42%
Vanilla bean paste or extract (see note on page 86)	9g	1 tablespoon	2.37%
Active dry yeast	4g	1 teaspoon	1.05%
Ground cinnamon	4g	1½ teaspoons	1.05%
Ground ginger	2g	1 teaspoon	0.53%
Ground nutmeg	1g	½ teaspoon	0.26%
Ground mace (optional)	1g	½ teaspoon	0.26%
Ground cloves	1g	½ teaspoon	0.26%
Unsalted butter, softened	225g	1 cup	59.21%
Sliced almonds	94g	1 cup	24.74%
Unsalted butter, melted, for dipping	450g	4 cups	
Powdered sugar, for dusting			

Make the preferment: In a medium bowl, add the bread flour, water, and yeast and mix by hand for 2 minutes to combine. Cover the bowl with a tea towel or linen and set aside at room temperature to ferment for 12 hours.

Make the soaked fruit mix: In a medium bowl, combine the dried cherries, raisins, candied orange peel, and candied lemon peel. Pour the orange juice over the mixture to cover. Add more juice if needed to just barely but completely cover the fruit. Cover the bowl with plastic wrap and refrigerate overnight. Drain before adding to the dough.

Make the marzipan: In the bowl of a stand mixer fitted with the paddle attachment, combine the powdered sugar, almond flour, egg white, orange blossom water (if using), almond extract, and salt. Mix on low speed for 3 to 4 minutes, until the mixture is completely homogeneous and all of the sugar and flour have been absorbed. Divide the mixture in half and form each piece into a log about 6 inches long and 1 inch in diameter. Wrap the marzipan logs in plastic wrap and store in the fridge until you're ready to shape the bread.

Make the dough: In the bowl of a stand mixer fitted with the dough hook attachment, combine the preferment, bread flour, milk, sugar, spelt flour, egg yolks, salt, vanilla, yeast, cinnamon, ginger, nutmeg, mace (if using), and cloves. Mix on low speed for 3 to 4 minutes, until a dough forms. Increase the speed to medium and mix for another 10 to 12 minutes, until the dough is smooth, shiny, and one cohesive ball. Reduce the speed to low and add the butter in three additions, making sure each is completely incorporated before adding the next. Add the drained fruit and almonds and mix for another 2 minutes, or until the fruit and nuts are evenly dispersed. Remove the dough hook from the bowl and remove the bowl from the mixer.

Ferment: Cover the bowl with a tea towel or linen and let the dough ferment at room temperature for 2 to 3 hours. Fold the dough after 1 hour of fermentation, re-cover the bowl, and let the dough rest for the remaining hour or two. The dough is ready when it has doubled in size.

Shape and proof: Line a baking sheet with parchment.

Turn out the dough onto a lightly floured work surface and divide the dough in half; each half should weigh about 750 grams. Round each half tightly using a pre-shaping method (see page 50). Let the dough rest, covered with a tea towel or linen, for 20 minutes.

Lightly flour a work surface, then place the dough in the flour. With a rolling pin, roll each dough piece into an oval about 10 inches long, 6 inches wide, and 1 inch thick. Place a log of marzipan across each dough piece and fold the dough over it to create a smaller oval. Place each piece on the prepared baking sheet. Cover with a tea towel or linen and ferment at room temperature for another 1 to 2 hours, until the dough has doubled in size.

Bake, dip, and powder: Preheat an oven to 350°F.

Bake the stollen cakes for 35 minutes, or until they're a deep golden brown and reach an internal temperature of 200°F.

Continued

While the cakes bake, add the melted butter to a pan large enough to fit the stollen. Dip the hot baked bread completely in butter on both sides. Alternatively, you can brush the baked loaves generously with butter when they come out of the oven. The dipping method is better and traditional, but a bit messy and hot. Dealer's choice. Allow the stollen to cool. Dust heavily with powdered sugar, slice, and serve.

Bee Sting Cake

Unlike the cakes you came across in Chapter 1, this dense, chewy cake is yeasted (aka fermented). A little bit more work than throwing together a batter? Sure. But next-level delicious? Definitely. Yeasted cakes have been around for much longer than what we consider to be "traditional" cakes, and while they're not as common anymore, I love the idea of capturing that complexity of flavor and texture in a cake. In this case it's a German dessert (Bienenstich Kuchen) that gets a baked-on topping of honey and almonds, and is then sliced open and filled with pastry cream–whipped cream hybrid.

Makes 1 (9-inch) cake

For the Cake:

Ingredient	Weight	Volume	Baker's %
Total flour			100.00%
>>All-purpose whole-wheat flour or regular all-purpose flour	260g	2 cups	100.00%
Unsalted butter	60g	⅓ cup	23.08%
Whole milk	113g	⅓ cup	43.46%
Active sourdough starter	115g	½ cup	44.23%
Large egg yolks	55g	3 each	21.15%
Sugar	24g	2 tablespoons	9.23%
Honey	18g	1 tablespoon	6.92%
Fine sea salt	1g	¼ teaspoon	0.38%
Almond extract	1g	½ teaspoon	0.38%
Cooking spray, for greasing			

For the Topping:

Ingredient	Weight	Volume	Baker's %
Sugar	75g	⅓ cup	125.00%
Unsalted butter	60g	¼ cup	100.00%
Honey	20g	1 tablespoon	33.33%
Fine sea salt	1g	¼ teaspoon	1.67%
Sliced almonds		¾ cup	125.00%
Heavy cream	16g	1½ tablespoons	26.67%

Continued

For the Filling:

Ingredient	Weight	Volume	Baker's %
Cold water	30g	2 tablespoons	6.67%
Powdered gelatin	6g	2 teaspoons	1.33%
Whole milk	450g	1¾ cups plus 1½ tablespoons	100.00%
Granulated sugar	160g	¾ cup plus 2 tablespoons	35.56%
Large egg yolks	100g	6 each	22.22%
Cornstarch	20g	2 tablespoons plus 2 teaspoons	4.44%
Fine sea salt	3g	¼ teaspoon	0.67%
Almond paste	100g	½ cup	22.22%
Unsalted butter	50g	¼ cup	11.11%
Vanilla bean paste or extract (see note on page 86)	10g	1 tablespoon	2.22%

Mix the cake: In a small saucepan over low heat, melt the butter. Add the milk and gently warm to about 80°F. This should be slightly warm to the touch but not hot. Transfer the mixture to the bowl of a stand mixer fitted with the dough hook attachment and add the flour, sourdough starter, egg yolks, sugar, honey, salt, and almond extract. Mix on low speed until everything is incorporated, about 4 minutes, scraping down the sides of the bowl and underneath the dough to ensure there are no dry pockets of flour.

Ferment: Pre-shape the dough into a tight round (see page 50), cover with a tea towel or linen, and let ferment in a warm area for 3 hours. The dough is ready when it has grown by about a third and feels light and airy to the touch.

Line a 9-inch springform pan or regular round cake pan with parchment and coat with cooking spray. Press the dough into the lined pan, cover with a tea towel or linen, and let ferment in a warm area again for 1½ hours. It should about double in size.

Make the topping: When the cake is ready to bake, make the topping. In a small saucepan over medium heat, add the sugar, butter, honey, and salt. Cook gently until the mixture comes to a simmer and the sugar has dissolved, about 7 minutes. Whisk in the almonds and cream and set aside.

Bake: Preheat the oven to 350°F.

Prick the cake all over with a fork to allow the syrup to penetrate the cake. Pour the topping evenly over the cake. Bake for about 35 minutes, or until the topping is golden brown. If you used a springform pan, run a knife around the edge of the cake and remove the collar while the cake is still warm from the oven. If you used a regular cake pan, allow the cake to cool completely, then run a knife around the edge of the cake before removing from the pan. The cake should be completely cool before moving on to assembling it with the filling.

Make the filling: In a small bowl, combine the cold water and gelatin and set aside to bloom for 5 minutes. You will know it's ready when the gelatin has a absorbed all of the water and has swollen in the dish. In a medium saucepan over medium-high heat, add the milk and heat slowly to a boil while you prep the remaining filling components.

In a medium bowl, combine the sugar, egg yolks, cornstarch, and salt and whisk until smooth, about 2 minutes.

When the milk has come to a boil, slowly and gradually whisk it into the egg mixture. The key to avoid scrambling the eggs is to add the milk in a slow, steady stream while whisking constantly to temper the eggs. Return the egg and milk mixture back to the pan and add the bloomed gelatin. Bring the pan to a boil over high heat, whisking constantly. Reduce the heat just slightly to medium-high and boil for 3 minutes, continuing to whisk. The mixture will be quite thick.

Pour the custard into the bowl of a food processor, add the almond paste, butter, and vanilla, and process until very smooth. Let the mixture cool for 30 minutes before assembling the cake.

Assemble the cake: Cut the cooled cake horizontally through the middle, creating two even rounds. Set the top round aside and place the bottom round back in the cake pan. Pour the filling over the bottom round of the cake. (Doing this in the cake pan will help keep the pastry cream from running out the sides of the cake while it cools.) Replace the top round and let the pastry cream cool and set completely. Remove the cake from the pan and serve.

Buckwheat Canelés

Canelés are pastry frickin' magic. Technically challenging and difficult to make, yeah, but a really worthwhile project. They're like an egg custard that you bake in a mold lined with beeswax paper and clarified butter so they end up with this caramelized sugar shell that encases this really soft perfumy middle. Normally we'd add rum to the mix, but for this version we're going with bourbon to complement the buckwheat, which in turn complements the deep, almost-burnt sugar flavor of the pastries. I also like that we're using beeswax as part of the production and that buckwheat happens to be really good for bees and other pollinators, but maybe that's just me.

Note: While there's a decent amount of room for play with the recipes in this book with regard to swapping in different grains, you need to stick with a fine flour for these. With the long bake time, any chunks in oat or a bran flour will sink to the bottom of the canelé and you won't get the same sort of glossy shell.

Also, to make canelé you'll need special copper molds. They are expensive but super worth this endeavor. You could buy only a few of them and bake the batter in batches.

Makes 24 canelé

Ingredient	Weight	Volume	Baker's %
Total flour			100.00%
>>Buckwheat flour	200g	1¾ cups	100.00%
Whole milk	880g	3½ cups	440.00%
Heavy cream	100g	⅓ cup plus 1 tablespoon	50.00%
Unsalted butter, melted	50g	¼ cup	25.00%
Granulated sugar	440g	2¼ cups	220.00%
Fine sea salt	2g	½ teaspoon	1.00%
Large egg yolks	140g	7 each	70.00%
Large egg	55g	1 whole	27.50%
Vanilla bean paste or extract (see note on page 86)	20g	2 tablespoons	10.00%
Bourbon	150g	⅔ cup	75.00%
Clarified butter (see page 119)	200g	1 cup	100.00%
Beeswax	80g	⅓ cup	40.00%

Continued

In a medium saucepan over medium heat, combine the milk and cream and heat to 175°F. Remove the pan from the heat and let the mixture cool to 120°F.

In a large bowl, combine the flour and butter. Rub the mixture between your hands using a back-and-forth motion for 15 minutes. You are trying to coat the flour very evenly with the melted butter. Add the sugar and salt.

In a medium bowl, combine the egg yolks, whole egg, and vanilla and whisk until smooth.

Pour half of the cream mixture into the flour mixture and whisk for just 2 or 3 seconds. Add all of the egg mixture and whisk for another few seconds. Add the remaining cream mixture and whisk for another few seconds. It's OK if the batter isn't completely homogeneous, but it should be most of the way there. The goal is to not overbeat the batter at any point, or the pastries will gain too much structure and will puff out of the molds when baking. Refrigerate the batter overnight. When it comes out of the fridge, add the bourbon and whisk for 2 seconds to combine.

Preheat the oven to 365°F.

In a small saucepan over low heat, melt the clarified butter and beeswax, occasionally swirling the pan to combine. Pour a small amount into each canelé mold, tilting and swirling the pan to evenly coat each mold. Flip the molds over to drain any excess beeswax mixture back into the pan, then set the pan down with the mold openings facing up. Fill the molds almost to the very top with batter, leaving very little headspace. Bake for 55 minutes, until the pastries are flush with the top of the mold, deep brown, and very caramelized. Carefully remove the canelés from the molds while still hot, making sure to hold the hot mold with a towel or oven mitt to avoid burning yourself. Let the pastries cool for at least 15 minutes on a wire cooling rack. These are best enjoyed warm.

Oat Madeleines

Light, fluffy, and slightly crisp madeleines are a delight to have with some coffee in the afternoon, or morning, or really whenever. This recipe was developed for one of our Bread Camps by a pastry chef and friend of mine, Meg Galus, who says that adding oat flour to her madeleine recipe made them taste like butterscotch. This recipe will work equally well using other alternative flours like buckwheat.

Note: To make these as the French intended, you'll want to invest in a madeleine tray in order to honor this pastry's distinctive shape. Also, these are best eaten within minutes of coming out of the oven.

Makes about 24 madeleines

Ingredient	Weight	Volume	Baker's %
Total flour			100.00%
>>Cake flour	50g	⅓ cup plus 2 tablespoons	52.63%
>>Oat flour	45g	⅓ cup plus 1 tablespoon	47.37%
Unsalted butter, plus more for greasing	85g	⅓ cup	89.47%
Honey	15g	2 teaspoons	15.78%
Vanilla bean paste or extract (see note on page 86)	5g	1 teaspoon	5.26%
Large eggs	110g	2 whole	105.26%
Granulated sugar	80g	⅓ cup plus 1 tablespoon	84.21%
Baking powder	6g	1½ teaspoons	6.31%
Fine sea salt	3g	½ teaspoon	3.15%

Melt the butter in a small saucepan over medium-low heat. Continue cooking the butter as it simmers, until browned, about 8 minutes. Strain out the solids through a fine-mesh strainer or cheesecloth into a medium bowl. Add the honey and vanilla and whisk to combine. Set aside.

In the bowl of a stand mixer fitted with the whisk attachment, combine the eggs and sugar. Whip on high speed for 5 or 6 minutes, until the mixture is at the ribbon stage. In other words, the mixture should be light and fluffy, and when you pull the whisk out of the mixture and let some of the batter drizzle over the bowl, it should remain in ribbons before settling back into the mixture.

Continued

In a medium bowl, add the cake flour, oat flour, baking powder, and salt and whisk to combine. Add this mixture to the batter and mix on low speed until just combined, 1 to 2 minutes. Drizzle the brown butter mixture into the batter and continue mixing on low speed until just combined, another 1 to 2 minutes. Transfer the batter to a piping bag or large zip-top plastic bag and chill for several hours or overnight.

Grease a tray of madeleine molds with butter and place the tray in the freezer until ready to use, which will help prevent the madeleines from sticking once they're baked.

Preheat the oven to 350°F.

Pipe the batter into the prepared molds, filling them just over three-quarters full. (If you're using a zip-top bag, just snip off one corner to create a makeshift piping bag. Also, you could just use a spoon to dollop the batter into the molds, but piping is going to be a lot cleaner.) Bake for 10 to 12 minutes, until golden. Enjoy immediately.

Introduction to Laminated Dough

Laminated pastry, or pastry dough that's cut with layers of butter, is the key to flaky croissants, danishes, and kouign amann. As the water content of the butter turns to steam during baking, the layers of dough puff up, leaving you with light, buttery goodness. The way you achieve this is not only by folding the dough and butter together, but also by maintaining the perfect temperature of your butter. It needs to be warm enough to be pliable, but cold enough so that it'll create the steam effect in the oven. Otherwise you'll end up with heavy, greasy pastry. The ideal temperature for your butter as you laminate is right around 59° or 60°F. While it'll be a different temperature than your dough, it should have the same texture—it should give a little when pressed on, but firm. Here are the fundamentals of laminating.

Shaping the Butter

Let your butter soften at room temperature for about 1 hour. Place the butter between two sheets of parchment paper that are slightly larger than your desired finished dimensions of the butter sheet.

Use a rolling pin to press firmly on and/or beat the butter until it's pliable and starts to flatten, then roll out the butter to your desired size. You can then use the edge of a bench scraper to help smooth and square your edges. Do this by holding the butter in place with one hand while pressing the flat edge of the scraper up against the edge of the butter with the other. Keeping your sheet of butter between the two pieces of parchment, carefully transfer it to the fridge while you prepare your dough. Just be sure to bring the butter's temp back up to 59° or 60°F before working it into the dough, which you can do by having it sit at room temperature for a few minutes.

Locking in Layers

Different types of pastries call for different numbers of "lock-ins," or initial layers when you first put together the dough and butter. This ultimately yields a different number of layers in the final product (along with the number of folds, which we'll get to in a moment). For example, croissants call for a two-layer lock-in, while danishes call for a one-layer lock-in. This will be specified in the recipe; here's how you do it:

One-Layer Lock-In: Take your shaped butter out of the fridge and set aside. Flour your pastry dough and the table. Use a rolling pin to roll the pastry to the same length but twice the width of your butter. It should be about ¼-thick—the same thickness as the butter. Use a dry pastry brush to brush off as much excess flour as you can.

Peel off one layer of the parchment paper from the butter and discard. Lay the butter on the pastry so that their edges meet and they're matching in length. Gently press the butter into the dough, then remove the top layer of parchment paper and discard. Use a knife to cut the excess width of the dough away from the butter, then drape that piece of dough over the butter to form a sort of butter sandwich. Gently tuck the dough over any bits of butter that are overhanging.

Sprinkle flour beneath the dough and over the top. With the short edge of the rectangle closest to you, use a rolling pin to start gently rocking back and forth over the dough until you feel that the butter wants to move. Gradually apply more pressure to coax the dough back to its original ¼-inch thickness. When you're done, you should be able to run your hand over the dough without feeling any "islands" or cracks in the butter.

Continued

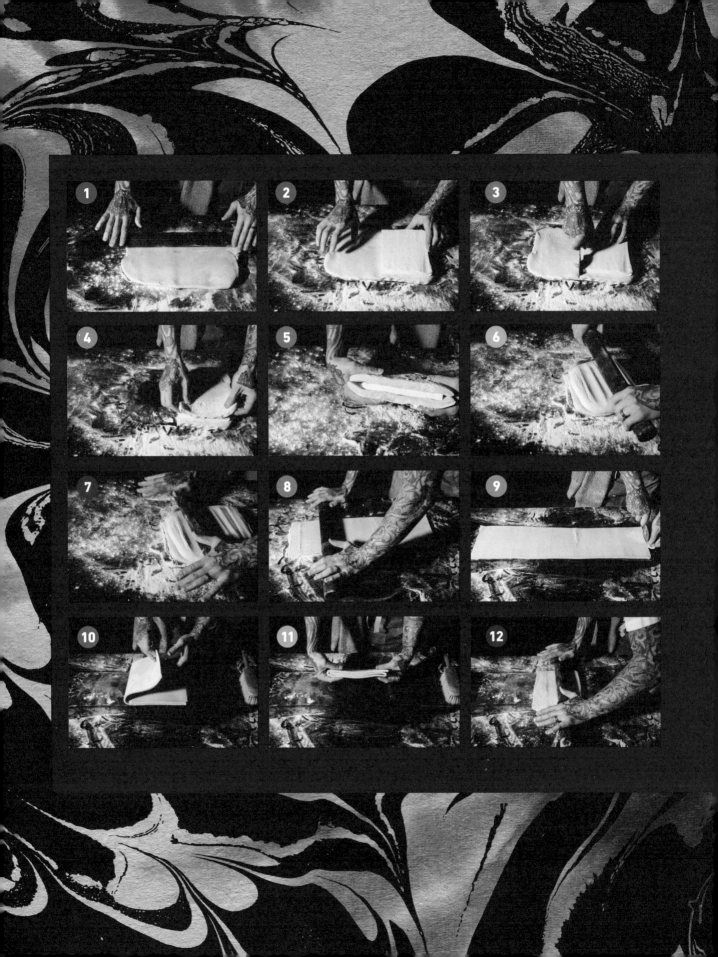

Feel for where the butter stops at the short edges and trim away any excess dough with a knife. Check what you've trimmed—you should be able to see a layer of butter between two layers of dough. If you skip this step, that little bit of extra dough in your lamination will end up having a doughy pocket no matter how long it's baked for.

Now you're ready to fold.

Two-Layer Lock-In: Take your shaped butter out of the fridge and set aside. Flour your pastry dough and the table. Use a rolling pin to roll the pastry to the same length but 1⅓ to 1½ times the width of the butter. It should be about ¼-inch thick—the same thickness as the butter. Use a dry pastry brush to brush off as much excess flour as you can.

Peel off one layer of the parchment paper from the butter and discard. Lay the butter on the pastry so that their edges meet and they're matching in length. Gently press the butter into the dough, then remove the top layer of parchment paper and discard. Fold the excess dough over the butter and brush off any excess flour. Then take the other end of your rectangle with your dough and butter and fold it so it meets the other edge, as though you're folding a letter. So now you're starting off with two layers of butter.

Sprinkle flour beneath the dough and over the top. With the short edge of the rectangle closest to you, use a rolling pin to start gently rocking back and forth over the dough until you feel that the butter wants to move. Gradually apply more pressure to coax the dough back to its original ¼-inch thickness. When you're done, you should be able to run your hand over the dough without feeling any islands of butter.

Feel for where the butter stops at the short edges and trim away any excess dough with a knife. Check what

you've trimmed—you should be able to see a layer of butter between two layers of dough. If you skip this step, that little bit of extra dough in your lamination will end up having a doughy pocket no matter how long it's baked for.

Now you're ready to fold.

Folding the Dough

Different pastries call for different folds and a different number of them—for instance, danishes use three letter folds, kouign amann uses two books folds. This is what yields the delicate layers of butter that you want in a laminated pastry. It will also determine the internal structure of your croissants; more folds will yield a tighter, more uniform crumb, while fewer folds will lead it to be more open and airy inside.

Book Fold: Fold in one short end of your dough about 2 inches. Fold the other short end of your dough to meet that first folded edge. Brush off any excess flour. Then take a short end once more and bring it to meet the other edge, folding the dough in half to make a "book." Situating the dough with a short end closest to you, once again roll the dough into a ¼-inch-thick rectangle, trim the edges, and fold again as directed in the recipe.

Letter Fold: You're essentially just folding up your rectangle of dough as you would a piece of paper when sending a letter: Take a short edge and fold it over about two-thirds of the way. Take the second short edge and fold it all the way to the other edge. Situating the dough with a short end closest to you, once again roll the dough into a ¼-inch-thick rectangle, trim the edges, and fold again as directed in the recipe.

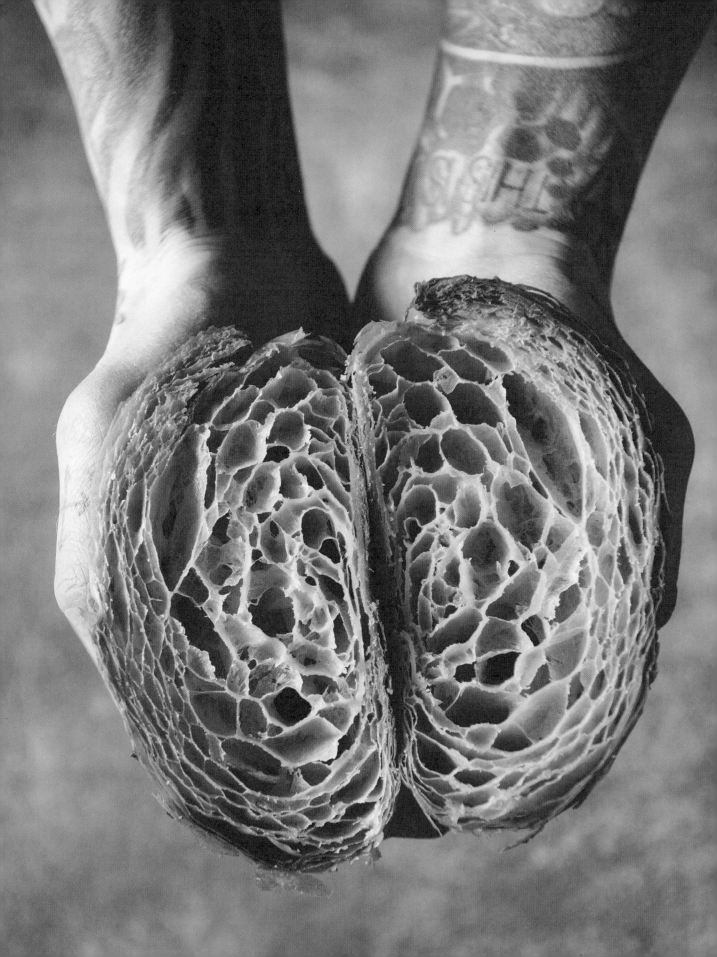

Whole-Wheat Croissants

This is a straight-from-the-bakery recipe. It's just too good to change. And frankly, there are few shortcuts when it comes to making great croissants. By using a preferment and a sourdough starter and a more complex fermentation on these, you're building tons of complexity in the dough to complement the whole grains. And by doing all that work up front, you can take a less-is-more approach when it comes to laminating the croissants because the flavor is already there. If you were to take away the butter and the sugar, what are you left with? The dough. The reason I find a lot of people's croissants are lacking in flavor is because they're focusing more on the lamination than the fermentation, so the dough will have a lot of richness from the butter, but none of the extra dimension or tang that fermentation will give you.

Makes 10 croissants

For the Preferment:

Ingredient	Weight	Volume	Baker's %
Total flour			100.00%
>>Bread flour	35g	¼ cup	100.00%
Water	35g	2 tablespoons	100.00%
Active dry yeast	0.5g	¼ teaspoon	1.33%

For the Dough:

Ingredient	Weight	Volume	Baker's %
Total flour			100.00%
>>Bread flour	425g	3¼ cups	79.81%
>>Whole-wheat flour	110g	¾ cup	20.19%
Whole milk	240g	1 cup	45.07%
Water	80g	⅓ cup	15.02%
Active sourdough starter	75g	⅓ cup	14.55%
Honey	55g	⅓ cup	9.86%
Unsalted butter, melted	25g	2 tablespoons + 1 teaspoon	5.16%
Fine sea salt	12g	1 tablespoon plus 1 teaspoon	2.25%
Active dry yeast	5g	2 teaspoons	0.94%
Unsalted butter rolled out to a 6-by-10-inch rectangle, for lamination (see page 273)	330g	3 cups	61.97%

Continued

For the Egg Wash:

Ingredient	Volume
Large egg	1 whole
Water	1 tablespoon

Make the preferment: In a medium bowl, add the bread flour, water, and yeast. Mix by hand until completely combined, about 2 minutes. Cover with a tea towel or linen and set aside at room temperature to ferment for 12 hours.

Mix the dough: In the bowl of a stand mixer fitted with the dough hook attachment, add the preferment, bread flour, milk, wheat flour, water, sourdough starter, honey, melted butter, salt, and yeast. Mix on low speed until a cohesive dough forms with no dry spots of flour, about 3 minutes. Increase the speed to medium and mix for another 10 minutes, or until a smooth and shiny dough forms. Remove the dough hook from the bowl and remove the bowl from the mixer.

Ferment: Cover the bowl with a tea towel or linen and let the dough ferment at room temperature for 1 hour. At the end of the hour, fold once, re-cover the bowl, and refrigerate overnight.

Laminate the dough: Laminate the dough and butter sheet with a two-layer lock-in and perform two letter folds (see page 275). Let the dough rest, covered, for 1 hour in the refrigerator before shaping.

Shape and proof: Line a baking sheet with parchment paper.

Roll the dough into a rectangle that is 9 inches long and as wide as you can roll it for the dough to be ¼ inch thick. Trim the edges on all sides of the dough. Cut a strip of dough that is 9 inches long and 4 inches wide. Then run your knife from the top left corner of the rectangle to the bottom right so you have two tall, thin triangles. Beginning at the base of a triangle, roll up the dough to meet the tip of the triangle. Continue rolling until the tip is underneath the pastry, place the rolled croissant on the prepared baking sheet, and cover with a tea towel or linen. Repeat with the remaining croissants, leaving room on the baking sheet for the pastry to expand.

Proof for 1 to 2 hours, or until just about doubled in size. Be aware of your ambient temperature—if your room is above 85°F, your butter will melt. Below

70°F and these will take forever to proof. Aim for the sweet spot of 80°F. What you want to see are the layers beginning to pull apart, and when you shake the tray, the croissants should jiggle a little like panna cotta.

Bake: Preheat the oven to 400°F.

In a small bowl, whisk together the egg and water. Brush the egg wash over the pastries. Place the croissants in the oven and immediately reduce the oven temperature to 375°F. (We in the trade call this "oven spring"—the initial higher heat gets the croissants to really pop, then the lower heat helps them bake through and dry out just the right amount.) Bake for 20 to 30 minutes, until the croissants are a deep golden brown. Let cool before serving.

RIFF

◇◦◇

Chocolate Croissants

20 to 25 pieces semisweet chocolate batons (2 per croissant)

Roll out the dough as above. Cut the dough into rectangles that are 3 inches long and as wide as your chocolate sticks (usually around 4½ inches). Place two chocolate sticks on the dough, separating the dough into equal thirds. Take the bottom short edge of the dough and fold it up and over the first chocolate stick, so it lands just about in the middle of the two sticks. Bring the top edge of the rectangle up and over the second chocolate stick to the middle so that it sits just on top of where you placed the bottom edge. Place the croissants seam-side down on the prepared baking sheet and proof for 1 to 2 hours, until just about doubled in size. You'll want to see the layers pulling apart and the dough having taken on a panna cotta–like jiggle when you shake the ban. Bake as described above.

Cornmeal Danishes

Danishes have a similar ideology to croissants in terms of the sweet-flaky factor, but their middle should be denser—more like a brioche. By using cooked cornmeal in the dough, you're not only getting that naturally buttery sweet corn flavor that's complemented by the rich pistachio pastry cream, you're also harnessing the unctuous creaminess of a polenta. Consider this recipe to be a sort of Master's Degree in pastry—you'll be reaching for a lot of your (hopefully now-familiar) baking tools such as making a porridge, baking in stages, adding a sourdough starter, laminating the dough, and working with filling.

Makes 12 danishes

For the Polenta:

Ingredient	Weight	Volume	Baker's %
Total flour			100.00%
>>Fine cornmeal	80g	½ cup	100.00%
Water	240g	1 cup	300.00%
Fine sea salt	1g	¼ teaspoon	1.25%

For the Dough:

Ingredient	Weight	Volume	Baker's %
Total flour			100.00%
>>Bread flour	480g	3¾ cups	100.00%
Active sourdough starter	200g	1 cup	41.67%
Large eggs	55g	1 whole	11.46%
Whole milk	110g	½ cup	22.92%
Sugar	60g	⅓ cup	12.50%
Unsalted butter	18g	1 tablespoon plus 1 teaspoon	3.75%
Fine sea salt	10g	1½ teaspoons	2.08%
Active dry yeast	5g	1 tablespoon plus 1 teaspoon	1.04%
Unsalted butter rolled out to an 8-by-11-inch rectangle, for lamination (see page 273)	450g	2 cups	

Continued

For the Pastry Cream:

Ingredient	Weight	Volume	Baker's %
Whole milk	450g	1¾ cups plus 1½ tablespoons	100.00%
Granulated sugar	160g	¾ cup plus 2 tablespoons	35.56%
Large egg yolks	100g	6 each	22.22%
Cornstarch	20g	2 tablespoons plus 2 teaspoons	4.44%
Fine sea salt	3g	¼ teaspoon	0.67%
Pistachio paste	100g	½ cup	22.22%
Unsalted butter	50g	¼ cup	11.11%
Vanilla bean paste or extract (see note on page 86)	10g	1 tablespoon	2.22%

For the Egg Wash:

Ingredient	Volume
Large egg	1 whole
Water	1 tablespoon

Make the polenta: In a medium saucepan over medium heat, add the water, cornmeal, and salt and mix with a wooden spoon to thoroughly combine. Bring to a boil, stirring often to prevent scorching. Reduce the heat to a simmer and cook until the polenta is very thick, 3 to 4 minutes after it comes to a boil. Pour the polenta onto a baking sheet and let cool to room temperature.

Mix the dough: In the bowl of a stand mixer fitted with the dough hook attachment, add the cooled polenta, bread flour, sourdough starter, milk, sugar, egg, butter, salt, and yeast. Mix on low speed until a cohesive dough forms with no dry spots of flour. Increase the speed to medium and mix for another 10 minutes to develop dough strength, until a smooth and shiny dough forms. Remove the dough hook from the bowl and remove the bowl from the mixer.

Ferment: Cover the bowl with a tea towel or linen and let the dough ferment at room temperature for 1 hour. At the end of the hour, fold once, re-cover the bowl, and place in the refrigerator overnight.

Make the filling: In a medium saucepan over medium heat, add the milk and slowly bring it to a boil.

Meanwhile, in a medium bowl, combine the sugar, egg yolks, cornstarch, and salt. Whisk until smooth, about 2 minutes.

While whisking continuously, slowly pour the hot milk over the egg mixture. The key to avoid scrambling the eggs here is to add the milk in a slow, steady stream while whisking constantly to temper the eggs.

Set the pan back over high heat and whisk constantly as you bring the mixture to a boil. Reduce the heat to medium-high and cook for 3 more minutes, continuing to whisk constantly. The pastry cream base should be quite thick at this point. Pour the thickened custard into the bowl of the food processor, add the pistachio paste, butter, and vanilla, and process until very smooth. Let this mixture cool for 30 minutes or overnight (covered, in the refrigerator) before using.

Laminate the dough: Laminate the dough and butter sheet with a single-layer lock-in and perform three letter folds (see page 275). Let the dough rest, covered, for 1 hour in the refrigerator before shaping.

Shape and proof: Line a baking sheet with parchment paper.

On a lightly floured surface, use a rolling pin to roll the dough to ¼ inch thick. Cut the pastry into twelve 4½-inch squares. From here you have some shaping options:

Danish shape: Square

- **Square:** An easy shape that works for most fillings is to start with a 4½-inch square piece of dough. Take each corner and fold it over, having the point of each corner almost touch in the center of the square. Place your filling in the center of the pastry after the corners have been folded.

- **Pinwheel:** At each corner of a pastry square, cut a line that runs diagonally toward the center of the square, but not quite to the center. Do the same at each corner. Lift the left "flap" at each corner to meet at the center, creating a pinwheel shape. Dollop about a tablespoon of filling on top.

- **Bearclaw:** Start with a 4½-inch square of dough. Place 2 tablespoons of filling in the center of the dough. Fold the dough over the filling, having the flat edges meet and form a rectangle with the filling encased in dough. Press on all sides of the dough to seal it. With a small knife, cut four times through the long edge where the two layers of dough form the seal. Gently pull the sides of the dough back from the uncut side of the pastry, fanning out the cuts you just made. You've now made a bearclaw! (See photos on page 284).

Danish shape: Pinwheel

Continued

Bake: Preheat the oven to 400°F. Arrange the shaped and filled danishes on the prepared baking sheet, spaced to allow room for the pastry to roughly double in size. Cover and proof at room temperature for 1 to 2 hours.

In a small bowl, make the egg wash by whisking together the egg and water. Brush the mixture over any exposed dough not covered by filling.

Place the pastries in the oven and immediately reduce the heat to 375°F. Bake for 20 to 30 minutes, until the danishes are deep golden brown and fragrant. Let cool before serving. Store any leftovers in an airtight container on the counter for up to 2 days.

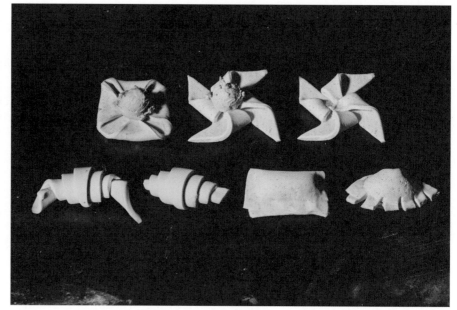

Danish shape: Bearclaw   Various danish shaping options

Maple Rye Kouign Amann

Translated as "butter cake" and pronounced "queen a-mahn," this old-school mash-up of a croissant and a palmier is probably one of the most mind-blowing pastries I've ever had. The first time I tried one and had to wrap my head around its crispy, sugary, kinda salty shell that's filled with melted-sugar goo, my only thought was, *Holy crap, what is that, how can I make it, and can I have more? Oh, and obviously, How can I put my own spin on it?* I immediately reached for rye flour because of the way it plays so nicely with caramelized sugar, perfumed it with maple syrup, and then added some ground fenugreek, an herb that has a surprisingly maple-y flavor. The effect is "pancake" but a million times better. Like the other laminated dough recipes, this one is definitely a skill builder, but there are few steps here that you haven't done before, and I assure you that your time will be more than well spent.

That said, one element you have not come across yet is working with gold yeast. This type of yeast is considered to be "osmotolerant," meaning it will still ferment well in the presence of a lot of sugar—which this recipe most definitely has. Normally high amounts of sugar will lock up the available active water in a dough, which yeast needs. But not this yeast.

Note: You can of course use a proper kouign amann mold, which looks a lot like an oversized muffin tin. Or you can use an oversized muffin tin, a regular muffin tin, 4-inch silicone baking molds, or twelve 4-inch ring molds that are at least 2 inches deep set on a baking sheet.

Makes 12 pastries

Ingredient	Weight	Volume	Baker's %
Total flour			100.00%
>>Bread flour	485g	3¾ cups	84.35%
>>Rye flour	90g	¾ cup	15.65%
Water	300g	1¼ cups	52.17%
Active sourdough starter	170g	¾ cup	29.57%
Maple syrup	95g	⅓ cup	16.52%
Unsalted butter, plus more for greasing	20g	1½ tablespoons	3.48%
Fine sea salt, plus more for sprinkling	13g	2¼ teaspoons	2.26%
Ground fenugreek	10g	1 tablespoon	1.74%
Saf-Instant Gold yeast or active dry yeast	6g	1¼ teaspoons	1.04%
Unsalted butter rolled out to an 8-by-11-inch rectangle, for lamination (see page 273)	450g	2 cups	
Granulated sugar, for sprinkling	100g	½ cup	

Continued

Mix the dough: In the bowl of a stand mixer fitted with the dough hook attachment, combine the bread flour, water, sourdough starter, maple syrup, rye flour, butter, salt, fenugreek, and yeast. Mix on low speed until a cohesive dough forms with no dry spots of flour. Increase the speed to medium and mix for another 10 minutes, until a smooth and shiny dough forms. Remove the dough hook from the bowl and remove the bowl from the mixer.

Ferment: Cover the bowl with a tea towel or linen and let the dough ferment at room temperature for 1 hour. At the end of the hour, fold once, re-cover the bowl, and place in the refrigerator overnight.

Laminate the dough: Laminate the dough and butter sheet with a single-layer lock-in and perform two book folds (see page 275). Roll out the dough again as if to perform a third book fold, but before folding, dust the entire surface heavily with sugar and lightly with salt. Fold the ends in as you would for the first steps of a book fold, repeat the heavy layer of sugar and light layer of salt, and complete the book fold. Let the dough rest, covered, for 1 hour in the refrigerator before rolling it out and shaping the pastries.

Shape and proof: Rub your molds of choice (see note) with butter and set aside.

Roll out the dough to ⅓ inch thick. Dust the work surface with sugar. Place the entire piece of dough into the sugar and dust the top with sugar. With the rolling pin, gently press the dough into the sugar, being careful not to press so hard that you tear the dough.

Cut the sheet of dough into twelve 4-inch squares, unless you're using a standard muffin tin, in which case your squares should be 3 inches. Fold each corner of the pastry to the center, then transfer the pastry to a cup of the mold. Cover with a tea towel or linen and proof for 2 hours. The pastries won't so much double in size as they'll fill out and get a little more snug in their molds. They'll also look a little syrupy as the sugar draws out moisture from the dough—this is normal and fine.

Bake: Preheat the oven to 425°F.

Place the pastries in the oven and immediately reduce the heat to 375°F. Bake for 30 minutes, or until the pastries are deeply caramelized and fragrant. Allow to cool slightly before removing from the molds. Cool for another 15 to

Laminating the dough

20 minutes before enjoying. Store any leftovers in an airtight container on the counter for up to 3 days. Reheat at 350°F for 7 minutes, then let cool slightly before digging in.

Rye Phyllo Pies

Back when I worked at Taxim, a Greek restaurant in Chicago, I would make a frickin' *ton* of hand-stretched phyllo dough. And one of my secrets was to add some rye flour because of the elastic, extensible quality it lends. It served me well because the goal is to basically make a giant, super thin dough that you add your fillings to (in this case, chopped ramps and feta for a riff on spanakopita, or spinach pie).

Making phyllo calls for going big: big on time because, remember, the longer you let dough rest, the more slack and stretchy it gets. And big on grease, because you're going to be melting butter with olive oil and schmearing that stuff all over everything—your table, your hands, your dough. Reason being: You're going to massage the dough until it gets nice and thin for filling, parceling, and baking.

Makes 11 (100-gram) hand pies

For the Dough:

Ingredient	Weight	Volume	Baker's %
Total flour			100.00%
>>Bread flour	400g	3 cups	66.67%
>>Rye flour	200g	1⅔ cups	33.33%
Whole milk	400g	1⅔ cups	66.67%
Large egg	110g	2 whole	18.33%
Fine sea salt	12g	2 teaspoons	2.00%
Cooking spray, for greasing			
Extra-virgin olive oil	1 cup, plus more if needed		
Unsalted butter, melted and cooled	1 cup, plus more if needed		
Sesame seeds	as needed		

Continued

For the Filling:

Ingredient	Volume
Extra-virgin olive oil	as needed
Chopped ramps or leeks	5 cups
Minced garlic	3 tablespoons
Fine sea salt and freshly ground black pepper	to taste
Fresh lemon juice	3 tablespoons
Grated lemon zest	2 tablespoons
Large egg, beaten	1 whole
Crumbled feta	½ cup

For the Egg Wash:

Ingredient	Volume
Large egg	1 whole
Water	1 tablespoon

Mix the dough: In the bowl of a stand mixer fitted with the dough hook attachment, add the bread flour, milk, rye flour, eggs, and salt. Mix on low speed for 3 to 4 minutes, until thoroughly combined with no dry flour remaining. Increase the speed to medium-high and mix for another 10 to 12 minutes, until very smooth and shiny. Let the dough rest for 15 minutes.

Portion: Coat a baking sheet with cooking spray. Turn out the dough onto a lightly floured work surface and divide it into eleven equal pieces; each piece should weigh about 100 grams. Gently round each piece by hand and place them on the prepared baking sheet. Cover with a tea towel or linen and let the dough rest at room temperature for at least 1 hour and up to 4 hours. You want the dough to be very relaxed and able to stretch very thin.

Make the filling: In a large pan over medium heat, heat a teaspoon or two of oil. Add the ramps and cook until soft, 5 to 7 minutes. Add the garlic and sweat for another 2 to 3 minutes. Season with salt and pepper, add the lemon juice, and reduce until most of the liquid has evaporated, about 2 minutes. Remove the pan from the heat, add the lemon zest, and toss to combine. Let the mixture cool while you whisk the egg in a small bowl. Add the egg and crumbled cheese to the mixture and stir to combine. Set aside.

Assemble the pies: Line two baking sheets with parchment.

In a medium bowl, add 1 cup of olive oil and 1 cup of melted butter and stir briefly to combine. Scoop a generous amount of the fat mixture onto a clean work surface. Rub the fat into the surface and coat your hands with it as well. Place a piece of dough on the greased surface and add another small scoop of the fat mixture on top. Massage the oiled dough into the work surface using a gentle, round swirling motion while applying pressure to start flattening the dough against the counter. Once the disk is about 6 inches in diameter, stretch the dough as thin as you can by running your hands from the center of the dough toward the edges, going for more of a rectangular shape at this point. If you feel your hands getting dry, dip them in the fat mixture again. Continue running your hands from the center of the dough out to the edges until the dough is very thin and completely transparent. Some tearing of the dough is OK, as the tears will be covered up as you roll the pie.

Place about ⅓ cup of filling along the long edge at the base of the dough and roll the dough around the filling, continuing to roll the dough and pulling and stretching it into a thin rope as you roll up to the top of the dough. Pick up the rope from the center with your thumb and forefinger and hold the two ends of the rope with your other hand as you twist with the hand you picked up the dough with. Continue twisting the dough so it coils in on itself into a knotted pastry. Transfer the pastry to one of the prepared baking sheets and repeat with the remaining dough and filling. Limit 6 pastries per baking sheet to leave ample room for baking.

Bake: Preheat the oven to 325°F.

In a small bowl, beat the egg and water. Brush the pies with the egg wash and sprinkle sesame seeds over the top. Bake the pies for 40 to 45 minutes, until golden brown. Let cool slightly before serving.

Rye Puff Pastry Galette de Rois

Puff pastry is one of those special things that you can do just about anything with—roll it up and make palmiers (a sweet, flaky French cookie), cut it into squares and bake it on top of broccoli-cheese soup, wrap up mini wieners . . . you get the idea. In this case, I'm using it as the base for a galette de rois, or a "king cake," which is essentially a giant frangipane sandwich.

Note: It is traditional, though optional, to place a single bean or an almond randomly into the frangipane before baking. The person who receives this in their piece is declared the King or Queen of the evening. You decide what that honor comes with.

Makes 1 (10-inch) galette

For the Puff Pastry:

Ingredient	Weight	Volume	Baker's %
Total flour			100.00%
>>Bread flour	450g	3½ cups	80.40%
>>Rye flour	110g	1 cup	19.60%
Cold water	280g	1 cup plus 3 tablespoons	50.00%
Softened unsalted butter	56g	¼ cup	10.00%
Fine sea salt	11.2g	2 teaspoons	2.00%
Fresh lemon juice	5.6g	1 teaspoon	1.00%
Unsalted butter rolled into an 8-by-6-inch rectangle for lamination (see page 273)	450g		

For the Frangipane:

Ingredient	Weight	Volume
Pastry cream (page 282)	½ recipe	(omit pistachio paste)
Powdered sugar	100g	¾ cup plus 2 tablespoons
Unsalted butter	100g	½ cup
Almond flour	65g	⅔ cup
Large egg	55g	1 whole
Large egg yolk	20g	1 each
Cornstarch	20g	2 tablespoons plus 2 teaspoons
Almond extract	3g	1 teaspoon
Vanilla bean paste or extract (see note on page 86)	3g	1 teaspoon
Fine sea salt	1g	¼ teaspoon

For the Egg Wash:

Ingredient	Volume
Large egg	1 whole
Water	1 tablespoon

Mix the dough: In the bowl of a stand mixer fitted with the dough hook attachment, add the bread flour, cold water, rye flour, softened butter, salt, and lemon juice. Mix on low speed for 4 minutes, or until the mixture is thoroughly combined and no dry spots of flour remain. The dough will be quite stiff.

Transfer the dough to a baking sheet and, using your hands, flatten the dough into a rectangle measuring about 8 by 15 inches. Cover with plastic wrap and refrigerate for 2 hours.

Make the frangipane: In the bowl of a food processor, add the pastry cream, powdered sugar, butter, almond flour, whole egg, egg yolk, cornstarch, almond extract, vanilla, and salt. Process until a smooth batter forms. Scoop the batter into a piping bag fitted with a large round tip or a large zip-top plastic bag. Refrigerate until ready to use.

Laminate the dough: Laminate the dough and butter sheet with a single-layer lock-in and perform five letter folds (see page 275). Be sure to perform no more than two folds at a time and rest the dough, covered, in the refrigerator for at least 1 hour between working the dough. When done, let the dough rest, covered, in the refrigerator for at least 1 more hour, or overnight.

Assemble: Line a baking sheet with parchment.

Lightly flour a work surface. Use a rolling pin to roll the pastry to about ⅛ inch thick, aiming for a rectangle shape about 11 by 21 inches. Cut out one 10-inch circle from the sheet of pastry. Reserve the remaining pastry dough and transfer the pastry disk to the prepared baking sheet.

Pipe a 9-inch circle of frangipane over the disk of dough, filling in the circle but leaving an empty 1-inch ring at the edge of the pastry, which will become a sealable crust. If you like a lot of filling, you could do two layers of frangipane. In fact, it's pretty good, so maybe go ahead and do that. If you're going the surprise-bean/almond route (see note), this is when you'd add it.

Continued

Dip a pastry brush in a bit of water and lightly moisten the edge of the dough. Set aside.

Cut an 11-inch disk from the sheet of remaining pastry. Drape it over the frangipane, pressing lightly at first to remove any air pockets, then more firmly on the outer ring where the two doughs will meet to seal nicely. Cover and refrigerate for at least 1 hour before baking. If you'd like to serve this warm, refrigerate until about an hour and a half before baking.

Bake: Preheat the oven to 425°F.

In a small bowl, whisk the egg and water. Brush the pastry with the egg wash and, if desired, lightly etch a decorative design on top using the tip of a knife or a razor. Additionally, cut four to six 1-inch slits through the pastry to release steam as the galette bakes.

Place the pastry in the oven and immediately decrease the temperature to 400°F. Bake for 30 to 40 minutes, until the pastry is deeply golden, puffy, and fragrant. Serve warm or at room temperature. If you do use an almond or bean, remind your guests to be on the lookout and not choke on it.

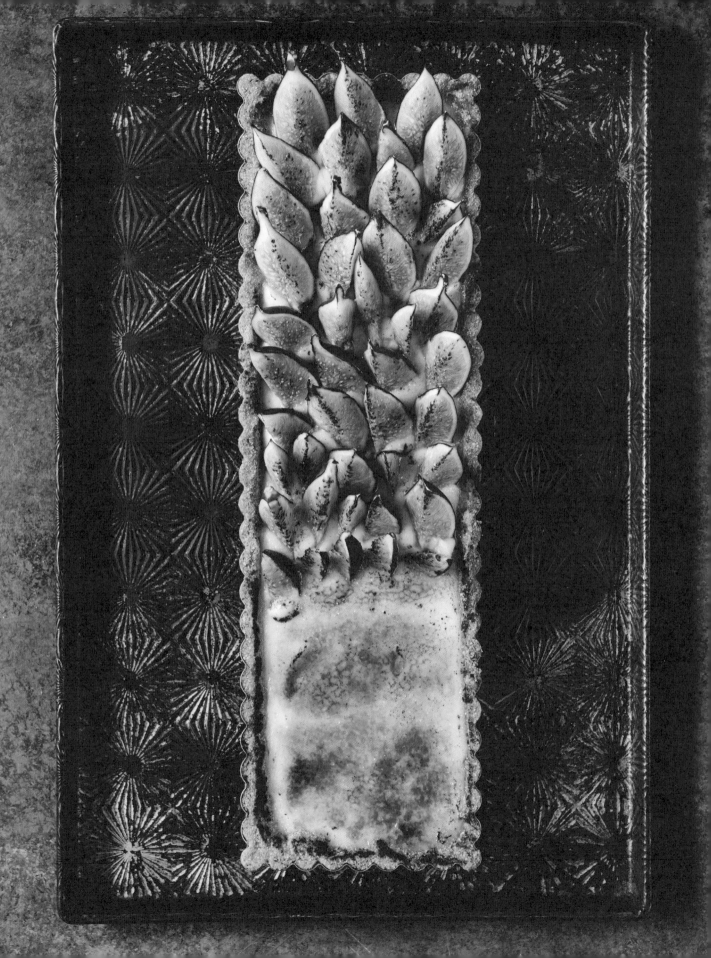

Sorghum Shortbread Fig Tart

The quintessential shortbread tart crust is buttery and sandy—exactly what you get when inviting sorghum into the mix. To help it really shine and show off the versatility of this crop, I also add sorghum syrup to the pastry cream. A sibling of the sorghum grain, sorghum syrup tastes a lot like honey that's been hanging out in a barn—treacly sweet, with just a hint of funk. If you'd prefer a more traditional sweetener, local honey will work just fine. I like topping this tart with brûléed figs because the deep richness of the sorghum pastry cream plus the earthiness of the fruit plus the smokiness of the burnt sugar is a damn fine combination. That said, any fresh soft fruit in season will get the job done.

Note: I like to use a 14-by-5-inch pan for this, but a 9-inch round one is fine, too.

Makes 1 tart

For the Shortbread Crust:

Ingredient	Weight	Volume	Baker's %
Total flour			100.00%
>>Sorghum flour	260g	2 cups	63.41%
>>All-purpose flour	150g	1 cup + 2 tablespoons	36.59%
Cooking spray, for greasing			
Unsalted butter	225g	1 cup	54.88%
Granulated sugar	100g	½ cup	24.39%
Fine sea salt	2g	½ teaspoon	0.49%

For the Sorghum Pastry Cream:

Ingredient	Weight	Volume	Baker's %
Whole milk	450g	1¾ cups plus 1½ tablespoons	100.00%
Sorghum syrup	200g	⅔ cup	35.56%
Large egg yolks	100g	6 each	22.22%
Cornstarch	20g	2 tablespoons plus 2 teaspoons	4.44%
Fine sea salt	3g	¼ teaspoon	0.67%
Unsalted butter	50g	¼ cup	11.11%
Vanilla bean paste or extract (see note on page 86)	10g	1 tablespoon	2.22%

Continued

For the Topping:

Ingredient	Volume
Figs	20
Sugar	½ cup

Make the shortbread: Coat a tart shell with cooking spray.

In the bowl of a food processor, combine the sorghum flour, butter, all-purpose flour, sugar, and salt and process until a dough forms, 2 to 3 minutes.

Lightly flour a work surface and turn out the dough. Use a rolling pin to roll the dough to about ¼ inch thick. Place the dough in the prepared tart shell and press it into place around the edges. Trim off any excess dough from the top of the tart pan (which you could also use to patch any places that may need more dough.) Place the tart shell on a baking sheet and refrigerate for 30 minutes.

Bake the shell: Preheat the oven to 350°F.

Prick the bottom of the chilled tart shell all over with a fork. Bake for 20 to 25 minutes, until the shell is golden brown and crisp. Set aside to cool.

Make the pastry cream: In a medium saucepan over medium heat, slowly bring the milk to a boil. Remove from the heat.

In a medium bowl, combine the sorghum syrup, egg yolks, cornstarch, and salt and whisk until smooth, about 2 minutes. Continue whisking as you slowly pour the hot milk over the egg mixture. The key to avoid scrambling the eggs here is to add the milk in a slow, steady stream while whisking constantly to temper the eggs.

Set the pan back over high heat and whisk constantly as you bring the mixture to a boil. Reduce the heat to medium-high and cook for 3 more minutes, continuing to whisk constantly. The pastry cream base should be quite thick at this point. Whisk in the butter and vanilla and pour the thickened custard into the baked tart shell. Gently place plastic wrap directly on the surface of the pastry cream and refrigerate for at least 3 hours or overnight.

Top the tart: Cut the figs in half lengthwise down the meridian, not the equator. Cut each half into three wedges lengthwise so they are crescent-shaped. Place the figs pointed-side up into the pastry cream and repeat with more figs until the entire surface of the cream is covered. Dust the figs generously with sugar, brûlée with a torch, and enjoy.

Sourdough Pizzelles

Way back when, I used to work at Culver's, a burger and ice cream chain in the Midwest. What always reminds me of that time is the smell of waffle cones baking, or in this case, waffle cones' flat alter ego, the pizzelle. It's the signature scent of ice cream shops everywhere, and it doesn't get more warm and fuzzy than that. These pizzelles get a complexity bump from incorporating a sourdough starter (a great way to use up more of the excess that would otherwise be thrown away). They don't get sour necessarily, just richer. For that reason, you can also use this recipe to make straight-up waffle batter, which you can ferment in the fridge overnight and pour into the waffle maker in the morning. You can thank me later for the way your house will smell after baking these—and for changing your life when you add a scoop of **Malted Grain Ice Cream** (page 300).

Note: You will need a pizzelle maker for these, but as mentioned earlier, you could instead just turn these into ice cream-topped waffles. Breakfast be damned.

Makes 24 pizzelles

Ingredient	Weight	Volume	Baker's %
Total flour			100.00%
>>Active sourdough starter	500g	4 cups	100.00%
Whole milk	100g	⅓ cup plus 1 tablespoon	20.00%
Large egg	55g	1 whole	11.00%
Melted unsalted butter	50g	¼ cup	10.00%
Raw sugar	50g	¼ cup	10.00%
Vanilla bean paste or extract (see note on page 86)	10g	1 tablespoon	2.00%
Fine sea salt	8g	1½ teaspoons	1.60%
Baking soda	7g	2 teaspoons	1.40%

Heat a pizzelle maker or waffle iron while you make the batter.

In a large bowl, add the sourdough starter, milk, egg, butter, sugar, vanilla, salt, and baking soda. Whisk to combine until completely homogeneous, about 2 minutes.

Add a 2-tablespoon scoop of batter into each section of the hot pizzelle or waffle iron. Cook until golden brown, 3 to 4 minutes. Allow the pizzelles to cool for a few minutes before serving so they crisp up. Or, if desired, roll the freshly cooked pizzelle into a cone shape while it's still warm, let cool, and fill with ice cream. Store any leftovers in an airtight container for up to a week.

Malted Grain Ice Cream

Erika Chan, the pastry chef at the Publican, developed this recipe for one of my Bread Camps, and the reason I included it here is because I want you to see how you can use grains in ways other than as flour. What you're doing in this case is steeping malted grain (sold at brewery supply stores) into an ice cream base, which will impart its naturally sweet-grain flavor—not dissimilar to the effect you get from cereal soaking in milk. It's a technique that you can use any time you're making a custard, such as for panna cotta or crème brûlée. And this ice cream wouldn't be half bad on many of the baked goods in this book, especially the Oat Galette with Seasonal Fruit (page 97) or the Sourdough Pizzelles (page 299).

Note: You'll see that ice cream stabilizer is optional in this recipe; it will improve the texture of your ice cream but is not necessary for success. I turn to my friend and pastry chef Dana Cree for all things ice cream. In her book *Hello, My Name Is Ice Cream,* Dana explains that while "stabilizer" has a bad reputation, in this context "ice cream stabilizer" is a combination of milk protein, starch, and pectin that work in tandem to prevent water crystals from forming in your ice cream, resulting in a smoother, creamier dessert.

Makes 1 quart

Ingredient	Weight	Volume	Baker's %
Whole milk	450g	1¾ cups plus 2 tablespoons	100.00%
Heavy cream	280g	1¼ cups	62.22%
Malted grain	60g	⅓ cup	13.33%
Sugar	140g	¾ cup	31.11%
Glucose syrup	45g	¼ cup	10.00%
Milk powder	30g	¼ cup	6.67%
Ice cream stabilizer (optional)	4g	2 teaspoons	0.89%
Fine sea salt	3g	½ teaspoon	0.67%

In a large saucepan over medium-high heat, combine the milk and cream. Whisk as the mixture heats and comes to a simmer. Add the malted grain, remove the pan from the heat, cover, and set aside to steep for 1 hour.

In a medium bowl, add the sugar, glucose, milk powder, stabilizer (if using), and salt and whisk to combine. Set aside. Prepare an ice bath in a large bowl and set this aside as well.

Strain the grains from the milk mixture and return the pot to the stove over medium-high heat to bring to a boil. Add the sugar mixture and bring back to a simmer, whisking constantly. Continue simmering for 1 minute. Remove the pan from the heat and strain the mixture into a large bowl set over the ice bath. Once the mixture cools completely, cover the bowl with plastic wrap and refrigerate overnight.

Use an ice cream maker to churn the mixture according to the manufacturer's instructions. Pack the ice cream into a freezer-safe container and freeze until solid, about 4 hours.

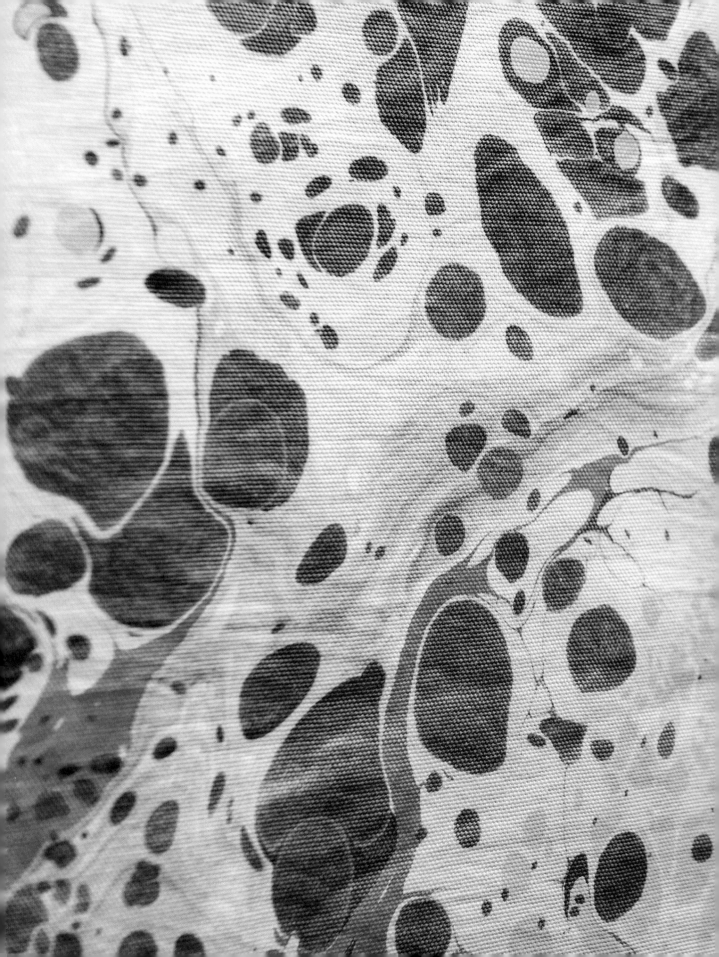

PART III

Digging Deeper

Troubleshooting and Taking Things to the Next Level

Fermentation Experimentation

ALL OF THE RECIPES IN THIS BOOK DESCRIBE THE RECOMMENDED length of time you should ferment your dough, and at what (rough) temperature. This is based on my experience and understanding of how these two variables—time and temperature—will affect the final outcome of your bread. However, my goal for you is to understand *why* these times and temps look the way they do. In doing this, you'll be able to have a more instinctive feel for what your dough needs and why. Which means more confidence, flexibility, and predictability in the face of the great fermented unknown.

Making bread is all about controlling your variables. We start with controlling what we put into the mix and in what ratio, in order to develop good gluten and dough strength, as well as proper hydration of the dough. Then we have to nurture the young dough into a mature one full of character, flavor, and culture. We do that by curating proper fermentation of the dough. We have ultimately three variables when talking about fermentation itself:

- *Available food* (sugar) for fermentation: This is determined by the amount of starter added to the mix. If we add too much (more yeast and bacteria) to our dough, it will break down and digest the flour too quickly, developing too much acid before expelling enough gas to leaven the bread properly. If we add too little, it will not ferment quickly enough. Remember, as the dough sits, it will relax—that is the nature of how gluten works. The more relaxed the dough, the less gas it will trap. The dough will become too relaxed to trap the gas necessary for leavening and could take an extremely long time to develop flavor. Keep your starter between 10 and 20 percent of your total dough weight if developing recipes yourself, or follow the recipes in this book for guidelines.

- *Temperature* (rate of fermentation): Desired dough temperature is a major tool for success when talking about bread baking, for professional bakers and home bakers alike. We aim for 78° to 82°F depending on the time of year and ambient temperature of the bakery. Bacteria and yeast are more active at warmer temperatures (75° to 90°F; yeast starts dying at 120°F), which means they will break down and digest the available food (flour) at a faster rate. They are less active at cooler temperatures (65° to 70°F) and, while still active, ferment at a much slower rate. A dough mixed to 80°F can be ready in about 3 hours of bulk fermentation, whereas a dough mixed to 70°F can take 6 hours to be ready. Below 50°F you're not going to get much yeast activity at all.

- *Time* (length of fermentation): Time and temperature have an inverse relationship in fermentation. As temperature goes up, your fermentation time needs to go down. As temperature goes down, your length of time to ferment the dough needs to increase.

The key to good bread dough is maintaining a balanced control of these three variables. We know that as the dough ferments, it builds acid and will expand (leaven) due to the gases given off during fermentation. We also know that developing too much acid will weaken our dough, but also that if we don't catch enough of the gas our bread will be dense. Our goal is to develop enough acid to be flavorful, while leavening it enough to be palatable. If you follow the recipes in this book, the ratio of starter to the rest of the dough will be proper. But as you also know, life sometimes isn't as simple as following a recipe, and no two bakes are exactly the same. Which brings me to:

Maintaining a Baking Log

The best way to hone your fermentation skills is to keep a log. You want to track the room temperature, temperature of water used, final dough temperature, total bulk fermentation time, and final (individual loaves once shaped) fermentation time. Also keep a notes section and write down your experience with the dough. It can look something like this:

Bread Type:	Sourdough	Dough made on {Date}:

Room Temp:

75°

Water Temp:

80°

Final Dough Temp:

80°

Bulk Fermentation Time:

3 Hours

Individual Fermentation Time Once Shaped:

2 Hours

Notes:

Mixed in morning, kitchen was cool at first but rose in temp as morning went on.

Used starter 3 hours after feeding. Gave 3 stretch and folds throughout 3-hour bulk fermentation period.

Room was closer to 78°F once bread was shaped.

Bread Type:

Dough made on {Date}:

Room Temp:

Water Temp:

Final Dough Temp:

Bulk Fermentation Time:

Individual Fermentation Time Once Shaped:

Notes:

Bread Type:

Dough made on {Date}:

Total Proof Time:

Bake Temperature:

Final Bake Time:

Crust:

Crumb:

Tasting Notes:

If you make more than one dough, you can add more rows.

You can keep your notes as detailed as you want, because all the little things when making bread dough can add up to something big. For example, panettone is so finicky I always play holiday music when mixing it, just to be safe.

Calculating Desired Dough Temperature

Sooner or later you're going to get to the point where you want to intentionally control the temperature of your dough, rather than just track what temperature it comes out at once it is mixed. Why? Because when you have the ability to control this variable, then you're able to bake consistent loaves in any setting, versus just reacting to what might come at you. Often this has to do with the weather outside. Cooler days in the bakery mean we mix our doughs warmer so they ferment properly. The heat of the summer means we mix cooler so we don't hate our lives when dough is exploding everywhere. We do this by calculating our desired water temperature. All of the recipes in this book suggest doing this, so maybe that's something you're ready to add to your baking-tool repertoire.

To determine your water temperature, you need to know the rest of the variables having an effect on temperature of the dough:

DDT   Desired dough temperature

WT   Water temperature

FT   Flour temperature

ST   Starter temperature

RT   Room temperature

FF   Friction factor

We then use the following formula to determine desired dough temperature:

$$WT = DDT \times 4 - (FT + ST + RT + FF)$$

And here's the kicker: To accurately calculate the water temperature you should be using for your dough, you'll need to make the same dough more than once. This is because of the FF above, something called the friction factor. This is the amount of heat added to the dough during the mixing process. This number will be large (30 to 40) if you are using an electric mixer or small

(5 to 10) if mixing by hand. This will be pretty consistent once you figure it out for that dough and that mixer. The way to do this is to solve for FF instead of WT, so on your first mix you will take the temperature of the water, flour, starter, and room. Your friction factor will be unknown and initially your dough temp will be unknown. Take the temperature of the flour, starter, room, and water used and mix your dough until you are happy with it. Then take the temperature of the dough once you are done. Lastly, use the following formula:

$$FF = DDT \times 4 - (FT + ST + RT + WT)$$

Say we have the following temperatures:

Dough temperature = 79

Flour temp = 70

Starter temp = 78

Room temp = 72

Water temp = 75

Our formula will be this:

$$\text{Friction factor} = 79 \times 4 - (70 + 78 + 72 + 75)$$

$$\text{Friction factor} = 316 - (295)$$

$$\text{Friction factor} = 21$$

We now have the friction factor for this dough and this mixer. In the future, we can control our dough temperature in advance of mixing. Say it is winter and our kitchen is cool. We want to mix our dough warmer than usual in order to have it ferment better in a cool room, so we choose to mix to 82°F. We still take the temperature of the flour, starter, and room.

Desired dough temperature (we choose) = 82

Flour = 68

Starter = 75

Room = 68

Friction factor = 21 (We already calculated this, and it should remain constant.)

We now solve for the water temperature we want to use in our mix:

$$WT = DDT \times 4 - (FT + ST + RT + FF)$$

$$WT = 82 \times 4 - (68 + 75 + 68 + 21)$$

$$\text{Water temp} = 328 - (232)$$

$$\text{Water temp} = 96$$

We will use 96°F water in our mix. But you should still take the temperature of the dough once you are finished! We want to control the temperature the dough comes out at in order to control our fermentation, but you need to verify it is the correct temperature! If the dough comes out *cooler* than you desire, you will need to *increase* fermentation time. If the dough comes our *warmer* than you desire, you will *decrease* fermentation time. Make sure to keep notes in your log. Here's a good starting point: For every degree you are up or down from your desired temp, you should increase or decrease your fermentation time by 7 minutes. So if your desired temperature is 80°F and your dough comes out at 76°F, you should increase your fermentation time by 28 minutes. If your desired dough temperature is 80°F and your dough comes out at 82°F, decrease your fermentation time by 14 minutes.

I know this might seem like a lot of extra work, and you will notice that I intentionally do not call for a lot of these processes in the bulk of the book. But with practice, time, and increasing comfort working with dough, you'll find that this extra layer of attention to detail yields an even better product. And what can be more rewarding than even more delicious bread?

Baker's Percentages and Building Your Own Recipes

Bakers use a way of expressing a recipe (what we call a formula) called baker's percentage. In this way of writing recipes, all ingredients are expressed as a ratio relative to the amount of flour used, or in cases where there is no flour in the recipe, the main ingredient (such as milk in a pastry cream). By doing this, we are able to easily scale the recipes up or down to suit the needs of production and have the product remain the same.

Let's start easy. Here is a super basic sourdough bread recipe:

Ingredient	Weight	Baker's %
Bread flour	1000 grams	100%
Water	750 grams	75%
Active sourdough starter	200 grams	20%
Salt	20 grams	2%

In this recipe, bread flour is the only flour we are using and is expressed as 100% (as it always is when treated as the main ingredient). Water is 75%, which means for every 1000 grams of flour, there will be 750 grams of water. Starter is 20%, so for every 1000 grams of flour, there will be 200 grams of starter. Salt is 2%, so for every 1000 grams of flour, there will be 20 grams of salt.

Now, take a look at the next recipe. This is the same formula, meaning we have the same ratio of ingredients. The weights are different, so we technically have a different recipe, but we are making the same bread, just more of it. To find the weights we will use, we take the flour weight that we want and multiply it by the percentages of each ingredient. In this case, we are using

2500 grams of flour. So to find water, we multiply 2500 × 0.75, which gives us 1875 grams.

Ingredient	Weight	Baker's %
Bread flour	2500 grams	100%
Water	1875 grams	75%
Active sourdough starter	500 grams	20%
Salt	50 grams	2%

Next, we will add another flour. Remember, flour is always 100%, so if we use more than one flour in a recipe, we express those as follows:

Ingredient	Weight	Baker's %
Total Flour	1000 grams	100%
Bread flour	800 grams	80%
Wheat flour	200 grams	20%
Water	750 grams	75%
Active sourdough starter	200 grams	20%
Salt	20 grams	2%

As you can see, the water, sourdough starter, and salt are still expressed as a ratio in comparison to the total flour. Bread flour and wheat flour are broken down and expressed as a ratio of total flour, but they must always add up to 100% (80% + 20% = 100%).

So how is this used in practice? In the bakery, we need to calculate the amount of dough we need each day to fill our orders. If I have orders for 40 loaves of sourdough, and each loaf is going to weigh 900 grams, I need 36 kilograms of dough. I then update a recipe to make sure I have more than that amount of dough weight.

For those of us who are baking at home, not at a bakery, using baker's percentages is useful when creating recipes. When I am coming up with a bread recipe, I am always thinking of an end texture in mind, which is going to come from the total hydration from water or any ingredient added that contains water (butter, milk, eggs, etc.) and the flours used. I then think about fermentation flavors and, finally, how I'll fit this into production. Do I want this to be a crusty loaf with whole-grain-forward textures and flavors? Do I want this bread to be able to be made in one day because that is how it will fit best in production, or would I rather be able to make the bread one day and then bake it the next? Should I add any extra sweetness to the bread, or will the fermentation add enough sugar? Do I want the bread to be soft and supple with a closed crumb?

Overall, I design recipes while thinking about final hydration, fat content, sweetness, fermentation, production methods, and, lastly, any mix-ins or garnishes that would be appropriate.

Here are a few ratios and general rules of thumb for creating some common breads:

General rules for all dough recipes

- Do not preferment more than 30% of your total flour weight. It will cause your dough to deteriorate.

- Whole grains absorb more water than white flour. If the flour in your formula is all whole-grain flour with no white flour, increase your water by 10% to 15%. If your formula contains half the flour weight in whole-grain flour, increase your water by 5% to 7%.

- Do not be afraid of salt. Even if you prefer a low-sodium diet, or less-salty foods, do not just omit the salt! It plays an important role in fermentation and dough development.

- Your ingredients and ratios are the building blocks for your bread. Where your bread gains character and life is during the fermentation process, so always take into consideration *time* and *temperature* when you are thinking of your bread recipes.

- Your "total hydration" includes more than just water:

Common ingredients and their water contents

Ingredient	Water Content
Egg white	87.6%
Milk	87%
Whole egg	76%
Cream	58%
Egg yolk	48%
Molasses	22%
Honey	17%
Butter	15%

How to use this in practice

Say you are making a milk bread recipe. It may look something like this:

Ingredient	Weight	Baker's %
Flour	1000g	100%
Milk	700g	70%
Salt	20g	2%
Yeast	5g	0.5%

What is our total hydration? We take the milk weight (700 grams) and multiply that by the water content percentage in the table above to find the total water content: $700 \times 0.87 = 609$ grams of water. So even though this recipe has 700 grams of milk in it, and is technically 70% hydrated, the dough will *feel* and *behave* like it is 60.9% hydrated.

Here is an example of a more complex recipe and how we would calculate that hydration:

Ingredient	Weight	Baker's %
Flour	1000g	100%
Milk	600g	60%
Honey	100g	10%
Butter	100g	10%
Salt	20g	2%
Yeast	5g	0.5%

So in this recipe, we have milk, honey, and butter all contributing to the overall hydration of the dough. We can calculate our total hydration as follows:

$$\text{Milk} = 700 \times 0.87 = 609 \text{ grams}$$

$$\text{Honey} = 100 \times 0.17 = 17 \text{ grams}$$

$$\text{Butter} = 100 \times 0.15 = 15 \text{ grams}$$

Added up, we have $609 + 17 + 15 = 641$ total grams water, so this dough will behave as if it is 64.1% hydrated.

This also works if we are making a dough with water and adding honey as a sweetener:

Ingredient	Weight	Baker's %
Flour	1000g	100%
Water	750g	75%
Honey	150g	15%
Active sourdough starter	150g	15%
Salt	20g	2%

So in this recipe we have water and honey contributing to the hydration. We take honey $(150 \times 0.17) = 25$ grams of water. Our total hydration becomes $750 + 25 = 775$ grams of water, so we have a total dough hydration of 77.5%.

Lean Doughs

Lean doughs contain only flour/grain, water, leavening (sourdough starter or yeast), and salt.

Ingredient	Acceptable baker's % ratio	Notes
Total flour	100%	This line must always be 100%. You can break down that 100% into more than one type of flour, but all the flour added up must equal 100%.
Water	57–90% is acceptable. Sourdough bread will usually be more like 75–85% total.	This is a big ratio, but this, along with the types of flour used, is what will make the largest difference in lean breads' flavor and texture. Remember to adjust your *total* hydration based on your ingredients used.
Active sourdough starter (if using)	10–20%	This ratio will leaven bread. The reason you may want to use more or less will depend on the rate at which you want to ferment your bread, or the temperature at which you will be fermenting. If your kitchen is notoriously warm in the summer months, use less starter because the warm environment will encourage your dough to ferment quickly. It is the opposite in winter.
Active dry yeast (if using)	0.5–2%	More yeast means faster fermentation
Salt	1.5–2.5%	Salt will not only season your bread but also control fermentation rate and improve gluten structure. More salt will restrict the fermentation rate, causing your dough to take more time to ferment.
Chunky garnish (nuts, seeds, etc.)	0–25% total	Use up to 25% total if using more than one type of nut or seed.
Herbs and spices	0–3%	Herbs and spices go a long way in bread, so usually less than 3% is necessary to perfume the bread.

General rules for lean dough recipes

- Your fermentation time and temperature, along with your flour and hydration choices, will be most apparent in this style bread.

- An autolyse (see page 123) is recommended for this type of bread.

- If mixing higher-hydration (75%+) doughs, it is recommended to withhold a small amount of the water and incorporate it after the autolyse.

- Incorporate nuts, seeds, herbs, spices after mixing to the desired gluten quality, before bulk fermentation.

Enriched Doughs

Enriched doughs are called such because they are "enriched" by the addition of things like butter, eggs, milk, or oil. Enriched doughs are softer than lean doughs, with a more closed cell structure to their crumbs.

Ingredient	Acceptable baker's % ratio	Notes
Total flour	100%	This line must always be 100%. You can break down that 100% into more than one type of flour, but all the flour added up must equal 100%.
Total hydration	57–90% is acceptable. Sourdough bread will usually be more like 75–85% total.	This is a big ratio, but this, along with the types of flour used, is what will make the largest difference in lean breads' flavor and texture. Remember to adjust your *total* hydration based on your ingredients used.
Eggs	0–75%	Remember when using eggs that you are gaining more than just moisture—you are gaining fat and protein. The proteins in eggs will affect the texture of the finished product. Generally you will not use eggs as the only liquid in a bread.
Fat (butter, olive oil, etc.)	0–20% for common enriched doughs, 50–80% for brioche	More fat will inhibit gluten development and also require more leavening power or time. Brioches are loaded with enrichment, so plan to use 50–80%; for an enriched bread for sandwich bread or challah, use up to 20%.
Sweetener (honey, sugar, molasses)	0–15% for general added sweetness in an enriched dough, 15–35% for very sweet breads	With higher amounts of sugar, make sure to switch to Saf-Instant Gold yeast. This type of yeast isn't affected by the fact that high amounts of sugar will pull active water from the dough and create an environment not conducive to yeast activity. You can also "train" your sourdough starter to be osmotolerant by adding 20 percent sugar to your feed.
Active sourdough starter (if using)	15–25%	This ratio will leaven bread; keep in mind that enriched doughs require more leavening power. The reason you may want to use more or less will depend on the rate at which you want to ferment your bread, or the temperature at which you will be fermenting. If your kitchen is notoriously warm in the summer months, use less starter because the warm environment will encourage your dough to ferment quickly. It is the opposite in winter.
Salt	1.5–3.5%	Salt will not only season your bread but also control fermentation rate and improve gluten structure. More salt will restrict the fermentation rate, causing your dough to take more time to ferment. The salt ratio should be higher when increasing the amount of enrichment, such as a significant amount of butter or eggs.
Active dry yeast (if using)	0.5–3%	More yeast means faster fermentation.
Chunky garnish (nuts, seeds, chunks of cheese, etc.)	0–25% total	Use up to 25% total if using more than one type of nut or seed.
Herbs and spices	0–3%	Herbs and spices go a long way in bread, so usually less than 3% is necessary to perfume the bread.

General rules for enriched dough recipes

- Your fermentation temperature is still very important in enriched doughs. Higher than 85°F will create greasy products if using butter as fat.

- An autolyse is not needed for this type of bread.

- If mixing breads with higher amounts (15%+) of fat, it is recommended to withhold the fat until good gluten strength is developed in the dough. Incorporate the fat from a softened state on slow speed until fully incorporated in the dough.

- Sugars will also soften the dough.

- Reduce baking temperatures for doughs with added sugar as they will caramelize more quickly.

- As enrichment increases, so should yeast/leavening and salt.

- It will be easier to be successful with enriched sourdough products if a small (0.25 to 0.5%) amount of commercial yeast is also added to the dough.

- Incorporate nuts, seeds, herbs, spices after mixing to the desired gluten quality, before bulk fermentation.

General Reference for Fermentation Times

Once you have developed your dough, use these guidelines for proofing times:

- As dough temperature and/or room temperature increases, *shorten* your bulk and individual fermentation time.

- As dough temperature and/or room temperature decreases, *increase* your bulk and individual fermentation time.

Use these times as guidelines. Always look for signs of proper dough development and proofing to guide your breadmaking decisions. Generally doughs will double in size during bulk fermentation, and just under double in individual fermentation.

Type of bread	Bulk fermentation time	Individual fermentation time
Lean (sourdough leavened)	3–4 hours at 75°F	1–2 hours at 75°F, then often refrigerated overnight
Lean (commercial yeast)	2 hours at 75°F	1 hour at 75°F
Enriched (sourdough leavened)	6–8 hours at 75°F	3–4 hours at 75°F
Enriched (sourdough leavened with added yeast)	3–4 hours at 75°F	1–2 hours at 75°F
Enriched (commercial yeast)	2–3 hours at 75°F	1–2 hours at 75°F
Brioche (sourdough leavened)	4–5 hours at 75°F, then refrigerate overnight	5–6 hours at 75°F once shaped
Brioche (commercial yeast)	2–3 hours at 75°F, then refrigerate overnight	3–4 hours at 75°F once shaped

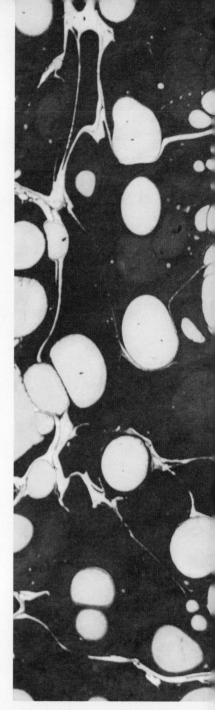

Troubleshooting: Help, Everything's on Fire!

THERE ARE ALWAYS GOING TO BE TIMES WHEN THINGS JUST DON'T go your way. Remember, this takes practice! And at the end of the day, it's about the journey.

I forgot to incorporate salt at the right time. The solution to this will depend on how much time has passed since you were supposed to add the salt. If it's been 30 minutes to an hour, just go ahead and squeeze it in right away and restart your bulk fermentation time. If it has been longer than that (2+ hours), you've got a couple options:

- *Option 1:* If the dough still feels strong, you can incorporate the salt now and reduce your bulk fermentation time slightly to compensate for the time you've already given it.

- *Option 2:* If the dough does not feel strong when you check on it, such as tearing very easily, it may be best to use the dough as pâte fermentée. This is a method of using old dough to leaven new dough. In this case, you'll be using the unsalted dough to leaven new bread, and this time you will remember to include the salt. You'll end up with more dough and bread than you wanted, but sometimes you need to just double down and commit to being a bread head.

I forgot to incorporate the sourdough starter at the right time. There is nothing more frustrating than realizing you've forgotten the starter in a mix. Luckily, since there is no fermentation happening, you can simply add it as soon as you remember, making sure to squeeze the dough by hand to incorporate it fully. Watch for breakdown of the dough, though—if you work it too much at this stage, you could destroy the gluten matrix and create weak dough. If that happens, stick to baking a pan bread with this mix.

I've overmixed my dough. You'll know you've overmixed if your dough is stringy—think taffy in the summertime. It will also likely be warm or even hot to the touch. But be careful not to mistake the extensibility of a high-hydration sourdough for overmixing. It's also very difficult to overmix if you're mixing by hand.

Anyway, doughs that have been overmixed will not make spectacular hearth loaves, but if you're determined not to throw away your dough and start again, here's what I suggest:

1. Refrigerate the dough for the first hour of fermentation. Give it a fold, then finish your bulk ferment at room temp. I would also suggest reducing your bulk proof time by about 45 minutes.
2. If you can pre-shape your dough and then get it into a loaf pan or onto a baking sheet, great. If not, just pour the dough into the pan or tray to make a focaccia-style bread.

I've undermixed my dough. This one is a lot easier to deal with. If you have undermixed or short-mixed your dough, just fold it more frequently during bulk fermentation. The extra folds will develop the required structure for your bread. For example, if your dough does not come to full gluten when you think it should have and you normally give the bread one fold after an hour, give it two or three folds every 30 to 45 minutes until you are happy with the bulk ferment.

My dough is too warm. This is not the end of the world unless your dough's temp is above 120°F, at which point you've killed your yeast and will need to start over. If you are in the upper 80s to mid 90s, while not a desired dough temp, a simple solution is to refrigerate the dough for the first hour of bulk fermentation. Fold it after that hour, then finish your bulk fermentation at room temp. Remember to reduce the shaped fermentation time by about half as well.

My dough is too cold. Once you've caught the baking bug, you'll start to do this thing where you'll wave your arms around while walking through your house, trying to feel for the warmer and colder areas. When your dough is too cold (70°F or below), this is the time to whip out that knowledge of your home's hot spots. Bulk ferment your dough on top of your radiator, in the kitchen with the oven turned on for added warmth, in a sunny corner of your living room, or somewhere that is going to add some gentle heat to your mix. You can also choose to drastically increase (I'm talking hours, not minutes) your bulk fermentation time. Remember, if you've added the sourdough starter, it will get there! It's just a matter of time.

My dough was strong when it came out, but now it's shredding. This is a sign of too much acid in your dough. Your dough temperature may be too warm, or your starter may have been overfermented, which creates a buildup of organic acids. You'll want to handle this loaf gently when shaping. Simple, gentle folds to shape the bread will be key. Shape into a basket, then refrigerate immediately. And use a very gentle hand when scoring, so it's more shallow than normal. The loaf may be smaller than normal, but it could still retain its shape and be salvageable.

My shaping didn't go as well as I wanted it to. By this I mean that it may have torn during shaping or the dough looks kind of uneven. Well, at least it'll still probably taste good, right? You can try to gently handle and coax the proofed loaf into a more pleasing aesthetic, or you can try to score the bread in a way that accentuates the unique shape your bread has chosen. Or you can full-on embrace it. Like my mom says, "You're going to be your own worst critic." If you don't point out that the bread is misshapen, no one will notice or care!

I forgot to score my bread. Well, that's just a shame. You got all the way to the end to not finish strong! But if you manage to remember soon enough (like less than a few minutes after your bread's been in the oven), you can try scoring ASAP. If it's been longer, you're just going to have to live with it. My guess is you won't make that mistake twice.

My bread is gaining too much color too quickly. If your loaf looks like toast or appears to be baked through but has not yet reached an internal temp of 200°F, drop the oven temp to about 325°F and continue baking until the loaf is fully baked through. If it continues to pick up color, make an aluminum foil tent and place it over the loaf to keep it from getting darker. In the future, start your bake at a lower temp for this particular bread.

My bread is not gaining enough color. This is a sign of a lack of available simple sugars in your bread. After all, bread gains color in the first place because of the Maillard reaction, or the caramelization of sugars. So if your bread doesn't gain color, or caramelize, you need to make sure some of those sugars are still available at the end of your fermentation and into the bake cycle. While there's not much you can do to remedy that fact once the bread is baking, you can increase your oven temperature to coax it into gaining color. In the future, reduce your bulk fermentation time and/or your individual fermentation time. The longer you ferment your dough, the more the bacteria will break down the starches (complex sugars) into simple sugars. Eventually the yeast will break down and ferment all of those simple sugars.

Acknowledgments

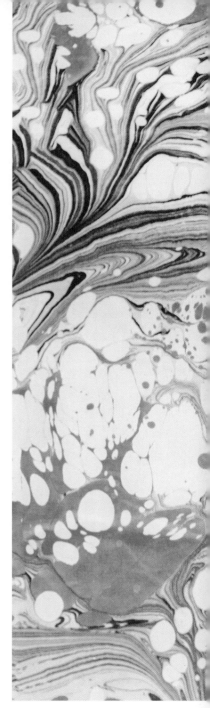

THIS BOOK HAS BEEN SEVERAL YEARS IN THE MAKING, AND I consider myself lucky to have so many people to thank for helping create it along the way. I hope that because of these thoughtful, talented, and dedicated people this book becomes greater than the sum of its parts, just as I feel I am made a better person for having known them.

First, thank you to Paul, who as a chef, mentor, and friend, pushed me to write this book in the first place, and for teaching me to make each day "better and better, every day better."

Thank you to Marty, Jill, Harold, Gary, Paul, and Lou. The dedication, knowledge, and passion each of you bring to your parts in agriculture and food production, and the humility with which you share that knowledge with me, is truly appreciated. You are the people that are making the world and our food systems better each day. I know farming and food production is often a thankless job, so even if no one else says it, let me say it here: thank you, thank you, thank you.

Thank you to my coauthor, Rachel, without whom this book would not be what it became. Your thoughtful approach to writing, ability to synthesize my sometimes (often) rambling discourses on bread and baking, and polite but firm way of sticking to a deadline is nothing short of a wonder to work with.

Thank you to Emily, Mollie, and Janelle; all three of you had such smooth professionalism and worked seamlessly to bring the vision for this book to life in the midst of a pandemic. The creativity, ingenuity, and talent with which you executed this project was astounding.

Thank you to Janis, you gave this first-time author the trust, time, and attention I needed to be comfortable writing a book. Thank you for never giving up on getting this book out there.

Thank you to Melanie Tortoroli and her team at W. W. Norton: Steve Attardo, Jessica Murphy, Devon Zahn, Will Scarlett, and Meredith McGinnis. Melanie, your guidance and patience throughout the process was monumental, and I'm sure way more difficult because you had to do it all remotely. The way everyone embraced the creativity of this project from design to layout and verbiage was inspiring. It truly takes a village to create a book!

Thank you to the teams that helped put this together: Paul Nielsen for design, Karen Wise for copyediting (when I saw you had an appreciation for the Dead, I knew we had the right person!), and Lynne Cannon for proofreading. There was so much more that went into this process than I knew, and I now have a much greater appreciation for cookbooks and the work you all do!

Thank you to the Publican Quality Bread team, for testing recipes, for supporting me while I took the time needed to write this book, and for always cranking out some of the best bread in the city.

Thank you to my parents, John and Laurie. Without your love and support, I would not be where I am today. Dad, baking with you on the weekends while growing up is a cherished memory—especially reaping the rewards of toasted rye bread with cheddar at the end. Your thoughtfulness and dedication as a father has moved me more than you know. Mom, your wild nature and "don't-tell-me-no" attitude to just get up and do what is in your heart is inspiring, whether that is opening your cafés or moving to another state in your 50s without a job or home, just to camp and experience the adventure.

And last but most important, thank you to my wife, Kayla. You are the most important person in my life and I cherish the love and support you give me each day. You are a patient, kind, caring, and beautiful person who I am lucky to share my life with. I love you.

Index

Note: Page references in *italics* indicate photographs.

A

acetic acids, 57, 58
alleopathic effect, 30
all-purpose flour, about, 39, 40
almond flour
    Frangipane, 293
    Marzipan, 259–61
almonds and almond paste
    Bee Sting Cake, 263–66, *265*
    Stollen, 259–62, *262*
Anson Mills, 30
Appam, 220–22, *221*
Appam, Egg, *221*, 222
apples
    Apple and Peanut Loaf, 133–34
    Spelt and Apple Muffins, 105–6
Artisan Grain Collaborative, 35
Asparagus, Spring Onion, and Fresno
    Pepper Pizzas, *208*, 217
autolysis (autolyse), 46, 123

B

Bacon-Rye Cheese Rolls, 253–55, *255*
bacteria, in sourdough, 57, 58
bagels
    Bagels, *192*, 193–95
    Cornmeal and Jalapeño Bagels, 196
    Rye and Blueberry Bagels, 196

baguettes
    Multigrain Baguette, 152–55, *153*
    scoring dough for, 54
    shaping dough for, 49–52
baker's percentages, 25, 313–21
baking log, 306–10
Banana Bread, Buckwheat, 86–87
basil
    Margarita Pizzas, 212, *212*
batards
    scoring dough for, 54
    shaping dough for, 52–53
Bee Sting Cake, 263–66, *265*
bench scraper, 45, 51
benne seeds. *See also* sesame seeds
    Carolina Gold, *140*, 141–43
biga, defined, 20
Biscuits, Whole-Wheat, 114–15
bleaching agents, 29
Blondies, Sorghum, 103–4
Blueberry and Rye Bagels, 196
Bob's Red Mill, 30
boules
    scoring dough for, 54
    shaping dough for, 53
bourbon
    Buckwheat Canelés, 267–69, *268*
bowls, mixing, 43

bowl scraper, 45
branch-chain amino acids, 33
bread, baked, storing, 55
bread flour, about, 40–41
bread making. *See also* flour; grains
    anticipating inconsistent results, 16
    autolyse method, 46, 123
    baker's percentages, 25, 313–21
    desired dough temperature (DDT),
        310–12, 324–25
    environmental variables, 15–16
    equipment and tools, 43–45
    fermentation experimentation, 305–12
    glossary of terms, 19–21
    new baking manifesto, 17
    note on recipe yields, 25
    soaker method, 122
    troubleshooting, 323–26
    viewing recipes as guidelines, 16
bread making techniques
    baking the dough, 54–55, 326
    mixing the dough, 46–48, 324
    scoring the dough, 53–54, 325
    shaping the dough, 48–53, 325
bread pans, 44
Brioche, Wheat, 250–52
Brockman-Cummings, Jill, 27
Brownies, Buckwheat, *88*, 89–90, *90*

buckwheat, about, 38

buckwheat flour
> Buckwheat and Thyme Loaf, 138–39
> Buckwheat Banana Bread, 86–87
> Buckwheat Brownies, 88, 89–90, 90
> Buckwheat Canelés, 267–69, 268

bulgur, as cracked wheat substitute, 40

bulk fermentation, 21, 324–25

butter
> Buckwheat Canelés, 267–69, 268
> Cornmeal Danishes, 280, 281
> Frangipane, 293
> Maple Rye Kouign Amann, 285–87, 287
> Rghaif, 226–28
> Rye Phyllo Pies, 288, 289–91
> Rye Puff Pastry Galette de Rois, 292–93
> Whole-Wheat Croissants, 276, 277–79

Butternut Squash Filling for Rghaif, 228

C

cake flour, about, 40

cakes
> Bee Sting Cake, 263–66, 265
> Whole-Wheat Sponge Cake with Honey Buttercream Frosting, 117–19, 118

Calvel, Raymond, 46

Canelés, Buckwheat, 267–69, 268

carbon dioxide, 57, 58

cardamom
> Buckwheat Brownies, 88, 89–90, 90

Carolina Gold, 140, 141–43

Cashew and Peach Loaf, 130–31, 132

Celery Root and Rosemary Pizzas, 213

Challah, Oat Cinnamon-Raisin, 76, 77–79

Challenger Breadware, 35

Challenger cast-iron bread pan, 44

charnushka seeds
> Farmer's Favorite, 159–61, 161

Seeded Pumpernickel, 148, 149–51

cheese
> Bacon-Rye Cheese Rolls, 253–55, 255
> Celery Root and Rosemary Pizzas, 213
> Cornmeal and Jalapeño Bagels, 196
> Farinata, 190–91, 191
> Giardiniera and Goat Cheese Focaccia, 82, 85
> Khachapuri, 238–40, 239
> Margarita Pizzas, 212, 212
> Rye Phyllo Pies, 288, 289–91
> Sunchoke, Blue Cheese, and Rosemary Focaccia, 82, 85

cherries
> Millet Porridge and Cherry Loaf, 135–37, 137
> Stollen, 259–62, 262

chickpea flour. See Farinata

chiles
> Asparagus, Spring Onion, and Fresno Pepper Pizzas, 208, 217
> Chile Oil, 201–2
> Chile Polenta Loaf, 144–47, 145
> Cornmeal and Jalapeño Bagels, 196

chocolate
> Brown Butter Wheat Chocolate Chip Cookies, 108, 109–10
> Buckwheat Brownies, 88, 89–90, 90
> Chocolate Croissants, 279
> Honey Wheat Graham Cracker S'Mores, 111–13

ciabatta
> Roasted Garlic and Mashed Potato, 173–75, 174
> Ryebatta, 176–77
> Sorghum and Rosemary Ciabatta, 178, 179–80

cinnamon
> Oat Cinnamon-Raisin Challah, 76, 77–79
> Spiced Rye Cookies, 107, 108

Stollen, 259–62, 262

citrus fruit and peel
> Citrus Curd, 100–101
> Stollen, 259–62, 262

clay baker, 44

coconut
> Appam, 220–22, 221

commercial mills, 29

cookies
> Brown Butter Wheat Chocolate Chip Cookies, 108, 109–10
> Spiced Rye Cookies, 107, 108

corn, dried heirloom, about, 38

Cornbread, Heritage, 91–92

cornmeal
> baking with, 38
> Chile Polenta Loaf, 144–47, 145
> Cornmeal and Jalapeño Bagels, 196
> Cornmeal Danishes, 280, 281
> Cornmeal Whoopie Pies, 93–95, 95
> Heritage Cornbread, 91–92

couches (linen cloths), 44

cracked rye
> Seeded Pumpernickel, 148, 149–51
> substitutes for, 37
> Volkornbrot, 232, 233–34

cracked wheat
> Multigrain Seed Mix, 152
> substitutes for, 40

croissants
> Chocolate Croissants, 279
> Whole-Wheat Croissants, 276, 277–79

crop rotation, 30

crumb, defined, 19

Crumpets, Whole-Wheat, 116

crust, defined, 19

cumin
> Butternut Squash Filling for Rghaif, 228
> Spelt, Cumin, and Walnut Ring Loaf, 181–83, 183

Curd, Citrus, 100–101

D

Danishes, Cornmeal, *280*, 281

desired dough temperature (DDT),
310–12, 324–25

digital scale, 43

digital thermometer, 44

Dinner Rolls, Oat, 73–75, *75*

Doughnuts, Oat, 100–102, *102*

E

eggs
Egg Appam, *221*, 222
Khachapuri, 238–40, *239*

elasticity, defined, 20

English Muffins, Rye, 80–81

enriched doughs
baker's percentages, 319–20
mixing, 47–48

Ensaïmada, 229–31, *231*

equipment and tools, 43–45

ethanol, 57, 58

extensibility, defined, 20

F

Farinata, 190–91, *191*

Farmer's Favorite, 159–61, *161*

Farmhouse Sourdough, *124*, 125–26

fermentation experimentation, 305–12

Fig Tart, Sorghum Shortbread, *296*, 297–98

fine sea salt, 45

flax seeds
Farmer's Favorite, 159–61, *161*
Multigrain Seed Mix, 152
Seeded Pumpernickel, *148*, 149–51
Volkornbrot, *232*, 233–34

"float test," 62

flour. *See also* wheat flour; *specific types
of flour*
high-quality, sourcing, 35
protein percentages, 40–41
storing, 41

focaccia
Giardiniera and Goat Cheese
Focaccia, *82*, 85
Rye Focaccia, *82*, 83–85
Sunchoke, Blue Cheese, and
Rosemary Focaccia, *82*, 85

FODMAPs, 33

Frangipane, 293

Frosting, Honey Buttercream, Whole-
Wheat Sponge Cake with, 117–19,
118

fruit. *See also specific fruits*
Oat Galette with Seasonal Fruit, *96*,
97–99
Stollen, 259–62, *262*

G

Galette, Oat, with Seasonal Fruit, *96*,
97–99

Galette de Rois, Rye Puff Pastry, 292–93

Garlic, Roasted, and Mashed Potato
Ciabatta, 173–75, *174*

Giardiniera and Goat Cheese Focaccia,
82, 85

ginger
Sorghum Blondies, 103–4
Spiced Rye Cookies, 107, *108*
Stollen, 259–62, *262*

gliadin, 20, 46

gluten
defined, 20
high-gluten flour, 41
how it is formed, 46, 58
structure created with, 20

glutenin, 20, 46

gluten intolerance, 33–34

glyphosate, 29, 33

Graham Cracker, Honey Wheat, S'Mores,
111–13

grains. *See also specific types*
cracked, substitutes for, 122

soaker method, 122
types of, 37–40
whole, cracking, 122

grape method for sourdough starter, 60

H

herbs. *See* basil; rosemary; thyme

Heritage Cornbread, 91–92

high-gluten flour, 41

Hirzel Farms, 27

honey
Bagels, *192*, 193–95
Bee Sting Cake, 263–66, *265*
Honey and Sprouted Wheat Loaf,
166–68
Honey Marshmallows, 111–12
Honey-Oat Porridge Loaf, 162–64,
165
Honey Wheat Graham Cracker
S'Mores, 111–13
Whole-Wheat Croissants, *276*,
277–79
Whole-Wheat Pretzels, *204*, 205–7
Whole-Wheat Sponge Cake with
Honey Buttercream Frosting,
117–19, *118*

hydration, 60–61

I

Ice Cream, Malted Grain, 300–301

Illinois Stewardship Alliance, 35

inclusion, defined, 20

Injera, 223

J

Janie's Farm, 27

Janie's Mill, 27

K

Khachapuri, 238–40, *239*

King Arthur, 30

kitchen scale, 43

Kouign Amann, Maple Rye, 285–87, *287*

Kozma, Lou, 27

L

lactic acids, 57, 58

lame, 45

laminated dough, introduction to, 273–75

lean doughs

    baker's percentages, 317–18

    mixing, 47

leeks or ramps

    Rye Phyllo Pies, *288,* 289–91

levain, defined, 20

linen cloths, 44

M

Madeleines, Oat, *270,* 271–72, *272*

Malted Grain Ice Cream, 300–301

malted rye

    Malted Rye Bread, 127–29

    Volkornbrot, *232,* 233–34

    Whole-Wheat Pretzels, *204,* 205–7

Maple Rye Kouign Amann, 285–87, *287*

Marbled Rye, 169–72, *170*

Margarita Pizzas, 212, *212*

Marshmallows, Honey, 111–12

Marzipan, 259–61

millet

    about, 37–38

    Millet Porridge and Cherry Loaf, 135–37, *137*

    Multigrain Seed Mix, 152

mills

    commercial, 29

    small, buying flour from, 35

mixing bowls, 43

monoculture farming, 28

muffins

    Heritage Cornbread Muffins, 91–92

    Rye English Muffins, 80–81

Spelt and Apple Muffins, 105–6

Multigrain Baguette, 152–55, *153*

Multigrain Seed Mix, 152

Multigrain Sourdough, 156–58

Mushroom and Thyme Pizzas, 248

N

Naan, Rye, 199–200

Neapolitan Pizza Dough, Wheat, 214–15

Neapolitan Pizzas, Sungold and Church Bell Pepper, 216

nitrogen, 28

"NPK mentality," 28

nuts

    Bee Sting Cake, 263–66, *265*

    Peach and Cashew Loaf, 130–31, *132*

    Pistachio Pastry Cream, 282

    Spelt, Cumin, and Walnut Ring Loaf, 181–83, *183*

    Stollen, 259–62, *262*

O

oat flour

    Honey Wheat Graham Cracker S'Mores, 111–13

    Oat Doughnuts, 100–102, *102*

    Oat Galette with Seasonal Fruit, *96,* 97–99

    Oat Madeleines, *270,* 271–72, *272*

oats

    baking with, 39

    Honey-Oat Porridge Loaf, 162–64, *165*

    Multigrain Seed Mix, 152

    Oat Cinnamon-Raisin Challah, *76,* 77–79

    Oat Dinner Rolls, 73–75, *75*

    Spelt and Apple Muffins, 105–6

Oil, Chile, 201–2

onions

    Bacon-Rye Cheese Rolls, 253–55, *255*

Butternut Squash Filling for Rghaif, 228

    Rye English Muffins, 80–81

P

parathas

    Mashed Potato Parathas, 237

    Whole-Wheat Parathas, 235–37, *236*

pastry brush, 45

pastry cream

    Pistachio Pastry Cream, 282

    Sorghum Pastry Cream, 297–98

pastry flour, 40. *See also* whole-wheat pastry flour

Peach and Cashew Loaf, 130–31, *132*

Peanut and Apple Loaf, 133–34

pepitas

    Chile Polenta Loaf, 144–47, *145*

    Multigrain Baguette, 152–55, *153*

    Multigrain Sourdough, 156–58

peppers. *See also* chiles

    Shishito and Prosciutto Pizzas, *246,* 249, *249*

    Sungold and Church Bell Pepper Neapolitan Pizzas, 216

pesticides, 28–29, 33

phosphorus, 28

Phyllo Pies, Rye, *288,* 289–91

phytase, 34

phytic acid, 34, 58

Pide Bread, Whole-Grain Chile, 201–3, *203*

Pies, Rye Phyllo, *288,* 289–91

Pistachio Pastry Cream, 282

Pitas, Wheat, 197–98

pizza dough

    Sourdough Pizza Dough, *208,* 209–11

    Wheat Neapolitan Pizza Dough, 214–15

    Whole-Grain Roman-Style Pizza Dough, *246,* 247–48

pizzas
  Asparagus, Spring Onion, and Fresno
    Pepper Pizzas, *208,* 217
  Celery Root and Rosemary Pizzas,
    213
  Margarita Pizzas, 212, *212*
  Mushroom and Thyme Pizzas, 248
  Shishito and Prosciutto Pizzas, *246,*
    249, *249*
  Sungold and Church Bell Pepper
    Neapolitan Pizzas, 216
pizza stone, 43–44
Pizzelles, Sourdough, 299
polycropping, 32
poolish, defined, 20
poppy seeds
  Farmer's Favorite, 159–61, *161*
  Multigrain Seed Mix, 152
pork. *See* bacon; prosciutto
potassium, 28
potatoes
  Mashed Potato Parathas, 237
  Potato Fry Pockets, 256–57
  Roasted Garlic and Mashed Potato
    Ciabatta, 173–75, *174*
preferments, 20
Pretzels, Whole-Wheat, *204,* 205–7
proofing, 21, 324–25
proofing baskets, 44
Prosciutto and Shishito Pizzas, *246,* 249,
  249
Puff Pastry, Rye, Galette de Rois, 292–93
Pumpernickel, Seeded, *148,*
  149–51
Puri, 224–25

R

raisins
  Oat Cinnamon-Raisin Challah, 76,
    77–79
  Stollen, 259–62, *262*

ramps or leeks
  Rye Phyllo Pies, *288,* 289–91
Red Fife wheat, 32
Reding, Gary, 28
Rghaif, 226–28
rice
  Appam, 220–22, *221*
  baking with, 38
  Carolina Gold, *140,* 141–43
ring loaves, shaping dough for, 53
rolls
  Bacon-Rye Cheese Rolls, 253–55, *255*
  Oat Dinner Rolls, 73–75, *75*
  Roman-Style Pizza Dough, Whole-Grain,
    246, 247–48
rosemary
  Celery Root and Rosemary Pizzas, 213
  Sorghum and Rosemary Ciabatta,
    178, 179–80
  Sunchoke, Blue Cheese, and
    Rosemary Focaccia, *82,* 85
Roundup, 29, 33
ruler, 45
rye, cracked
  Seeded Pumpernickel, *148,* 149–51
  substitutes for, 37
  Volkornbrot, *232,* 233–34
rye, malted
  Malted Rye, 127–29
  Volkornbrot, *232,* 233–34
  Whole-Wheat Pretzels, *204,* 205–7
rye flour
  Bacon-Rye Cheese Rolls, 253–55, *255*
  Farmer's Favorite, 159–61, *161*
  Farmhouse Sourdough, *124,* 125–26
  fresh-ground, about, 37
  Khachapuri, 238–40, *239*
  Malted Rye, 127–29
  Maple Rye Kouign Amann, 285–87,
    287
  Marbled Rye, 169–72, *170*

Multigrain Baguette, 152–55, *153*
Multigrain Sourdough, 156–58
Rye and Blueberry Bagels, 196
Ryebatta, 176–77
Rye English Muffins, 80–81
Rye Focaccia, *82,* 83–85
Rye Naan, 199–200
Rye Phyllo Pies, *288,* 289–91
Rye Puff Pastry Galette de Rois,
  292–93
Seeded Pumpernickel, *148,* 149–51
sourcing, 37
Spiced Rye Cookies, 107, *108*
as substitute for cracked rye, 37
Volkornbrot, *232,* 233–34
Whole-Grain Chile Pide Bread,
  201–3, *203*

S

salt, 45, 46, 323
"San Francisco sourdough," 57
Sauce, Tomato, 212
scale, digital, 43
seeds. *See also specific seeds*
  Farmer's Favorite, 159–61, *161*
  Multigrain Baguette, 152–55,
    153
  Multigrain Seed Mix, 152
  Multigrain Sourdough, 156–58
  Seeded Pumpernickel, *148,* 149–51
"seed starter," 59
sesame seeds
  Carolina Gold, *140,* 141–43
  Farmer's Favorite, 159–61, *161*
  Multigrain Seed Mix, 152
  Rye Phyllo Pies, *288,* 289–91
  Seeded Pumpernickel, *148,* 149–51
  Toasted Sesame Loaf, *184,* 185–87,
    186
Shabazi spice blend
  Chile Oil, 201–2

shallots
    Mushroom and Thyme Pizzas, 248
    Rye English Muffins, 80–81
Shishito and Prosciutto Pizzas, *246*, 249, *249*
Shortbread Fig Tart, Sorghum, *296*, 297–98
Simply Local app, 35
S'Mores, Honey Wheat Graham Cracker, 111–13
soaker method, 122
sorghum
    about, 39
    Sorghum and Rosemary Ciabatta, *178*, 179–80
    Sorghum Blondies, 103–4
    Sorghum Pastry Cream, 297–98
    Sorghum Shortbread Fig Tart, *296*, 297–98
Sourdough Pizza Dough, *208*, 209–11
Sourdough Pizzelles, 299
sourdough starter
    creating, methods for, 58–60
    defined, 57
    feeding for everyday baking, 62–63
    "float test," 62
    forgetting to add at right time, 323–24
    health benefits, 33–34
    maintaining, 60–62
    neglected, remedies for, 63
    refrigerated, reviving, 61–62
    refrigerating, 61
    "seed starter," 59
    sourcing from bakery, 60
    storage guidelines, 63
    testing for readiness, 62
    what it does, 58
    when to discard, 63
spelt flour
    about, 39
    Carolina Gold, *140*, 141–43

Ensaïmada, 229–31, *231*
Heritage Cornbread, 91–92
Potato Fry Pockets, 256–57
Spelt, Cumin, and Walnut Ring Loaf, 181–83, *183*
Spelt and Apple Muffins, 105–6
Stollen, 259–62, *262*
using in place of all-purpose flour, 39
Spence, Paul, 32
Spence Farm, 27
Spiced Rye Cookies, 107, *108*
spider, 45
Sponge Cake, Whole-Wheat, with Honey Buttercream Frosting, 117–19, *118*
Spring Onion, Asparagus, and Fresno Pepper Pizzas, *208*, 217
Sprouted Wheat and Honey Loaf, 166–68
Squash, Butternut, Filling for Rghaif, 228
stand mixer, 43
Stollen, 259–62, *262*
Sunchoke, Blue Cheese, and Rosemary Focaccia, *82*, 85
sunflower seeds
    Farmer's Favorite, 159–61, *161*
    Multigrain Baguette, 152–55, *153*
    Multigrain Sourdough, 156–58
    Seeded Pumpernickel, *148*, 149–51
    Volkornbrot, *232*, 233–34

T

tangzhong, about, 253
Tart, Sorghum Shortbread Fig, *296*, 297–98
teff flour. *See* Injera
thermometer, digital, 44
thyme
    and Buckwheat Loaf, 138–39
    Mushroom and Thyme Pizzas, 248
Toasted Sesame Loaf, *184*, 185–87, *186*
tomatoes
    Margarita Pizzas, 212, *212*

Sungold and Church Bell Pepper Neapolitan Pizzas, 216
Tortillas, White Wheat, 241–43, *242*
Travis, Marty, 27, 32, 33
Travis, Will, 27
Turkey Red wheat, 32

V

Volkornbrot, *232*, 233–34

W

Walnut, Spelt, and Cumin Ring Loaf, 181–83, *183*
Warthog wheat, 32
wheat. *See also* wheat flour
    cracked, substitutes for, 40
    hard winter, about, 40
    industrial conventional, 28–29
    industrial organic, 29–30
    locally and sustainably grown, 30–33
    soft spring, about, 40
    varieties of, 39–40
wheat berries
    Honey and Sprouted Wheat Loaf, 166–68
wheat flour. *See also* whole-wheat flour; whole-wheat pastry flour; *specific flour types below*
    all-purpose flour, 40
    bread flour, 40–41
    cake flour, 40
    as cracked wheat substitute, 40
    and gluten intolerance, 33–34
    high-gluten flour, 41
    from industrial conventional wheat, 28–29
    from industrial organic wheat, 29–30
    from locally and sustainably grown wheat, 30–33
    pastry flour, 40
    storing, 41

types of, 40–41

White Wheat Tortillas, 241–43, *242*

White Bread, A Good, 68–69, *70*

white chocolate

Sorghum Blondies, 103–4

White Wheat Tortillas, 241–43, *242*

whole-wheat flour

Apple and Peanut Loaf, 133–34

Bagels, *192*, 193–95

Carolina Gold, *140*, 141–43

creating sourdough starter with, 58

Farmer's Favorite, 159–61, *161*

Farmhouse Sourdough, *124*, 125–26

Honey and Sprouted Wheat Loaf, 166–68

Honey Wheat Graham Cracker S'Mores, 111–13

Multigrain Baguette, 152–55, *153*

Multigrain Sourdough, 156–58

Peach and Cashew Loaf, 130–31, *132*

Puri, 224–25

Rghaif, 226–28

Sourdough Pizza Dough, *208*, 209–11

Toasted Sesame Loaf, *184*, 185–87, *186*

Wheat Brioche, 250–52

Wheat Neapolitan Pizza Dough, 214–15

Wheat Pitas, 197–98

Wheat Sandwich Loaf, 71–72

Whole-Grain Chile Pide Bread, 201–3, *203*

Whole-Grain Roman-Style Pizza Dough, *246*, 247–48

Whole-Wheat Biscuits, 114–15

Whole-Wheat Croissants, *276*, 277–79

Whole-Wheat Crumpets, 116

Whole-Wheat Parathas, 235–37, *236*

Whole-Wheat Pretzels, *204*, 205–7

whole-wheat pastry flour

Brown Butter Wheat Chocolate Chip Cookies, *108*, 109–10

Sorghum Blondies, 103–4

Whole-Wheat Sponge Cake with Honey Buttercream Frosting, 117–19, *118*

Whoopie Pies, Cornmeal, 93–95, *95*

wild yeast, 57, 58

Wilken, Harold, 27

"WTF flour," 33

Y

yeast, 57, 58

yogurt

Rye Naan, 199–200

Wheat Pitas, 197–98

Z

za'atar spice blend

Chile Oil, 201–2

zhoug

Chile Oil, 201–2

For information about permission to reproduce selections from this book, write to
Permissions, W. W. Norton & Company, Inc., 500 Fifth Avenue, New York, NY 10110

For information about special discounts for bulk purchases, please contact
W. W. Norton Special Sales at specialsales@wwnorton.com or 800-233-4830

Manufacturing through Imago
Book design by Faceout Studio, Paul Nielsen
Production manager: Devon Zahn

ISBN 978-0-393-86674-2

W. W. Norton & Company, Inc.
500 Fifth Avenue, New York, N.Y. 10110
www.wwnorton.com

W. W. Norton & Company Ltd.
15 Carlisle Street, London W1D 3BS

1 2 3 4 5 6 7 8 9 0